DISCARD

LOCATING LANGUAGE IN TIME AND SPACE

This is the first volume in a series entitled
QUANTITATIVE ANALYSES OF LINGUISTIC STRUCTURE
Under the general editorship of
William Labov
University of Pennsylvania
David Sankoff
Centre de Recherches Mathematique

LOCATING LANGUAGE IN TIME AND SPACE

Edited by

William Labov
Department of Linguistics
University of Pennsylvania
Philadelphia, Pennsylvania

ACADEMIC PRESS
A Subsidiary of Harcourt Brace Jovanovich, Publishers
New York   London   Toronto   Sydney   San Francisco

ACADEMIC PRESS, INC.
111 Fifth Avenue, New York, New York 10003

United Kingdom Edition published by
ACADEMIC PRESS, INC. (LONDON) LTD.
24/28 Oval Road, London NW1   7DX

Library of Congress Cataloging in Publication Data
Main entry under title:

Locating language in time and space.

(Quantitative analyses of linguistic structure
series)
    Includes bibliographies and index.
    1. Language and languages--Variation.
2. Linguistic change. I. Labov, William.
II. Series.
P120.V37L6   410   80--24396
ISBN 0--12--432101--1

PRINTED IN THE UNITED STATES OF AMERICA

80 81 82 83   9 8 7 6 5 4 3 2 1

CONTENTS

1

VARIATION IN THE GROUP AND THE INDIVIDUAL: THE CASE OF FINAL STOP DELETION   1
Gregory R. Guy

2

RANKING OF CONSTRAINTS ON /t,d/ DELETION IN AMERICAN ENGLISH: A STATISTICAL ANALYSIS   37
Helene Neu

7

FACTORS CONTROLLING THE ACQUISITION OF THE PHILADELPHIA DIALECT BY OUT-OF-STATE CHILDREN 143
Arvilla C. Payne

8

THE STRUCTURE OF A LONG-TERM PHONOLOGICAL PROCESS: THE BACK VOWEL CHAIN SHIFT IN SOULATAN GASCON 179
Penelope Eckert

9

A FALSELY REPORTED MERGER IN EIGHTEENTH-CENTURY ENGLISH: A STUDY IN DIACHRONIC VARIATION 221
Geoffrey Nunberg

LIST OF CONTRIBUTORS

Numbers in parentheses indicate the pages on which authors' contributions begin.

John Baugh (83), DEPARTMENT OF LINGUISTICS, UNIVERSITY OF TEXAS, AUSTIN, TEXAS 78712

Penelope Eckert (179), DEPARTMENT OF ANTHROPOLOGY, UNIVERSITY OF MICHIGAN, ANN ARBOR, MICHIGAN 48104

Gregory R. Guy, (1),* DEPARTMENT OF LINGUISTICS, UNIVERSITY OF PENNSYL-VANIA, PHILADELPHIA, PENNSYLVANIA 19104

Flora Klein (69), SCHOOL OF LANGUAGES AND LINGUISTICS, GEORGETOWN UNIVER-SITY, WASHINGTON, D.C. 20057

William Labov (251), DEPARTMENT OF LINGUISTICS, UNIVERSITY OF PENNSYLVANIA, PHILADELPHIA, PENNSYLVANIA 19104

Helene Neu, (37), SPEECH COMMUNICATIONS RESEARCH LABORATORY, LOS ANGELES, CALIFORNIA 90007; AND DEPARTMENT OF ROMANCE LANGUAGES, UNIVERSITY OF MICHIGAN, ANN ARBOR, MICHIGAN 48109

Geoffrey Nunberg (24), DEPARTMENT OF LINGUISTICS, UNIVERSITY OF CALIFORNIA, LOS ANGELES, CALIFORNIA 90027

Arvilla C. Payne (143), DEPARTMENTS OF SOCIOLOGY AND ANTHROPOLOGY, HOWARD UNIVERSITY, WASHINGTON, D.C. 20059

Shana Poplack (55),† DEPARTMENT OF LINGUISTICS, UNIVERSITY OF PENNSYLVANIA, PHILADELPHIA, PENNSYLVANIA 19104

Walt Wolfram (107), DEPARTMENT OF COMMUNICATION SCIENCES, UNIVERSITY OF THE DISTRICT OF COLUMBIA, WASHINGTON, D.C. 20001; AND CENTER FOR APPLIED LINGUISTICS, ARLINGTON, VIRGINIA 22209

* Present address: Department of Linguistics, University of Sydney, N.S.W. 2006, Australia.

† Present address: Center for Puerto Rican Studies, City University of New York, New York, New York 10019.

PREFACE

This first volume in the series *Quantitative Analyses of Linguistic Structure* is designed to present substantive findings that have emerged from recent research with quantitative techniques. The aim of the series is to publish those results of quantitative work that bear most directly on the fundamental problems of linguistic change and linguistic structure.

Earlier publications in this field have inevitably been concerned with questions of method. In addition to discussions of new techniques of data reduction and organization, a great deal of effort was expended in ideological discussions as to whether quantitative methods were possible, the place of quantitative information in a grammar, or even whether human beings could learn to do one thing more often than another. At one point, it seemed that the study of variation would adopt permanently the forensic style that is the lingua franca of the more scholastic areas of linguistics.

This has not happened. The field has matured to the point that the advantages and disadvantages of various methods of treating the data are recognized and related to each other. Researchers are free to concentrate upon the problem that they are confronting rather than on the suitability of the methods they are using. In the contributions of this volume and in those to come, one will find traditional statistical techniques, variable rule analyses, implicational scales, and graphic presentation of analyses, and graphic presentations of spatial data.

In general, these analyses and syntheses will be built on linguistic theory as it has emerged over many centuries. The categories and algebras constructed by qualitative analyses are normally the input to the quantitative analysis. The enterprise presented here is conceived as cumulative and progressive. No quantitative revolution is advertised. Rather, we see quantitative methods as the major route for resolving theoretical alternatives in a decisive way.

The emphasis on substantive issues of linguistic theory does not mean that questions of method are no longer relevant. The present growth and development of studies of variation is dependent on its integration into the larger framework of probability theory, and the development of computational methods for resolving complex problems. There is no reason to believe that advances in methods of analysis will not be equally important in the future, and the series will aim to provide source material in this area, including programs and documentation.

The QALS series will publish original papers, longer studies, and book-length monographs. The editors invite the submission of research reports in this area for consideration, and hope to provide the space needed to treat each topic in the detail required to substantiate the ideas being put forward.

William Labov

David Sankoff

INTRODUCTION

It is often said that a field of human knowledge begins with qualitative observations and advances toward quantitative techniques as it matures. This may also be the case with linguistics, where a special configuration of obstacles to quantitative analysis has been maintained until quite recently. Though linguistics sits squarely in the middle of the tripartite division into humanities, natural sciences, and social sciences, most linguists come into the field from the first area, where quantitative work is still rare—perhaps not without justification. We have been able to make extraordinary progress on a qualitative basis, for a number of reasons. Language seems to be the foremost example of a human activity that imposes qualitative categories on continuous fields, sharpening even further whatever discrete properties are the products of our perceptual apparatus. The speech community does show a considerable degree of homogeneity, and we have been able to advance quite rapidly by assuming that the introspection of any one native speaker fully represents that community (Labov, 1975). On the other hand, many of the early efforts to use quantitative methods have seemed to linguists less than marginal in their failure to make contact with the central concerns of linguistic theory (Chrétien, 1965).

But as it often happens, a strength can become a weakness, and a calm security drift gradually into dangerous ignorance. There is no need to document here the problems encountered by formal linguistics: the weakness of the data base, the instability of theoretical constructs, the inability to deal with the data produced by observation and experimentation, the many paradoxes and scholastic contradictions. The readers of this volume have been exposed to these matters. They are more likely to underestimate the strength of formal, algebraic approaches than to overestimate them. It must be emphasized that very few of the questions investigated in this volume could have been framed without a long history of formal statement and restatement. The research reported here will demonstrate clearly that the analysis of variation and boundary conditions is a powerful tool for resolving long-standing issues of linguistic theory. But this work is built on the foundations of discrete analyses: Linguists who cannot assimilate the issues posed by abstract phonology and syntax may not profit very much from the quantitative research presented here.

My coeditor of the series has pointed out to linguists more than once that the axioms of probability theory presuppose an algebra, and a field that has not developed an algebra cannot benefit from the multivariate techniques that he has provided or interpret linguistic variation in the light of probability theory. We cannot function without the closed sets provided by phonological features, morphological oppositions, grammatical categories, and phrase structures. Each of the contributions in this book uses such an algebra, and studies the distribution of choices within an exhaustive set of mutually exclusive features.

There are areas where this does not go as smoothly as others. Wolfram's study of a-prefixing in Appalachian English includes a search, a review, of all possible suggestions for semantic content of this grammatical feature, which would distinguish a-goin from goin'. He examines such features as *intermittent, continuous, and planned* aspect. This is quite remote from the precision of the phonological features that he has available. It is clear that quantitative analysis becomes more difficult as the arena becomes more abstract, and one must use considerable ingenuity to extend the domain of closed sets into semantic territory.

Many of the recent meetings and collections of papers on variations have been concerned with methods, beginning with the first NWAVE volume (Bailey and Shuy, 1973), and extending to *Language Variation* edited by Sankoff (1979), which might well have been considered the first in this series. The first two chapters in this volume do have a methodological bent; they deal with -t, d deletion, which continues to be the best stone for sharpening our analytical tools. Throughout the other chapters, there will be found a wide variety of quantitative techniques, from the simplest to the most sophisticated. In general, however, this volume is not focused on methods, but on the substantive issues that arise in the course of describing language and explaining language change.

The title of this volume, *Locating Language in Time and Space,* echoes the theme of the 1973 Linguistic Institute at Ann Arbor. It reflects the natural alliance of historical linguists, dialect geographers, and sociolinguists, and their joint investment in the exploration of the real world. In assembling the various studies found here, I hope to have demonstrated the strength of that alliance. The common theme is the analysis of boundary conditions: boundaries between historical stages, between neighboring dialects, between social groups; and internal boundaries as well, between phonemes, processes, grammatical categories, and morphemes. All of these investigations use quantitative methods to investigate the abruptness, regularity, and contour of the boundary in question, rather than taking all these as given. From the results of these various inquiries, we can see emerging the "orderly heterogeneity" that Weinreich identified a dozen years ago in *Empirical Foundations* (Weinreich, Labov, and Herzog, 1968).

None of these authors need an elaborate explication: They state clearly the issues they are dealing with, and what they have found. I will confine myself to pointing out what I know of the origins of each study, what seems to me new in their statements of the problem, the solution, and the methods used to find that solution.

Guy's study of -*t*, *d* deletion was originally motivated by an issue raised by Derek Bickerton in his criticism of variable rule analyses. Bickerton argued (1971) that it was impossible for human beings to learn to produce one linguistic form more often than another, and that therefore the consistent variation that we report must be the result of averaging individuals with different patterns. Guy, one of the most skilled users of the Cedergren–Sankoff Varbrule program, demonstrates for the Philadelphia community what we had seen in many individual systems. The variable constraints on -*t*, *d* deletion are reliably and regularly repeated for each individual, and Guy obtains the same result when he considers a great deal of data from one person or moderate amounts from many. At the same time, he shows the importance of the size of the data set, a point that had been urged on us many times by Sankoff: Gross constraints (like following obstruent versus following vowel) can be located with small numbers of tokens, but the finer regularities of the system (like the effect of a following glide versus a following vowel) emerge reliably only when we have 30 or so tokens in the smaller of the two cells being compared.

Guy's rich analysis also shows the difference between articulatory constraints that are predictable from our general knowledge of physiology and acoustics, and features of a more global character. In previous studies, Labov, Cohen, Robins, and Lewis (1968) grouped pause with the obstruents; Wolfram (1969) with the vowels; and Fasold (1971) found that black speakers in Washington treated pause like an obstruent. Guy finds a sharp difference between the New York and Philadelphia white communities in their treatment of this parameter: New York City treats following pause like an obstruent, Philadelphia like a vowel. Further research by our Project on Linguistic Change and Variation has shown that this abstract trait is geographically distributed: the closer to New York City a town is, the higher the pause factor; the closer to Philadelphia, the lower it is. Thus conditioning factors that can be analyzed in several different ways are also available for geographic and social differentiation. If linguists can see two sides of an argument, so can the speakers of the language.

Helene Neu's analysis of the same variable uses a straightforward statistical approach to one constraint at a time, to demonstrate the stability and generally of the basic -*t, d* pattern. She shows that one can use small amounts of data, taken under fairly formal conditions from a sizable number of people, and get reliable results. Her use of confidence intervals to demonstrate the significance of her findings is a technique that might well be adapted more widely. One of the most valuable features of Neu's paper is her clear illustration of the need to identify and segregate common words with skewed distributions. In our various reports on -*t, d,* we had neglected to report that we excluded *and,* since it is so very common and shows deletion at a high level. Neu does not take this for granted, but demonstrates the kind of distortion that results from including *and* in the main data set.

Our experience with -*t, d* deletion led us to expect that whenever a consonant was deleted, it would be deleted less often if it were a separate morpheme. The first studies of the aspiration and deletion of Spanish /s/ showed that this was not so: In fact, the plural /s/ was deleted more often than monomorphemic /s/—a paradox for those who believe that representational function controls all language variation. Chapter 3 presents Poplack's resolution of this paradox. She sharpens the paradox by demonstrating that the presence of an /s/ in a noun phrase string does not increase the probability of a following zero, but rather that /s/ triggers /s/, and zero triggers zero. Her ingenious use of the variable rule program goes considerably beyond any previous studies in this area, and shows that a simplistic approach to function will not do. Poplack is the first to go beyond morphological information in assessing the functional hypothesis, and the need to take into account syntactic, semantic, and cultural information as well.

Flora Klein's examination of the possible influence of English on Spanish shows how quantitative methods can go considerably beyond the limitations of contrastive analysis. She considers the progressive—common to both languages—and shows how a subtle influence can escape immediate observation. In this case, the effect of English cannot lead to forms that are different or distinct in any qualitative way from Spanish grammer, but a deeper examination of frequencies shows that the influence there has indeed altered the interpretive system based on expected meanings.

Such quantitative patterns can persist over long periods of time, even when they are not directly related to the communication of representational information. Chapter 6 contains John Baugh's complete analysis of the use of the copula by the Cobras in New York City. In my original discussion, "Contraction, deletion and inherent variability of the English copula" (1969), the Cobras appeared as the most extreme users of vernacular rules. But without the multivariate variable program, I was not able to analyze the constraints on their use of the copula without collapsing a number of categories. In the group dealing with the influence of following grammatical category, I made the mistake of combining predicate adjective and locative. The end result was a pattern that showed a perfect parallel between contraction and deletion for the following grammatical category, and this reinforced our conviction that Black English had drawn quite close to other dialects in the treatment of the copula. Baugh uses the variable program to disengage predicate adjective and copula, with a startling result that throws into high relief a quantitative residue of the creole history of Black English.

There is no chapter in this book that shows more dramatically the intimate relations between time and space than Baugh's reanalysis of the copula. Quantitative patterns can apparently preserve linguistic history over several centuries and several continents. This is one of many results that lead us to reformulate our notions of the relation of synchrony and diachrony. It is often said that synchronic analysis must ignore history, since children learn their language without reference to past history. We can look at the matter in exactly the reverse way: Children are from another point of view the perfect historians of language. They acquire a good part of past history, not in the qualitative categories of the sound system or the grammer, but in the detailed structure of quantitative relations that govern the use of these options.

The use of a-prefixing in Appalachian English appears to be another kind of historical residue. Given the bias of most linguists toward finding cognitive value throughout language, it is inevitable that some investigators will discover a meaning for any such grammatical particle. In his many other studies, Wolfram has discovered enough of the other kinds of patterns in language to allow him to consider calmly the possibility that there is no conceptual content for a given particle. With Wolfram, we might bear in mind that some particles are left over, and survive as "mere" stylistic variants. There is a great deal more in Wolfram's detailed analysis of a-prefixing, but more than anything else, it conveys to me the value of a patient and imperturbable scepticism in regard to the conceptual content of grammatical particles. A careful study of Wolfram's chapter may go a long way toward answering the fundamental question that must be raised about the analysis of tense and aspect particles: Why are there as many meanings as there are analysts?

Wolfram's analysis of a-prefixing shows his characteristic talent for looking at all sides of a question. The Cedergren–Sankoff program is used where it is called for, and more discursive analyses when they are needed. The judicious balance between quantitative and qualitative arguments is typical of Wolfram's work as a whole.

Chapter 7 reports a very substantial part of Arvilla Payne's inquiry into the acquisition of the Philadelphia dialect by children from other dialect areas. At the outset, this was an inquiry into the relative influence of parents and peers on the formation of a child's language. Payne located a bedroom community where the parents' dialect would have the maximum possibility of influencing the language of the child. Given the intimate knowledge of the Philadelphia system acquired by the Project on Linguistic Change and Variation, and a knowledge of the incoming systems as well, Payne was able to measure with some precision the degree of acquisition of a wide range of Philadelphia variables. The first results confirmed my earlier analysis in New York City (Labov, 1977): that second-generation speakers represent the dialect as well as third-generation speakers. In other words, children who enter the community before the age of 8 rapidly acquire the phonetic variables under the influence of their peers.

All this is quite true of the major features of the Philadelphia chain shifts: fronting, raising, diphthongization, and centralization. But it was startling to find that exactly the opposite was true for a different kind of phonological variable—the tensing of short *a*—which could only be learned if the child had parents born in Philadelphia. This fundamental distinction uncovered in Payne's work has played a major part in my own thinking about sound change (Labov 1979), and I would suggest that it is essential for anyone who would make general statements about the mechanism of linguistic evolution to be acquainted with Payne's results.

The last three chapters deal with sound change, the driving force behind linguistic evolution that is itself the center of so many paradoxes. Chapter 8 concerns a chain shift of unstressed /a/ → /o/ → /u/ in a Gascon dialect (the change that gives us *lingo* instead of *linga*). Penelope Eckert follows the strategy of our title better than any other author in the books: This shift is located as a stage in the development of the vowel system from late Latin to modern Gascon; it is placed in a transitional zone in the spatial dispersion of this process throughout southern France; and it is portrayed as a social process in the everyday language of the village of Soulan. This is the result of many years of participant observation by Eckert, who can provide us with the vivid view of the change in progress that we need to correct the more fragmentary information of the *Atlas Linguistique de France*. A number of the knottiest problems of representing chain shifts and their conditioning are attacked here, going considerably beyond the general principles set forth in our initial study, where Romance languages were represented only by secondary sources (Labov, Yaeger, and Steiner, 1972). Eckert's tables, maps, and quotations provide strong support for the rules of chain shifting that she sets out in conclusion.

The second study of sound change departs from the other major focus of Labov, Yaeger, and Steiner: near-mergers. In our investigations of change in progress, we were surprised to discover that minimal pair and commutation tests could show two kinds of contradictions between speech production and perception. Speakers often said that two sounds were different when they were pronounced the same. More interesting were cases where the productions of two vowels were reliably distinct, but speakers labeled them the same. We found six cases of such near-mergers: They generally involved close approximations of F1 and 100–150-Hz differences in F2. The possibility of such near-mergers helped to explain a number of anomalies in historical development: One of these was the reseparation of /ay/ and /oy/ in nineteenth-century English after a merger that is said to have lasted for over a century. In Chapter 9, Geoffrey Nunberg plunges into the evidence in a systematic way. In his first four tables, he shows that the history of English can provide enough data for quantitative analysis if it is approached with sufficient ingenuity and theoretical insight. Nunberg's proposals for the mechanism of near-merger and separation are of great importance for the interpretation of past and present sound changes. It is interesting to note that another of our early speculations on near-mergers in the history of English, the case of *meat–mate,* has been illuminated by James Milroy's discovery of the continued near-merger in Belfast (1979).

Six of these ten chapters have been associated with the Project on Linguistic Change and Variation in Philadelphia, supported by the National Science Foundation from 1972 to 1977; that support is gratefully acknowledged here. The last chapter deals with the central question approached by this research group. From 1973 to 1978, we searched for answers to the problem of the causes of sound change, looking for a solution to the embedding problem: How are sound changes embedded in the social structure? By identifying the innovators in sound change, we hoped also to locate the social pressures that govern the development and directions of the change, and explain the continual and mysterious renewal of sound change. I have written this chapter "The social origins of linguistic change" to present in a brief space the main findings that are reported in detail in Labov, Bower, Dayton, Hindle, Kroch, Lennig, and Schiffrin (1980). The chapter in this volume gives some indication of the logic of the operation, the various techniques of sampling the community, measuring vowels, normalizing the systems, regression analyses, and, ultimately, explanation of the results. It is by far the largest and most advanced sociolinguistic project that I have been associated with, and as much as any other, shows the power of quantitative analysis in attacking the central problems of language change.

References

Bailey, C.-J., and Shuy, R. (Eds.). 1973. *New ways of analyzing variation in English*. Washington, D.C.: Georgetown University Press.

Bickerton, D. 1971. Inherent variability and variable rules. *Foundations of Language,* 7:457–492.

Chrétien, C. 1965. Review of G. Herdan, "The calculus of linguistic observations." *Language,* 41:348–356.

Labov, W. 1969. Contraction, deletion, and inherent variability of the English copula. *Language,* 45:715–762.

Labov, W. 1977. The relative influence of family and peers on the learning of language. In R.

Simone and G. Ruggiero (Eds.), *Aspetti Sociolinguistici dell'Italia Contemporanea*. Rome: Bulzoni.

Labov, W. 1979. Resolving the neogrammarian controversy. Address to the Western Meeting of the LSA, Los Angeles.

Labov, W., Bower, A., Hindle, D., Dayton, E., Lennig, M., and Schiffrin, D. 1980. *Social determinants of sound change*. Final Report to NSF on SOC75-00245. Philadelphia: U.S. Regional Survey.

Labov, W., Yaeger, M., and Steiner, R. 1972. *A quantitative study of sound change in progress*. Philadelphia: U.S. Regional Survey.

Sankoff, D. (Ed.). 1978. *Linguistic variation: Models and methods*. New York: Academic Press.

Weinreich, U., Labov, W., and Herzog, M. 1968. Empirical foundations of linguistic theory. In W. Lehmann and Y. Malkiel (eds.), *Directions for historical linguistics*. Austin: University of Texas Press.

LOCATING LANGUAGE
IN TIME AND SPACE

1

Gregory R. Guy

VARIATION IN THE GROUP AND THE INDIVIDUAL: THE CASE OF FINAL STOP DELETION

Introduction

One of the enduring questions in linguistics has been the nature of the relationship between the individual and the group. The problem is rooted in the fact that language, while existing to serve a social function (communication), is nevertheless seated in the minds of individuals. This dichotomy is reflected many times in linguistic theory, from Saussure's *langue–parole* distinction right down to present-day argumentation in syntax, where a multiplicity of idiosyncratic dialects is invoked to account for divergence of syntactic judgments.

An important aspect of this issue is the definition of what exactly should be the subject matter of a linguistic description. Are we to write grammars of the speech of an individual, or of the language of a community of speakers? It is a necessary goal of linguistics to describe the most general object possible. However, the variation encountered at the level of "language" has led many linguists, in the pursuit of homogeneity, through successive subdivisions of the available data, until ultimately an ideal, variation-free idiolect becomes the "correct" object of attention.

It would appear, however, that the pursuit of homogeneity in this fashion is doomed to failure, because variation is to be found everywhere in language, even at the level of the idiolect. We are coming to accept variation as "inherent" in language and possibly even essential to it.

An example of such inherent variation is the process of consonant cluster simplification in English; more specifically, the variable rule by which final stops (especially /t,d/) in consonant clusters are deleted. This rule is very compelling; it affects virtually all speakers of English in all but the most self-conscious styles. It is intricately conditioned, but is rarely categorical.

We conducted a study of this variable as part of a research project focusing on linguistic change and variation in the Philadelphia speech community. The project was supported by the National Science Foundation and directed by William Labov. In this chapter, I will report the results of that study. I will also describe the methodology that we developed for the study of this type of systematic variation. Finally, I will use the results to draw some conclusions about the relationship between the group and the individual. This question will be attacked through the analysis of the STRUCTURE OF VARIATION—the proportions of different variants used, the conditioning effect of different environments, the hierarchy of constraints, patterns of style shifting and social stratification, etc. Such knowledge of the structure of variation is indispensable for the understanding of historical processes of linguistic change, as well as for the synchronic study of language and its social usage.

Background

Systematic description and analysis of variation in language was inaugurated with the study of linguistic variables (Labov, 1966). It was given a formal relationship to conventional generative grammar by the introduction of the concept of variable rules—as distinct from the conventional obligatory and optional rules—in Labov (1969). Another major advance came with the introduction of probability theory and the development of computer analysis techniques by H. Cedergren and D. Sankoff in 1972. Using the Cedergren–Sankoff program one can easily estimate from data the probabilistic effects of constraints on the operation of a variable rule. The techniques used to make this estimation, however, require fairly sizable amounts of data. Therefore, most of the early studies using this program had data bases that grouped individuals together, rather than keeping them distinct (see, for example, Cedergren, 1973; G. Sankoff, 1973). This procedure was appropriately criticized by Bickerton (1973a,b) and others, since it makes it difficult to tell whether the observed variation is in fact present in the speech of individuals, rather than being simply the artifact of lumping together disparate, but internally homogeneous, individuals.

This criticism raises again our original question in a slightly different form: Is variation in the speech community the result of the diversity of the group, reflecting the organization of society into a number of discrete lects within which variation is at a minimum, or is this variation present with identical uniform structures in the speech of every individual? The truth, as it usually does, no doubt lies somewhere between these two extremes. The Baileyan "wave model" (Bailey, 1973, 1974), in which all variation is automatically viewed as a stage of a change in progress, essentially adopts the former view, considering individuals, and rule environments, to be hierarchically organized, with change gradually diffusing through contiguous environments and contiguous people. For a given speaker, variation is confined to a few environments per rule and different speakers may be ranked according to which environments are variable and which categorical. Our development of the variable rule analysis in the present study has benefited from the questions raised by Bailey and Bickerton concerning individual differences, and attempts to deal with some of these issues empirically.

A variable rule accounts for patterned variation in language by positing that every possible constraint on the rule has an associated probability as to whether or not the rule will apply. For a given instance, the overall probability of rule application is obtained by multiplying (or summing) the effects of all the constraints present in the environment, and over the long run the proportions of the different variants used in a given environment should reflect this overall probability. In this approach categorical rules (or constraints) have probabilities of 1 or 0. Linguistic change is viewed simply as a change of the values of some or all of the constraint probabilities. "Reweightings" of constraints are easily described in numerical terms. Bailey's model for the evolution of a rule, like the models considered in Labov (1972a) is also easily describable in these terms: Initially the rule has a probability of 0 in all environments; then the probabilities gradually increase, at first in a few environments, then in others, until they arrive at 1, first for the earliest environments, then for the later ones. This course could also be reversed or arrested, yielding stable variable rules which persist for a long time. However, it is clearly unjustified to assert that all presently stable variable rules are stagnated relics of earlier changing ones, especially in the case of a rule such as the one we will posit for final /t,d/ deletion. In the absence of any historical or contemporary evidence of change, such an assertion is unfounded speculation. But in any case, the advantage of variable rule methods of analysis is that they can be applied to a variety of such models of historical processes.

The Cedergren–Sankoff variable rule program estimates the probabilistic effect of each constraint on a rule, based on observations of the use of different forms of a linguistic variable. Descriptions of the use and applications of the program can be found in Cedergren and Sankoff's basic paper in *Language,* and in a number of further studies (including Griffin, Guy, and Sag, 1973; Guy, 1974). I will briefly recapitulate some of the terminology developed in those papers.

Any use of the variable rule program must be modeled on some proposed variable rule, and the data are tabulated in terms of whether that rule applied or did not apply (e.g., for a deletion rule, a rule application means an absence of the variable in a position where it could have occurred). A FAC-

TOR is any constraint on the rule that can be stated in the environmental description of the rule. (For example, if the first member of a final consonant cluster is a sibilant, this has an effect on the rate of final /t,d/ deletion, so this is one of the factors we code for.) A FACTOR GROUP is the set of all the possible factors that can occur at a given location in the environment of a variable. For example, final /t,d/ deletion is conditioned by the nature of the following segment, so we code a factor group for following segment consisting of the factors K (consonant), U (liquid),[1] G (glide), V (vowel), Q (no following segment—mnemonically "quiet"). (The capital letters are the computer codes we have assigned to the individual factors, and will be used throughout the chapter as convenient abbreviations for them.) A FACTOR VALUE is the probability associated with a factor which is found by the Cedergren–Sankoff program. An INPUT PROBABILITY for a rule is the probability that the rule will apply regardless of environmental constraints.

Final Stop Deletion: A Typical Variable Rule

Final consonant clusters in English that end in stops undergo a variable, conditioned process of simplification which we will describe as a final stop deletion rule. In running speech a speaker can leave out many such stops without producing incomprehension or evoking social opprobrium. The rule can be characterized roughly as

(1) $\$ \rightarrow \langle \emptyset \rangle / C \_ \#\#$

The vast majority of the stops that fall under the scope of Rule (1) happen to be /t/s or /d/s. Relatively few words in English have final consonant clusters ending in velar or labial stops, and most of those that do are cases of /sp, sk, lp, mp, lk, ŋk/. Only the apical stops can cluster with a full range of preceding consonants, including other stops. These distributional facts make it difficult to test the full range of possible deletions implied by Rule (1), since data are comparatively sparse on the labials and velars. Therefore we will restrict our quantitative study to the examination of a rule of final /t,d/ deletion, of the following form:

(2) $t,d \rightarrow \langle \emptyset \rangle / C \_ \#\#$

Although we have confined our attention to cases of word-final clusters, this rule should probably be extended to include clusters before # boundaries as

---

[1] We used "U" as the symbol for liquids in the following environment factor group to distinguish it from the "L" used as the symbol for laterals in the preceding environment factor group.

well, since we do find deletion in words such as *directly* and *expects*. Furthermore we have chosen to exclude from this rule any consideration of deletion of final /t,d/ after vowels. This process is very common for many black speakers, and possibly should be considered as a part of this same rule, but we found no unambiguous instances of it for any of our white speakers.

There are of course several other rules of consonant deletion in English. Standard English permits, among others, the following processes: combining two successive occurrences of a consonant into a single one (e.g., *black cat* = /blækæt/), deleting /t/ (and sometimes /p/ or /k/) from an *sts* cluster, leaving a long /s·/, as in *linguists* = /lingwis·/, and processes of assimilation as in *i's, tha's,* and *wha's.* Many nonstandard dialects have more extensive processes, such as VBE's final stop deletion after vowels and /l/-deletion after vocalization (e.g., *self-help* = /sef hep/). Most of these other processes also appear to be variable rules, and warrant studies in their own right.

Rule (2) as it stands incorporates none of what we know about patterned variation in the application of the rule. A number of previous studies of the rule have demonstrated that it is conditioned by such factors as whether the cluster is mono- or bimorphemic, whether a following word begins with a vowel or a consonant, *etc.* To incorporate this information, we will treat this phenomenon within the variable rule framework that has been outlined.

Studies of /t,d/ deletion have been undertaken in a variety of research contexts by Labov (1967); Labov and Cohen (1967); Labov, Cohen, Robins, and Lewis (1968); Wolfram (1969, 1971); Fasold (1972); and others. Table 1.1 summarizes the various factors that were considered in those studies and in the present one. All of the studies show considerable agreement as to the major conditioning effects on /t,d/ deletion. The conditioning factors found were the following:

1. *Grammatical Conditioning.* Many of the clusters ending in /t,d/ found in English are the result of suffixing a /t/ or /d/ representing the past tense morpheme *-ed* onto a verb ending in a consonant (e.g., *walked, fished, rained*). Such bimorphemic clusters are much more resistant to the /t,d/ deletion rule than are monomorphemic clusters (as in *expect, mist, mind*), possibly because the result of the rule would be to produce forms that were indistinguishable from present tense forms (except in the third person singular). This may be expressed as a variable conditioning on the rule according to the presence or absence of a morpheme boundary in the cluster.

A further complication is introduced, however, by those irregular verbs that have in the past tense both a vowel change AND an alveolar stop suffix, such as *tell–told, sleep–slept, leave–left,* and possibly also *go–went.* We have termed these verbs "ambiguous," referring to the ambiguity in classifying them as strong or weak verbs. They do have the inhibitory inflectional boundary before the /t,d/ (although another possible analysis suggests that they have a + boundary rather than a #), but they also have another indication

TABLE 1.1
Constraints on -t,-d Deletion: Comparison of Six Studies

	Grammatical status	Preceding environment	Following environment	Other linguistic constraints	Style	Social factors
Labov, 1967	M,P		K,V			Race
Labov & Cohen, 1967	M,P		V,~V		Casual, careful	Social class
Labov, Cohen, Robins, & Lewis, 1968	M,A,P	Obs, Son	V,~V			
Wolfram, 1969	M,P	Stop, Son, Fric	K,~K		Interview, reading	Age, race, social class, sex, racial isolation
Fasold, 1972	A,P	Fric, Son	K,V,Q	Stress		
Guy, 1974	M,A,P	S,$,N,L,F	K,U,G,V,Q	(Articulatory complexity)	Casual, careful	Geographic background

of the past tense morpheme elsewhere in the word, so that deleting the /t,d/ would not produce the communicative hazards that it would in regular "weak" verbs.

Other grammatical possibilities, which we have largely ignored, are derivational boundaries (such as the analysis of *past* as /pæs+t/, but see the parenthetical note in the preceding paragraph), and the possibly morphemic status of the /t,d/ in *first* and *second*, where they could be considered as reflexes of a dental suffix meaning "ordinal number." In the preliminary study we did investigate the *-ed*'s that occur in past participles accompanied by auxiliaries separately from those that occur in simple past tense forms, but we found no significant difference between the effects of the two types.

The earlier studies of final /t,d/ deletion all reported that grammatical conditioning had a significant effect on the rule. Labov (1967), Labov and Cohen (1967), and Wolfram (1969) considered only the monomorphemic versus bimorphemic types. Labov, Cohen, Robins, and Lewis (1968) found a three-way distinction between monomorphemic, ambiguous, and bimorphemic clusters. Fasold (1972) treated only the past tense forms, but distinguished ambiguous and bimorphemic types. Having isolated these three major grammatical classes of clusters, we set up a factor group for our variable classes of clusters, we set up a factor group for our variable rule analysis consisting of the factors M (monomorphemic cluster), A (past tense of ambiguous verb), P (past tense of regular weak verb). The expectation was that the factor values for this group would be ordered $M > A > P$, that is, that M words would have a higher probability of deletion than A words, which would in turn have a higher probability than P words.

2. *Conditioning by Following Segment.* The segment (if any) that follows the /t,d/ cluster in the speech stream has been shown to have a considerable effect on the /t,d/ deletion rule. The rule is promoted by following consonants and inhibited by following vowels. (In the latter case, resyllabification frequently appends the /t/ or /d/ to the beginning of the next word, yielding, for example, /pɪk tʌp/ for *picked up.*) Thus the general effect of the rule is to produce CVC syllable structures. Consonants and vowels are known to have these same sorts of effects on other rules; for example, in most "r-less" dialects of English prevocalic /r/ is retained whereas preconsonantal /r/ is lost.

The finer structure of this conditioning can be examined by distinguishing—essentially on an articulatory and acoustic basis—four classes of following segments (which can be further characterized by means of distinctive feature notation), namely: consonants [+cons, −voc], liquids [+cons, +voc], glides [−cons, −voc], and vowels [−cons, +voc]. If the features [+cons] and [−voc] in a following segment favor the rule, and their binary opposites disfavor it, then glides and liquids, each having one favoring and one disfavoring feature, should show effects on final /t,d/ deletion that are intermediate between consonants (with both favoring features) and vowels (with both disfavoring features).

It is, of course, also possible to have no following segment at all, that is, silence or pause. This has no distinctive analysis in terms of the two features mentioned above, hence no obvious (or "inherent") position in the effect hierarchy of the four segmental classes. It has been treated in several different ways by previous investigators.

In the three studies in which Labov was involved, the practice was to distinguish only two categories for this environment: following vowel and following nonvowel. Thus consonants, liquids, pauses (and possibly glides?) were grouped together in opposition to vowels. Wolfram (1969) took a different approach, distinguishing consonants (presumably including liquids) from nonconsonants (which expressly included pauses). Fasold (1972) distinquished three groups—consonants, vowels, and pauses—and he reported that for his speakers pause was similar in effect to consonant. In the present study we used a factor group for following environment that consisted of five factors: K (consonant), G (glide), U (liquid), V (Vowel), Q (pause).[2]

3. *Conditioning by Preceding Segment.* The previous studies have all indicated that the preceding consonant in the cluster also influences the probability of final /t,d/ deletion. Deletion generally seems to be more probable after /s/ than after other consonants. There are, of course, a variety of ways to analyze and classify the consonants, but it appears that manner of articulation is the classificatory dimension most relevant to this rule.

Labov, Cohen, Robins, and Lewis (1968) used a two-way classification: obstruents (stops and fricatives) versus sonorants (nasals and liquids). Wolfram (1969) used a three-way distinction: fricatives, stops, and sonorants (nasals and laterals). Fasold's approach was similar to Wolfram's, except in the choice of the distinctive features to distinguish the three classes. (The other studies did not address themselves to this issue.) For the present study we adopted a five-way analysis: S (sibilants), F (nonsibilant fricatives), N (nasals), $ (stops), and L (laterals). As cases of deletion after /r/ were rare or nonexistent, we decided to consider postvocalic /r/ as being essentially a vowel for purposes of this rule. Hence no provision is made for it in this factor group and L is represented entirely by /l/ in the data. This approach has proved adequate for our present study, but not totally satisfactory, and is open to possible revision.

The above are the most powerful constraints on the /t,d/ deletion rule. Other subsidiary linguistic constraints have also been noted; for example:

4. *Stress.* Unstressed syllables are more likely to be subject to final /t,d/ deletion than are stressed ones. Fasold examined this and found it to be a

---

[2] It might be considered theoretically more desirable to have used three separate factor groups ([±seg], [±cons], [±voc]) to specify the following environment. This was avoided because the distinctive feature analysis is essentially derivable from the present approach, yet it requires 6 factor codes (in 3 groups) to specify only 5 classes of following environments.

fourth-level constraint. We did not consider stress in the present study, as most of our tokens are under primary or secondary stress.[3]

5. *Rate of Speech*. Probability of deletion apparently increases in proportion to the rate of speech. We did not examine this variable since we have not yet developed a simple, reliable system for measuring and coding rate of speech in natural conversation.

6. *Length of Cluster*. There appears to be a higher probability of deletion for words with triple clusters (e.g., *mixed, next, instinct, lapsed, risked, edged*), than for those with only double clusters (*mist, filled, rift, expect, mind*). However, as words in the former category are somewhat rare (and predominantly past tense verbs) we did not examine this question quantitatively.[4]

7. *Articulatory Complexity of Cluster*. The rule also appears to be affected by what could be labeled the articulatory complexity of the cluster. The measure that I developed for this is the number of changes in point of articulation that are required to execute the cluster. We would consider an /st/ cluster, with no change in point of articulation, to be easier to produce than an /ft/ or /kt/, which each involve one change. Furthermore, we would consider a /kst/ (one change) to be simpler than an /skt/ (two changes). This measure can be extended to include the point(s) of articulation of the initial consonant(s) of the following word (if any). This extended measure has a range from 0 (as in *missed out*) to 4 (as in *asked Brown*). Such a concept helps to explain why *asked* (2 changes) is overwhelmingly produced as /ast/ (0 changes) or in the metathesized form /akst/ (1 change) rather than in the full form or (if something is to be deleted) the form with a deleted /t/, /ask/ (1 change).

We analyzed some of our data using this coding system, and the results tended to confirm the hypothesis nicely. However, this is certainly a very low-level constraint, and the great increase in the complexity of the coding and computer analysis which this system required was not justified for the main body of the study by the limited increase in accuracy which it made possible.

8. *Style*. The rule is affected by style shifting, and is less likely to apply in more formal styles. Both Wolfram (1969) and Labov (1967) studied the effect of style. We have studied it quantitatively for some speakers; the results will be discussed in what follows.

9. *Social Factors*. This rule is certainly affected by social factors. The

---

[3] I have examined the data of several individuals for a stress effect without using the computer program, and found it to be minor in comparison to the effects described above. However, uncontrolled stress differences may account for a small portion of the differences between individuals reported in Table 1.3.

[4] This is also a minor constraint, and is partly accounted for by the articulatory complexity measure.

most thorough treatment of this aspect is Wolfram (1969). He reports effects for the following factors: age, sex, race, social class, and racial isolation.[5] Labov and Cohen (1967) also report differences between social classes. In the present study, we will discuss some age, race, and geographic background factors.

The /t,d/ Deletion Rule and the Study of Variation

Some of the implications of the /t,d/ rule have already been discussed in Labov (1972b) and elsewhere, but certain points bear repetition and expansion. As Labov notes, the rule in its most general form is "an excellent candidate for a pan-linquistic grammar" (1972b, p. 82). Written in the form

$$(3) \qquad [+\text{cons}] \rightarrow \langle \emptyset \rangle \ / \ \langle +\text{cons} \rangle \ \langle \emptyset \rangle \ \_\_ \ \#\# \left\langle \begin{matrix} +\text{cons} \\ -\text{voc} \end{matrix} \right\rangle$$

it applies to a number of processes in languages other than English. Kiparsky has suggested that perhaps /t,d/ deletion and other such processes should not be considered as "rules of grammar" at all, but rather as "the result of general functional conditions impinging on speech performance"—an approach which would enable the linguist to avoid describing "language particular facts" about variation (1972, p. 233). However, as will be seen, there are aspects of this phenomenon that clearly defy "universal" or "functional" explanations.

Whether or not one wishes to consider final /t,d/ deletion as a rule such as (1), (2), or (3), the conditioning that it exhibits does reflect some well-accepted and compelling generalizations about language, such as that CVC syllables are more common (less "marked") than CVCC, and that full morphemes are less likely to be deleted than parts of morphemes. The phonological constraints on this process probably have a basis in the neurology and physiology of the human speech mechanism, and/or in the acoustic characteristics of speech and speech perception. (As an example of the latter, the high rate of deletion from /st/ clusters may well be partly accounted for by the spectral similarities of the [t] burst and the [s] noise.)

The grammatical constraints may indeed be based on primarily "functional" semantic considerations. Real problems of communication can arise if the past tense morpheme is frequently deleted in a system that generally places great emphasis on tense distinctions. There are many utterances where an -ed suffix is the only indicator of past tense and its deletion would produce a perfectly grammatical (but semantically unintended) "present

---

[5] Wolfram (1971) compares VBE and Puerto Rican speakers on this (and many other) rule(s), as well as investigating in detail many of the linguistic constraints.

tense'' string. Fortunately most discourses contain multiple indications of time reference; otherwise we would often be unable to distinguish ordinary present tense forms from past tense forms with /t/ or /d/ deleted. If final /t,d/ deletion were not grammatically constrained it might severely affect the mutual comprehensibility of many speakers. Such a problem might very well arise for some speakers of vernacular Black English who have near-categorical of final deletion /t,d/ in all preconsonantal environments, regardless of grammatical status (Labov *et al.*, 1968). The semantic effect is certainly mitigated by the richness of the VBE aspectual system, but there is in such a situation great potential for structural change, for reading problems, especially with the *-ed* suffix (Labov, 1967; Summerlin, 1972), for problems of being misunderstood by nonspeakers of the dialect, *etc.*

Structural change in the form of relexification may well have occurred for some monomorphemic words for some VBE speakers. They invariably produce such words as *test, desk* without the final stop, even producing plurals such as *tesses, desses.* For these speakers it may be correct to say that such final stops have been deleted right out of the lexicon, and that the underlying forms do not include the stop at all.[6]

Another significant aspect of this rule is the universality and uniformity of its force. It applies, to a greater or lesser extent, in virtually all native speakers of English in almost all social settings. I have noted its effect in the speech of university professors lecturing their classes, linguists delivering papers before the LSA, Nixon delivering the State of the Union message to Congress, etc. Labov (1972b) reports variable final /t,d/ deletion for 8 individuals from places as diverse as Sonora, Texas, and Lancaster, England, as well as for 11 members of a teenage Harlem peer group, the Jets. We may thus consider it quite general among all English speakers.

The ''uniformity'' of this rule across speakers lies not in absolute equivalence of rates of deletion in given environments, but rather in the ordering of the constraints within a factor group—for example, in the greater frequency of deletion before consonants than before vowels, in monomorphemic clusters than in bimorphemic ones, etc.

A rule of such force is a most instructive site for the study of variation in language. It demonstrates, first, that variation is inherent, and cannot be scrubbed out of our linguistic description by ever-finer subdivisions of the data. Even with 13 factors dividing the data into 75 possible environments, we find variation in 35–70% of those cells where it is possible (all filled cells except those with only one token, which must perforce exhibit either categorical deletion or categorical retention).[7] Second, as a consequence of

[6] However, even many speakers who have *tesses* as the plural of *tes'* have verb forms like *testing,* which would indicate that these final stops are still present in the underlying forms for such speakers.

[7] Furthermore, as more data are available on an individual, we find more and more cells exhibiting variation. Thus the 70% figure mentioned here is more typical of the larger data sets.

its uniformity, the figures obtained for groups (by adding together the data on individuals) are also uniform. The group norms are not just artifacts of the macrocosmic viewpoint, representing mere averages of a collection of widely scattered individual norms. Rather, they recapitulate the generally uniform norms of individuals.

I will present evidence for both of these assertions in what follows. At present, however, I should like to point out what this suggests for the study of variation.

For rules that do not exhibit significant differences between individuals, such as final /t,d/ deletion appears to be, Bickerton's criticisms of the study of group behavior (as opposed to the study of individuals) do not hold, and the "dynamic paradigm" methodology of constructing implicational matrices to model the spread of the rule through a community and through time is not particularly useful or insightful. Those methods seem to be more applicable to situations where there is independent evidence of historical or ongoing change.

Perhaps a modest taxonomy of problems in variation will be helpful. We can distinguish two relevant dimensions: (a) similarities and differences between individuals (within groups); and (b) similarities and differences between groups. (There are, of course, many different kinds of social groups which one might wish to examine—sex, age, ethnic group, etc.—but all of them can be accounted for by this same sort of taxonomy.)

Let us first consider cases involving the comparison of two different groups, each of which represents a sample of some speech community at a given point in space–time. In such a situation we can construct a four-celled table for comparisons of the structure of variation, shown in Table 1.2.

In Cell 1, variation is uniformly distributed throughout the community, as is partly the case for /t,d/ deletion. In Cell 2, there is variation that is different in its structure for the two different (but internally homogeneous)

TABLE 1.2
Types of Structures in Linguistic Variation

Comparing different individuals (within groups)	Comparing different groups	
	Similar	Different
Similar	1. Variable rule of uniform force	2. Social or geographic dialects
Different	3. Individually stratified linguistic variation	4. Combinations of 2 and 3, or true free variation

groups. Where these groups differed only in geographic location, we would have a case of dialect difference. If we were comparing different social classes, or geographically defined groups that also differed in their social makeup (as would be the case in a comparison, say, of Westchester County and New York City speakers), it could be a case of sociolinguistic variation. If we were comparing different age groups, it could be a case of sound change in progress. Certain aspects of final /t,d/ deletion would fall in Cell 2.

In Cell 3, where different groups show similar structures but there is a large variety of norms for the individuals within them, possibly even a different norm for each individual, there would be found variables that are "individually stratified," a "polylectal" situation where the group structure arises from the regular relationships among the lects. This is, of course, the situation that Bailey and Bickerton postulate for society as a whole. A typical example of this type of variation would be a post-creole continuum, where the interesting fact is not that the individuals differ, but that they can be arranged in a regular hierarchy. Of course, in a sense each lect may characterize a group in itself. The difference between such proposed groups and more conventional social groups is that the lectal grouping is impossible to define by reference to any extralinguistic social fact. Furthermore, socially defined groups are usually quite limited in number, whereas the number of possible lects often exceeds the number of individuals.

In Cell 4, one finds possible combinations of Types 2 and 3, and possible cases of true "free variation," and possible cases of individual stylistic differences mixed with intergroup differences.

Obviously, variable rule analysis of group data will only be appropriate for variation of Types 1 and 2. For Types 3 and 4, the analysis would have to begin with some treatment of individuals, possibly then scaling or grouping them in some way. The methods of implicational scaling are expressly designed for this purpose. Where data on individuals are sufficient, an alternative approach would be an initial variable rule analysis of the individuals with subsequent scaling. The constraints on the /t,d/ deletion rule show primarily Type 1 variation with some Type 2. Most residual variation between individuals is probably the product of insufficient data.

The Output of the Cedergren–Sankoff Program

The comprehensive results of our variable rule analysis of individuals using the Cedergren–Sankoff program are shown in Table 1.3.[8] For every individual, a factor value (probability that the rule will apply—or not apply—if the factor is present in the environment of a token) is given for each

[8] The appendix gives the results of a preliminary study, which is described in an unpublished manuscript by Guy.

TABLE 1.3
Factor Values for 18 Individuals

	Input	M	A	P	K	U	G	V	Q	S	$	N	F	L	Number of tokens
Philadelphians															
Vince V. 21, SP[a]	1.00	1.00	.99	.40	1.00	.73	.23	.22	.08	.88	.65	1.00	0.00	.45	201
Rose V. 47, SP	.80	1.00	.62	.50	1.00	.99	.83	.43	.14	.34	0.00	.80	.50	1.00	175
Dorothy B. 52, SP	1.00	1.00	.71	.53	1.00	.83	.51	.43	.03	.89	1.00	.73	.72	.51	260
Walt B. 21, SP	1.00	1.00	—	1.00	.89	1.00	.89	.65	.31	1.00	.35	.62	.45	0.00	145
Rose P. 58, SP	1.00	1.00	1.00	.43	.50	1.00	1.00	.85	.15	.50	1.00	1.00	—	0.00	48
Josephine P. 42, SP	1.00	.94	1.00	.53	.52	1.00	.36	.66	.43	.91	.76	1.00	.38	.94	109
Franny P. 14, SP	1.00	1.00	1.00	0.00	1.00	0.00	.55	.66	.44	1.00	0.00	.68	1.00	.61	68
Alice B. 48, CH	.99	1.00	.97	.40	1.00	.87	.53	.28	.05	.96	1.00	.65	0.00	.70	280
Joanne H. 27, CH	.93	1.00	.87	.10	1.00	.75	.57	.21	.04	1.00	.98	.72	1.00	.58	566
Karen A. 9, KP	1.00	1.00	1.00	.17	1.00	0.00	.53	1.00	.31	1.00	1.00	.44	—	.41	45
Mark W. 12, KP	.90	1.00	.34	.67	1.00	—	.93	.96	.52	.98	.71	1.00	—	.78	66
Bruce H., Jr. 10, KP	1.00	1.00	1.00	.25	1.00	1.00	.89	.52	.22	1.00	1.00	.39	0.00	.12	138
Kathy H. 8, KP	1.00	1.00	1.00	.17	1.00	—	0.00	.83	.11	1.00	1.00	.55	—	—	53
Philadelphia immigrants															
Joyce H. 32, KP	1.00	1.00	.72	.66	1.00	.34	.48	.42	.15	1.00	.33	.63	0.00	0.00	224
Bruce H., Sr. 36, KP	.79	1.00	.26	.94	.98	.55	1.00	.30	.08	.72	.48	.84	1.00	0.00	230
New Yorkers															
Chris A. 73	1.00	.60	1.00	.11	1.00	.75	.31	.34	.54	.94	.75	1.00	1.00	.78	129
Jacob S. 57	.77	1.00	.60	.41	.88	.52	1.00	.66	.85	1.00	.89	.83	0.00	.26	92
Leon A. 35	1.00	1.00	.70	.78	.46	.75	1.00	.38	.84	.44	.48	1.00	.69	0.00	95

[a] SP = South Philadelphia, CH = Cherry Hill, KP = King of Prussia.

constraining factor on which data was available. For a given environment, the probability that the rule will apply is obtained by multiplying together the factor values of all the factors present in that environment: Thus,

$$p = p_0 \times p_1 \times p_2 \times p_3 \times \cdots \times p_n$$

where p is the overall probability of rule application in a given environment, p_0 is an input probability,[9] and p_1, p_2, p_3, . . . , p_n are the probabilities associated with factors 1, 2, 3, . . . n in that environment.

The model whose formula I have just given is called the APPLICATION PROBABILITIES MODEL, as it is based on the probabilities that the rule will apply. As those who are familiar with it are aware, the Cedergren–Sankoff program also makes available for the analysis of any data set a NONAPPLICATION PROBABILITIES MODEL. In this second model,

$$p = 1 - [(1 - p_0) \times (1 - p_1) \times (1 - p_2) \times \cdots \times (1 - p_n)]$$

is the formula for the probability of rule application in a given environment. The program also supplies a chi-square measure of the goodness of fit of each model to the data. In our studies of final /t,d/ deletion we have found that the applications model almost always shows the lower chi-square value—the better fit. The fit of the nonapplications model is sometimes so poor as to obscure obvious relationships; it frequently picks out only the highest-ordered constraints. Therefore I have ignored it entirely in this chapter, and will report only the results of the applications model.

The final column of Table 1.3 reports for each individual the total number of tokens on which the results for them are based.

Analytical Methodology

The output of Cedergren–Sankoff variable rule analyses of a number of speakers will inevitably show some variety. Our results, presented in Table

[9] The input probability, p_0, is reported for each subject. As it was originally conceived, this value was intended to represent the probability that the rule would apply regardless of environment, and was supposed to serve as a collector for residual social variation. These ends have not been too well achieved in actual practice. Since p_0 is considered to be in the environment of every cell, for any set of data containing a cell showing categorical deletion, p_0 cannot be less than 1 (for the applications model). Otherwise, it would be impossible to predict accurately those categorically deleted cells, as an input probability value of less than 1 is equivalent to the statement that categorical rule application never occurs—every cell shows some retention of full forms. Since with the relatively small amounts of data we were able to obtain on our individuals it was almost inevitable that there should be several 0 out of 1 cells in every data set, the input probabilities are almost always at 1.00. Where they are not, it is more a measure of the largeness of the data set than the "overall pattern" of the speaker. The only way to overcome this problem is to have very sizable amounts of data in every cell.

1.3, are for certain factors very diverse. This presents several problems. On the practical side, there is the problem of trying to reduce this mass of numbers into a manageable, comprehensible form. More substantively, we want to know what it all means, how much of this diversity reflects actual differences between speakers, and how much is due to mere statistical fluctuation and smallness of sample size. Finally, we want to know how well the individuals mirror the behavior of the group, and vice versa. Answering this range of questions will require a variety of techniques. We have developed several which have proved to be very useful.

The first thing we had to know about the /t,d/ deletion rule was what regularities existed in the relationships between factors within factor groups (i.e., whether the value of M was always greater than the value of P, K always greater than V, etc.). This information was obtained from a pairwise comparison chart for all possible intragroup factor comparisons, which is prepared as follows (see Figure 1.1): A "1" is entered in the appropriate cell wherever the factor at the top of the column is GREATER than the factor to the left of the row. If two factors are equal, a "–" is entered in the relevant cell below the diagonal. Thus a speaker who had values K > G > U > V = Q would be entered as illustrated in Figure 1.1. In Figure 1.1, the K (at the top of the chart) is greater than all other factors, hence all the cells below it have a "1" entered. The U is greater than only V and Q, so only those two cells in the second column have "1" entered. Since V and Q are equal, we enter a "–" at the bottom cell of the fourth column, and so on. After all these comparisons have been entered for all speakers, we order the factors according to the most regularly observed pattern, so as to produce a chart with the maximum number of marks below the diagonal. The result for this study is shown in Figure 1.2. For the ordering shown in Figure 1.2, all the cells below the diagonal represent the preferred relationships, and any marks in the other half of the chart are deviations from the majority pattern. Furthermore, the farther a deviation is from the diagonal, the more deviant it will be considered.

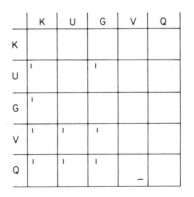

FIGURE 1.1 *Sample pairwise comparison chart.*

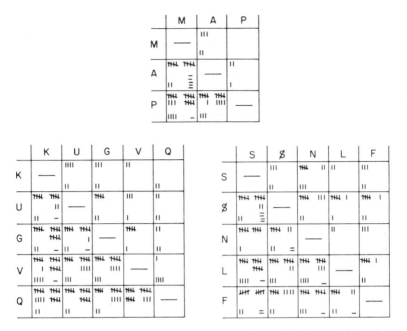

FIGURE 1.2 *Pairwise comparisons of factors. New Yorkers coded in lower left-hand corner of each cell.*

From such a display a summary of the pairwise comparisons can be obtained, as is shown in Table 1.4. The three numbers in each cell represent the number of people who had the factor written above the cell respectively greater than, equal to, or less than, the factor to the right of the cell. On the basis of these two displays we can establish a very strongly ordered relationship of M > A > P, and of K > U > G > V > Q. For the preceding environment factor group, a more weakly ordered relationship is found, with much larger numbers of deviations: S > $ > N > F > L (although the positions of N and F are somewhat questionable, and must be further examined).

There are several other obvious facts to be noted about Figure 1.2 and Table 1.4. In Figure 1.2 we observe the striking fact that most of the "deviant" relationships in the Q column are found for New Yorkers. This implies a dialect difference, which will be discussed further. Also in Figure 1.2 we note the large number of individuals who have M equal to A. We will discuss this "high-A dialect" at some length. Finally, in Table 1.4 it should be observed that although the ordering of a factor with respect to its immediately adjacent factors is not always very strong, ordering with respect to the second or third factor above or below it in the hierarchy is always quite good.

The question that now arises is, how many of the observed deviations from the regular (i.e., majority) pattern are due to small amounts of data on a

TABLE 1.4

Pairwise Comparison of Constraints on -t,-d Deletion for 19 Philadelphians and 4 New Yorkers[a]

M

10–5–3 / 2–0–2	A		
18–1–0 / 4–0–0	16–0–2 / 3–0–1	P	

K

12–1–4 / 2–0–2	U			
15–1–3 / 2–0–2	11–1–5 / 2–0–2	G		
16–1–2 / 4–0–0	14–0–3 / 3–0–1	14–0–5 / 3–0–1	V	
19–0–0 / 2–0–2	15–0–2 / 2–0–2	17–0–1 / 2–0–2	18–0–1 / 0–0–4	Q

S

12–4–3 / 2–0–2	$			
10–0–7 / 1–0–3	7–2–8 / 2–0–2	N		
10–2–3 / 2–0–2	9–0–6 / 2–0–2	10–0–3 / 3–1–0	F	
15–1–2 / 4–0–0	12–0–6 / 3–0–1	13–1–2 / 4–0–0	6–1–7 / 2–0–2	L

[a] Top line in each cell represents Philadelphians; bottom line in each cell represents New Yorkers. Each group of three numbers shows respectively the number of individuals who had the first factor greater than, equal to, and less than the second factor for that cell.

particular factor? For example, suppose we had a deviant value for F that was based on a data set that included plenty of data on all the other factors, but only 5 tokens of /ft/ or /vd/ clusters. The deviance of such a value would very likely be a result of insufficient data, and one would attribute much less significance to it than to a deviant F value that was based on, say, 35 tokens.

We can begin to answer this question with a version of the pairwise comparison chart that also includes a third dimension for number of tokens. This is done in Figure 1.3, which shows the comparisons of factor pairs plotted against the smaller number of tokens for the pair. For any pair x–y, a "1" is entered if $x > y$, a "–" is entered if $x = y$, and a "0" is entered if $x < y$. For example, if an individual had K > V, with 52 tokens of K and 35 tokens of V, a "1" would be entered in the K–V row at the 35th column (since, presumably, no comparison is stronger than its weaker link).

From Figure 1.3 it is immediately obvious that most of the deviations

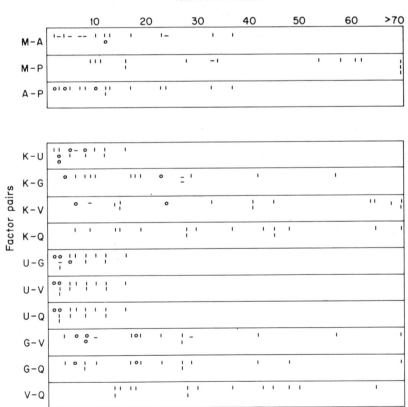

FIGURE 1.3 *Pairwise comparisons of factors by data quantity.*

TABLE 1.5
Percentage Distribution of Expected Orderings in Figure 1.3

Factor group	Number of tokens			
	0–5	6–15	16–35	36+
MAP	50%	73%	85%	100%
KUGVQ	56%	81%	80%	100%
N	8	15	13	9
	27	48	36	31

from the majority pattern for the grammatical status and following environment factor groups occur in the range below 10 tokens. Above 10 tokens there is 90% comformity with the expected pattern, whereas below 10 tokens only 63% of the relationships are as expected. Above 35 tokens, there is 100% conformity.[10] The percentage distribution of deviations is shown in Table 1.5.

These observations clearly demonstrate the inadequacy of statements based on small amounts of data. For this particular rule, an acceptable, reproducible level of accuracy is not obtained until each factor has at least 10 tokens representing it. Furthermore, each factor should be represented by, say, 4 or more cells; it would not be too useful to have 20 tokens on a factor, but all crammed into a single cell.

There are three ways to meet these requirements. First, one can limit the number of factors analyzed, concentrating on what appear to be the major effects, and ignoring (or preferably, combining with other factors) those factors with minimal amounts of data. Second, one could simply try to obtain sufficiently large volumes of speech from each informant. Most interviews reported for sociolinguistic surveys to date have been between 30 min and 1 hour long. For a good study of /t,d/ deletion, interviews of at least 2 hours are required. In our field work in Philadelphia, Payne developed techniques which yielded interviews of up to 3 or 4 hours in length, providing sufficient data for individual studies of a wide variety of linguistic problems (Payne, 1974).

A third way of obtaining sufficient data for a variable rule analysis is of course to lump together the data for several people. In some studies this will be the only possible way of obtaining sufficient data for a valid analysis. Hopefully the results reported here will shed some light on the question of

[10] For the preceding environment factor group, some deviations occurred at substantially higher levels of data quantity. This is probably due to the tertiary nature of these constraints and the smaller average differences between factor values in this group.

when such a procedure is appropriate, and when one of the other two mea-
sures will be required.

Another useful and instructive way to look at the data is the individual
accuracy chart, shown in Figure 1.4. The chart provides a more global measure of the behavior of individuals and its relation to overall data quantity. In
Figure 1.4 each individual has been plotted according to the total number of
tokens in his or her data set and the number of "correctly" ordered factor

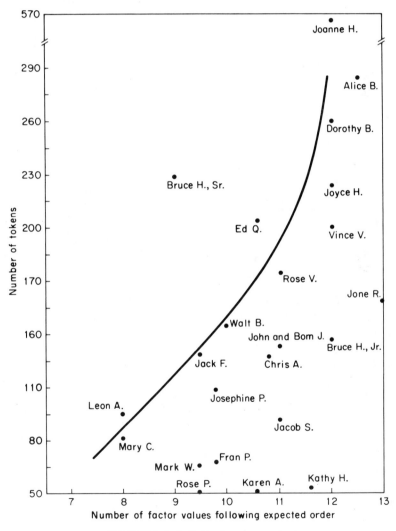

FIGURE 1.4 *Individual accuracy chart.*

values found in his or her variable rule program results.[11] (By "correctly ordered" I mean essentially "corresponding to the majority pattern.") For example, Joyce H. has 3 correctly ordered values in the MAP group, 4 in the KUGVQ group (U is too low), and 5 in SN$FL (the equivalence between F and L is not considered to be an incorrect ordering) for a total of 12 (see Table 1.3 for the numbers). Hence she is plotted on Figure 1.4 at the point for 12 correct values and 224 tokens.

Figure 1.4 clearly indicates a trend for improved reliability in factor values with increasing amounts of data. On the basis of such a trend we should be able to draw a line indicating the minimum level of accuracy to be expected in a data set of any given size. The curve drawn in Figure 1.4 may be taken as a rough approximation of such a line. Anyone above or to the left of that line would represent a significant deviation from the general pattern; there would be more deviations in their results than could be accounted for by mere random fluctuation, given the quantity of data available. It is interesting and instructive to note that the only people to the left of the line drawn in Figure 1.4 are non-Philadelphians, who presumably have different dialectal norms which account for some of their "deviations." (The worst level of "accuracy" [i.e., the maximum deviance] for the largest amount of data is Bruce H. Sr., who has the most eclectic dialect history of any of our subjects, having spent various portions of his youth in northeastern Pennsylvania, Newark, Philadelphia, and King of Prussia.)[12]

We have seen, then, that the individual accuracy diagram is a useful display which provides a quick way of estimating whether or not deviations from the norm in a set of factor values may be due to random fluctuation and insufficient data. But it must be borne in mind that this is a rather coarse measure. It is not corrected for any of the facts that might affect the significance or insignificance of the deviations, such as the quantitative magnitude of the incorrect orderings, which points are incorrectly ordered, and the amount of data on which an incorrectly ordered point is based. Frequently we find a set of "deviations" that are in a common direction and may have a linguistic explanation. Some of these have been corrected for in Figure 1.4,

[11] The following procedures were used to arrive at the values shown in Figure 1.4: Factors whose values were equal (to within ±.03) to that of a factor adjacent in the expected order were eliminated from consideration (they were considered neither "correct" nor "incorrect"); where an individual had less than 13 factors on which to base the abscissa of Figure 1.4, their number of correct points was adjusted upwards to reflect a base of 13 factors; to determine the number for the preceding environment factor group, only a partial ordering of the factors was used—$ was considered only in relation to S; L and F were not compared to each other; this was done as a partial correction for the tertiary nature of these constraints.

[12] Dialect history alone, however, probably does not account for the number of reversals of expected factor orderings found in Bruce H.'s results. Two of his deviant factors, A and F, had very small numbers of tokens. His results as a whole are somewhat unreliable in that the program did not "converge" (i.e., did not actually reach a final solution for a "best possible fit").

but others, such as the high F value which accounts for Joanne H.'s one incorrectly ordered point, have not been. The fact that the relationships in the MAP and KUGVQ factor groups are much more stable than those in the SN$FL group is not taken into account. This display of the results can be very useful, but one must be aware of its limitations.

So far our analysis has been strictly qualitative. Now we shall take a quantitative look at the actual numbers involved. Two types of graphic display suggest themselves. First, we can continue the pairwise comparisons developed in Figures 1.2 and 1.3 but using the numerical difference of the two values instead of just noting which is the larger. Plotting the difference against the smaller number of tokens for the pair (just as in Figure 1.3), we obtain a display such as those shown in Figures 1.5, 1.6, and 1.7. These quantitative factor pair charts should show values scattered over a wide range for small amounts of data (because of random fluctuation), but a narrowing down of the range for larger amounts of data, if what we are examining is at all stable. Generally speaking, the scatter of points should fall under a bell-shaped curve, whose peak would presumably represent the true behavioral norm, the ideal difference between the two factors being compared.

Figures 1.6 and 1.7 show such a pattern very nicely. For Figure 1.6, which compares the G and V factors, the width of the range is 1.48 below 20 tokens but only .73 above 20 tokens (and 7 of the 8 people above 20 tokens lie within a range of only .39). Similarly for Figure 1.7, which compares K and Q, the range width below 30 tokens is .8, whereas above 30 tokens it is only .16. What we also expect for such charts is that the individual values at the peak for maximum numbers of tokens should correspond closely to the values obtained from the amalgamated data for the whole group. This is the

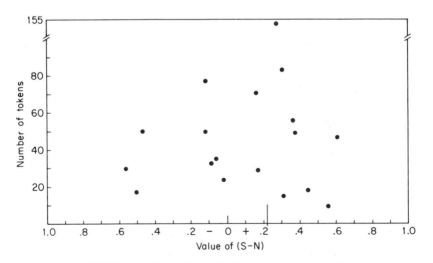

FIGURE 1.5 *Distribution of S–N values by data quantity.*

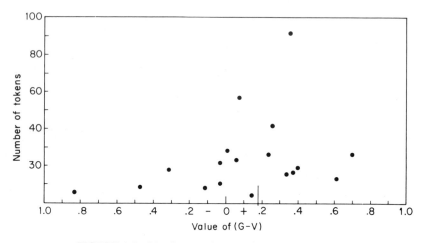

FIGURE 1.6 *Distribution of G–V values by data quantity*

case for Figures 1.6 and 1.7, where the vertical line indicates the group value. These constraint orders, K > Q, G > V certainly appear to be among the more stable relationships found for this rule.

The case is not as clear for Figure 1.5, however. There the comparison is for the factors S and N, which are not as "strictly ordered" as the pairs considered in Figures 1.6 and 1.7. The entire preceding segment factor group shows much greater variability and many more "incorrect orderings" than the other two factor groups, as can be readily seen in Figure 1.2 and Table 1.4.

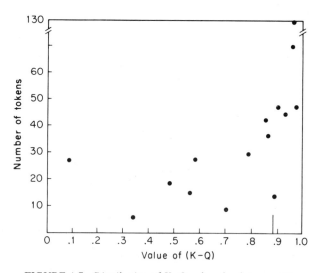

FIGURE 1.7 *Distribution of K–Q values by data quantity.*

Of course, this might be expected in a language such as English, where there is a very general tendency toward processes of anticipatory assimilation, and preceding environment is usually less significant for phonological rules than following environment. Because this factor group has less effect on the rule than the others, there tends to be a smaller average difference between factors in this group, which would produce more "overlapping" (apparent reversals of order) due to random fluctuation alone. All this is reflected in Figure 1.5, where the narrowing and peaking of the distribution occurs only above 50 tokens, if at all. It is possible that the group data in Figure 1.5 represents only an average value, rather than a behavioral norm toward which everyone should tend if we had sufficient data on them. It might be the case, however, that even Figure 1.5 would begin to peak if we had enough people with large amounts of data.

Another, perhaps more obvious, way to display the quantitative data is simply to plot all the individuals' values for a given factor against the number of tokens. This is done in Figure 1.9 for the P factor and Figure 1.8 for the A factor. If people are randomly fluctuating around a central value, the scatter of points in such a chart should also fall under an ordinary bell-shaped curve. This is essentially the case in Figure 1.9, with the notable exception of Joanne H., who clearly has a different norm for this factor. The other values shown on the chart, however, show with increasing numbers of tokens a convergence of the P value on a figure between .4 and .5, which is precisely where the P values for the group data fall. The scatter of points in Figure 1.8, however, is obviously quite different. There is clearly a bimodal distribution of values for the A factor, indicating two discrete norms for treating these

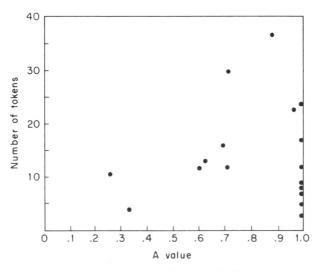

FIGURE 1.8 *Distribution of A values by data quantity.*

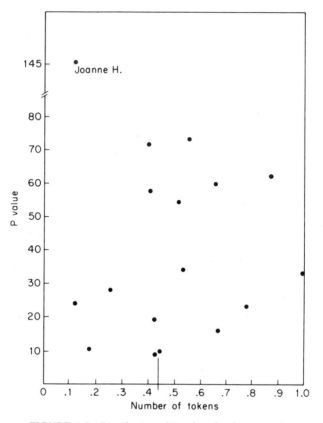

FIGURE 1.9 *Distribution of P values by data quantity.*

"ambiguous" verbs. It is significant that we find this bimodal distribution for precisely that factor for which our linguistic analysis suggests two possible interpretations. This pattern will be further discussed.

In using all these graphical methods, our goals are both methodological and substantive. As a practical matter, we wish to discover how much data is required in order to achieve a reasonable degree of reliability and accuracy in the factor values. In this regard, the figure of 30 tokens per factor seems to be an appropriate goal if reliable results are to be obtained.[13] But additionally, we wish to establish certain things about the relationship between the individual and the group: what the predominating relationships among factors are, how generally these are found in the speech of individuals, what central values there are, if any, toward which factor values for both groups and individuals tend when enough data is available, and whether there are differences between groups, such as social class or dialectal patterns.

[13] It is interesting to note that $N = 30$ is the approximate dividing line between "large" and "small" samples in statistics; below this figure different tests of significance (such as the t-test) must be used.

Analysis and Discussion

Social and Geographic Dialects

One of the most striking facts about Table 1.4 is the difference in the position of the Q factor between the New Yorkers and the Philadelphians. All 4 of the New Yorkers have Q greater than V; this is true of only 1 of the 19 Philadelphians. Two New Yorkers have Q greater even than K, whereas not one Philadelphian does. This is a clear example of a genuine dialect difference (Type 2 in the taxonomy presented in Table 1.2). For the New Yorkers, a following pause is like a following consonant in its effect on final /t,d/ deletion: It promotes it. This finding essentially corroborates Labov's practice in the original two New York studies of grouping Q together with K in opposition to V.[14] For the Philadelphians, however, Q is an extremely conservative environment, even more so than a following vowel.[15] (This can also be seen from Figure 1.7 which shows the amount by which K exceeds Q for the Philadelphians—for most of them this amount falls between .7 and .96, out of a maximum possible 1.0.) The group figures summarize this dialect difference:[16]

	K	V	Q
3 white New Yorkers	1.0	.56	.83
9 white Philadelphians	1.0	.38	.12

Let us consider the significance of this finding for linguistic theory. In all our studies, K and V are rigidly ordered, as are U and G where data on them is sufficient. The distribution of Q values, however, is highly variable, and to a certain extent bimodal. This tends to strengthen Labov's suggestion that the consonant–liquid–glide–vowel constraint hierarchy might be a universal one. The pause, however, is physically, acoustically, and functionally outside the K–U–G–V system, and therefore is susceptible to differing analyses by different speakers or dialects. Kiparsky's suggestion that observed patterns of variation might be accounted for by universal functional conditions

---

[14] However, Labov's New York City speakers were black, and there is evidence for a VBE pattern for this rule distinct from the SE pattern of middle-class whites, as will be discussed.

[15] This low-Q pattern was also found in a study of 8 white speakers from the southern and southwestern United States.

[16] The figures for the group of 19 Philadelphians illustrate the same point:

	K	V	Q
19 Philadelphians	1.00	.40	.19

But this group includes two black speakers (Johnny and Bom J.) who have Q values that are very high, although still the lowest in the factor group:

K	V	Q
1.00	.79	.75

is clearly untenable for a case such as the Q factor. Though it may one day be possible to explain the K–U–G–V pattern by reference to the sort of conditions Kiparsky has in mind, the effect of pause is arbitrarily defined for a given dialect—it must be learned by children acquiring a dialect, and must be accounted for in the grammar of a dialect. Clearly it is impossible to write "descriptively adequate" grammars that pay no attention to variation.

These facts about the dialectal differences in the effect of pause may account for the different treatments of it by Labov and Wolfram. As I have noted, Labov treats Q as being equivalent to K, whereas Wolfram treats it as being equivalent to V.[17] Fasold treats the three separately, and reports that K and Q are roughly equivalent. It may well be that Wolfram's speakers were predominantly of the low-Q type like the present sample of Philadelphians. However, the high-Q pattern appears to be typical of black speakers as well as of New Yorkers. Fasold's black Washingtonians, the black New Yorkers studied in Labov, Cohen, Robins, and Lewis, and the black Philadelphians that we have studied (cf. Note 16) all typically show high rates of /t,d/ deletion before a pause. If this is a general feature of Black English, Wolfram's speakers would be unusual in their divergence.

Uniformity

Table 1.6 shows the group values for

1. Seven South Philadelphians: Vince and Rose V., Dorothy and Walt B., and Josephine, Rose and Franny P.
2. Nine Philadelphia adults: the 7 people in Group 1 plus Joanne H. and Alice B.
3. An earlier "cosmopolitan" sample of 15 individuals from a variety of dialect regions, including some Philadelphians (Jack F., Jane R., Johnny and Bom J., and Mary C., none of whom appear in Groups 1 or 2)
4. Nineteen Philadelphians, including all the people in Group 2, all the Philadelphians in Group 3 plus 4 children and 1 adult from King of Prussia (a Philadelphia suburb—see Payne, 1974): Bruce H. Jr., Kathy H., Mark W., Karen A., and Joyce H.

Also in Table 1.6 we have repeated the figures for the one individual for whom we have very large amounts of data, Joanne H.[18] (Her data are also included in Groups 2 and 4.)

---

[17] These scholars presumably based their decisions on preliminary inspections of the data, which could possibly have been in error.

[18] The large quantities of data on Joanne H. and Alice B. were obtained by Payne during a study which was designed to collect on tape a substantial body of natural speech. Payne's method was to accompany the subject throughout most of a normal day, taping virtually everything the subject said in that time. This material was tremendously valuable for the present study, and has many other possible uses as well.

TABLE 1.6
Comparison of Group and Individual Factor Probabilities

	Input	M	A	P	K	U	G	V	Q	S	$	N	F	L	Number of tokens
1. 7 South Philadelphians	.80	1.00	.78	.51	1.00	.93	.58	.55	.20	1.00	.68	.88	.62	.67	1009
2. 9 Philadelphia adults	.86	1.00	.82	.39	1.00	.86	.56	.38	.12	1.00	.84	.78	.69	.66	1860
3. Cosmopolitan sample—15 speakers	.79	1.00	.91	.49	1.00	.89	.60	.36	.53	1.00	.86	.65	.44	.57	1931
4. 19 Philadelphians	.87	1.00	.97	.44	1.00	.77	.59	.40	.19	1.00	.81	.76	.46	.62	2886
5. Joanne H.	.93	1.00	.87	.10	1.00	.75	.57	.21	.04	1.00	.98	.72	1.00	.58	566

The close correspondence among the sets of figures in Table 1.6 is further indication of the striking uniformity of this rule. There is total unanimity as to the three factors that maximally promote the rule—M[onomorphemic], following K, and preceding S. For the two factor groups that are generally considered to contain the "highest order" constraints on this rule—grammatical status and following environment—there is no overlap whatsoever in the ranges of factor values within a group (except for the high-Q value in Group 3, which included high-Q speakers). The values for K–U–G–V in all data sets indicate that the [±cons] feature is unanimously given greater weight than the [±voc] feature. Only in the third factor group—preceding environment—is there much overlap in the ranges of factor values. But despite this overlapping, there is good agreement as to the ordering of the factors in the S$NFL pattern, excepting only that factor on which we have the least amount of data, F. Although the evidence from the individual analyses suggested that F should be placed between N and L in this hierarchy, only one of the group analyses shown in Table 1.6 shows that order. The other four factors in this group all follow the expected S–$–N–L order for all five data sets in Table 1.6, except for the reversal of $ and N in the first data set.

Besides F and Q, the only factors that show relatively wide ranges of values are P and V. These are respectively the most and second most conservative environments in their respective factor groups. It seems that the range of values that they display may be reflecting social class differences between the speakers. Apparently the most socially marked environments for deletion are the most conservative ones; middle class "respectable" speakers correct their /t,d/ deletion mainly by tending toward categorical retention in past tense and prevowel and prepause environments, while leaving their behavior in other environments unchanged. If such is the case the mark of a "proper" speaker will be a large difference between the factor values for the most and least conservative environments.

The high degree of correspondence between the group values and the individual values of Joanne H. is further evidence that speakers have essentially identical norms for final /t,d/ deletion, and that one only needs to obtain large amounts of data to demonstrate this fact. We feel that for most of the constraints on this rule (and other cases of "Type 1" variation) differences between individuals are primarily random perturbations due to paucity of data rather than real behavioral differences.

These results shed some light on some of the theoretical issues about variation that were discussed in the beginning of the chapter. As I mentioned, Bickerton and others have objected to the practice of using group data in studying variation. These writers assert that much of the "apparent variation" found in several variable rule analyses by other researchers using group data is the result of an inappropriate lumping together of different speakers and different conditioning environments. The primary orientation of this "dynamic paradigm" is toward producing "polylectal grammars" whose rules are categorical, or variable in at most only one or a few environments per speaker per rule. For a linguist working in this paradigm, persistence of massive variation is an indication that another conditioning factor or another way of dividing up the data must be found. As I have already suggested, such a search for the lect free of variation is inappropriate for many important areas of linguistic research. Further, the results of my investigations of data quantity indicate clearly that to subdivide the data too finely—by limiting the scope to individuals and multiplying the number of environments—is inherently self-defeating. Patterns and regularities in the data are obscured by such a procedure, rather than revealed. Such a procedure maximizes error as it minimizes cell size. This effect is further magnified by the practice (or requirement) of the dynamic paradigm that each different environment must be considered unitary (as they are each accounted for by a separate rule), rather than as the product of several independent effects (as is the case when a single variable rule is used to describe all environments). In the former case, a given item of data contributes information only about the cell it resides in, whereas in the latter case a datum can provide information about all the conditioning factors in its environment.

The High-A Lects

There is one factor in our data for which a study based on groups rather than individuals would be misleading, in just the way that Bickerton has suggested. The data on the A factor shown in Figures 1.2 and 1.3 are unusual in that a large number of people have the value of this factor equal to the M value (with both A and M equaling 1.00). A few even have A higher than M. Figure 1.8 shows the distribution of A values by numbers of tokens. It clearly indicates a bimodal distribution—one group clusters around .70; the other puts A at 1.00. Increased numbers of tokens have no effect on this pattern.[19] (Such a bimodal pattern for this factor was first suggested by the figures for four speakers reported in Labov, 1973.)

For this factor, the group values shown in Table 1.6 clearly do represent mere averages of distinct norms. This is the sort of situation where analyses of individuals are quite necessary. But there are indications that the high-A lect may be a social class and language acquisitional pattern, just as the high-Q pattern is a feature of geographic (and possibly ethnic) dialects. If such is the case, it might be possible to redefine homogeneous groups on the basis of extralinguistic facts.

[19] The fact that Joanne H., at .87 and 37 tokens, is rather lower than the other high-A speakers does not obscure this bimodal distribution. There is still a gap of .15 between her A value and the highest value in the low-A group (the .72 of Joyce H.) into which no one falls.

The linguistic significance of the two norms for the A[mbiguous] category is clear. The group with the lower value for A has apparently perceived the ambiguity of these /t,d/-final words, and retains them somewhat more than monomorphemic /t,d/'s (since they represent the -*ed* suffix), but somewhat less than those in regular past tense verbs (since the past tense morpheme is encoded elsewhere in the word). Alternatively, we could say that these speakers have analyzed the A words as having a + boundary before the /t,d/ and have assigned this boundary a restraining effect on the rule which is about half that of the # boundary in regular verbs.

The group with a high-A value, however, has apparently begun to obliterate this irregular class of verbs, and thrown its contents in with the ordinary "strong" (i.e., ablauting) verbs. Thus *sleep, tell, leave* are identified as vowel changing verbs with past tense forms *slep', tol', lef'* just like *swim– swam*. For some of these verbs there are even direct analogies with other strong verbs; for example *feed–fed* has the same vowel change as *sleep, keep, leave*. When the irregular verbs are analyzed in this way, their final *t*'s and *d*'s are either deleted preferentially or are not even entered in the dictionary form. In the latter case they would not actually undergo deletion because they are not there to begin with.[20]

A preliminary examination of the social distribution of the "high-A" dialect reveals two promising avenues for further research. First, the tendency to delete /t,d/ preferentially in the A category seems to be stronger in the children in our sample, as can be seen from the group figures for the four King of Prussia children studied:

	M	A	P
4 King of Prussia children	.96	1.00	.35

Second, among adults this pattern appears to be a characteristic of working class speakers, and is possibly socially stigmatized. Consider, for example, the four individuals in our sample who are probably lowest in socioeconomic status, Chris Andersen of New York City and the three members of the Porta family of South Philadelphia:

	M	A	P
Chris A., 73	.60	1.00	.11
Josephine P., 42	.94	1.00	.53
Rose P., 58	1.00	1.00	.43
Fran P., 14	1.00	1.00	.00

[20] For testing this hypothesis more fully it is sometimes useful to examine the nonapplications model provided by the Cedergren–Sankoff program. There we find that for most of those individuals for whom the applications model gives M = A = 1.0, the nonapplications model reports an A value even HIGHER than the M value. This indicates that for these speakers the ambiguous words are either subject to the deletion rule even more frequently than monomorphemic words, or else have relexified underlying forms that do not contain a final /t,d/.

If these tendencies are confirmed by further investigation, they w suggest the following: Among middle class children, the high-A lect may be stage in language acquisition; after a child has learned that there are vowel-changing verbs that take no -ed suffix, he generalizes this rule to all vowel-changing verbs, and only later learns the exceptions. Among some working class speakers, however, this rule may be pushing on to completion. It clearly represents an unmarking at some level of linguistic structure. If it is not stigmatized out of existence, it could point to a future direction of change of the standard dialect. Argumentation about these /t,d/'s being absent from the underlying forms is premature at this point, however, as even the most radical of the high-A speakers have at least a few of these /t,d/'s appearing in the favorable environments (before V or Q). (Note that a factor value of 1.00 does not imply 100% deletion when that factor is present in the rule environment; rather, it signifies that the factor favors deletion more than any other in its group.)

Style Shifting

We did not attempt to analyze style shifting for most of our speakers, as the analytical techniques we were using require large amounts of data. The methods developed by Labov for eliciting a range of styles in individual interviews obtain comparatively very small amounts of data on all styles other than the relatively careful general interview style. There were two speakers for whom clearly different styles were obtainable, however.

The first was Bruce H., Sr. Throughout the first half of his interview he was stiff, careful and formal, talking constantly about formal topics, especially religion. Then he went out on family business for half an hour; when he returned he was a considerably more relaxed subject, joking and laughing freely, and concentrating on different, less formal topics. The data from his interview was coded using an additional factor group for style, with the first half of the interview coded as careful and the second half as casual.

The other speaker was Alice B., whom Payne accompanied for an entire day, recording all her interactions with other people (as described in Footnote 18). For most of the day Alice was at her job at a travel agency, and the tape records her speaking to customers and ticket agents over the phone as well as conversing with her coworkers and friends. For her we distinguished two styles: All interactions with friends, family, and coworkers were coded as a casual style, and all interactions with customers and ticket agents (primarily over the telephone) were coded as a somewhat more formal, but still necessarily very friendly, style.

The results of the style factor group for these two speakers are as follows:

	Careful	Casual
Bruce H.	.74	1.00

	Business	Casual
Alice B.	.94	1.00

Both Bruce and Alice show less deletion in their more formal styles, though the difference between the two styles is clearly more substantial for Bruce than for Alice. It is interesting to note that the effect of style shifting on this rule is thus characterizable as a general upward or downward reweighting of the probabilities of deletion for all environments, rather than as involving different treatments for different environments, and this also tends to confirm the notion of a unitary variable rule as accounting for this behavior.

Conclusions

On the practical side, we feel we have developed a powerful and useful methodology for the analysis of certain types of variation with the Cedergren–Sankoff program. We have attacked the problem of data quantity directly—on the one hand we have tried to see what level of reliability can be expected from the available data, and on the other we have exploited the interview techniques developed by Payne and other members of our research group, techniques providing longer, richer interviews as well as continued access to people as more data is required.

On the substantive side, we have demonstrated that the /t,d/ deletion rule is omnipresent in a range of English speakers, and very stable and uniform with regard to its major constraints. It does show sensitivity to lectal differences in precisely those areas where a linguistic analysis would be ambivalent. Except for those differences, we suggest that it is a stable variable rule that is uniformly compelling on all speakers, and that any indications to the contrary would be due to insufficient data.

Finally, I would like to point out the similarities between the variable rule methods employed in the present study and the calculus for determining "environment weightings" developed by Bailey in *Variation and Linguistic Theory*. Bailey's method uses integral feature weights which are summed to yield weightings which impose an order on the possible environments for a given rule. Although this method is applicable to only a small number of factors and factor groups, it is basically similar in approach to the probabilistic variable rule techniques which Cedergren and Sankoff have developed and we have employed. It is very heartening to note this convergence of methodology among linguists engaged in the study of variation.

Appendix

TABLE 1.A.1

Factor Values from a Preliminary Study

	M	A	P	K	U	G	V	Q	S	$	N	F	L	Number of tokens
Philadelphians														
Jack F.,														
60, W Phila.	.94	1.00	.47	1.00	.47	1.00	.23	.29	.75	.38	—	1.00	.72	126
Jane R., 16,														
NE Phila.	.90	1.00	.90	1.00	.39	.36	.19	.15	1.00	.75	—	.85	.64	160
Johnny & Bom,														
25, W Phila.	1.00	.69	.22	1.00	.87	.90	.79	.75	1.00	.91	.74	.50	1.00	133
Mary C., 41,														
Dorothy, NJ	.60	0.00	1.00	1.00	0.00	0.00	.48	.34	.18	.54	1.00	.10	.49	81
Non-Philadelphians														
Ed Q., 63														
Ringoes, NJ	.82	1.00	.43	.63	1.00	.32	.29	.64	.77	1.00	.83	.16	.71	205
Coleman family,														
London	.83	.60	.60	.91	—	.43	.65	1.00	1.00	.25	.34	.19	.13	101
Mr. & Mrs.														
Billie W.														
Glasgow	1.00	.48	.34	.77	1.00	.43	.24	.48	.90	1.00	.49	.69	.42	445
Hawaiian boys	1.00	1.00	.59	1.00	.76	.76	.21	1.00	1.00	.57	—	—	.59	129
7 South & SW														
US whites	1.00	.66	.28	1.00	—	.65	.44	.35	.94	.93	.69	.75	.44	648
Cosmopolitan														
sample (all														
of the above)	1.00	.91	.49	1.00	.89	.60	.36	.53	1.00	.86	.65	.44	.57	1931

Acknowledgments

This research was supported by National Science Foundation Grant GS-36382X.

References

Bailey, C.-J. N. 1972. The integration of linguistic theory: Internal reconstruction and the comparative method in descriptive analysis. In R. P. Stockwell and R. K. S. Macaulay (Eds.), *Linguistic change and generative theory.* Bloomington: Indiana University Press.

Bailey, C.-J. N. 1973. The patterning of language variation. In R. W. Bailey and J. L. Robinson (Eds.), *Varieties of present-day English.* New York: Macmillan.

Bailey, C.-J. N. 1974. *Variation and linguistic theory.* Arlington, Va.: Center for Applied Linguistics.

Bailey, C.-J. N., and Shuy R. W. (Eds.). 1973. *New ways of analyzing variation in English.* Washington, D.C.: Georgetown University Press.

Bickerton, D. 1971. Inherent variability and variable rules. *Foundations of Language, 7,* 457–492.

Bickerton, D. 1973a. Quantitative vs. dynamic paradigms: The case of Montreal 'que.' In C.-J. Bailey and R. Shuy (Eds.), *New ways of analyzing variation in English*. Washington, D.C.: Georgetown University Press.

Bickerton, D. 1973b. On the nature of a Creole continuum. *Language, 49,* 640–669.

Cedergren, H. J. 1973. On the nature of variable constraints. In C.-J. Bailey and R. Shuy (Eds.), *New ways of analyzing variation in English*. Washington, D.C.: Georgetown University Press.

Cedergren, H. J., and Sankoff, D. 1974. Variable rules: Performance as a statistical reflection of competence. *Language, 50,* 333–355.

Fasold, R. 1972. *Tense marking in Black English*. Arlington, Va.: Center for Applied Linguistics.

Griffin, P., Guy, G., and Sag, I. 1973. Variable analysis of variable data. In Language in the context of space, time and society. *University of Michigan Papers in Linguistics, 1 (2)*.

Guy, G. 1975. Use and application of the Cedergren–Sankoff Variable Rule Program. In R. Fasold and R. Shuy (Eds.), *Analyzing variation in language*. Washington, D.C.: Georgetown University Press. Pp. 59–69.

Kiparsky, P. 1972. Explanation in phonology. In S. Peters (Ed.), *Goals of linguistic theory*. Englewood Cliffs, N.J.: Prentice-Hall.

Labov, W. 1966. *The social stratification of English in New York City*. Washington, D.C.: Center for Applied Linguistics.

Labov, W. 1967. Some sources of reading problems for Negro speakers of non-standard English. In A. Frazier (Ed.), *New directions in elementary English*. Champaign, Ill.: National Council of Teachers of English.

Labov, W. 1969. Contraction, deletion, and inherent variability of the English copula. *Language, 45,* 715–762.

Labov, W. 1972a. The internal evolution of linguistic rules. In R. Stockwell and R. K. S. Macaulay (Eds.), *Linguistic change and generative theory*. Bloomington: Indiana University Press.

Labov, W. 1972b. Where do grammars stop? In R. Shuy (Ed.), *Georgetown monograph on languages and linguistics, 25,* 43–88.

Labov, W. 1975. The quantitative study of linguistic structure. In K.-H. Dahstedt (Ed.), *The Nordic languages and modern linguistics 2*. Stockholm: Almgrist & Wiksell International.

Labov, W., and Cohen, P. 1967. Systematic relations of standard and non-standard rules in the grammars of Negro speakers. In *Project literacy reports 8*. Ithaca, N.Y.: Cornell University.

Labov, W., Cohen, P., Robins, C., and Lewis, J. 1968. *A study of the non-standard English of Negro and Puerto Rican speakers in New York City*. Cooperative Research Report 3288. (Vols. 1 and 2.) New York: Columbia University. (Reprinted by U.S. Regional Survey, 204 North 35th Street, Philadelphia, PA 19104.)

Payne, A. 1974. The re-organization of linguistic rules: A preliminary report. *Pennsylvania working papers on linguistic change and variation II (6)*.

Sankoff, G. 1972. A quantitative paradigm for the study of communicative competence. Presented to the Conference for the Ethnography of Speaking, Austin, Texas.

Sankoff, G. 1973. Above and beyond phonology in variable rules. In C.-J. Bailey and R. Shuy (Eds.), *New ways of analyzing variation in English*. Washington, D.C.: Georgetown University Press.

Summerlin, N. C. 1972. *A dialect study: Affective parameters in the deletion and substitution of consonants in the deep South*. Unpublished doctoral dissertation, Florida State University.

Wolfram, W. 1969. *A Sociolinguistic description of Detroit Negro speech*. Washington, D.C.: Center for Applied Linguistics.

Wolfram, W. 1971. *Overlapping influence in the English of second generation Puerto Rican teenagers in Harlem*. Final Report on OE Grant 3-70-0033(508). Washington, D.C.: Center for Applied Linguistics.

2

Helene Neu

RANKING OF CONSTRAINTS ON /t,d/ DELETION IN AMERICAN ENGLISH: A STATISTICAL ANALYSIS

Introduction

Phonological variation is an inherent characteristic of continuous speech. Much of this variation is systematic and can be captured by phonological rules. Work stemming from Labov (1969) has proposed the notion of variable rules to account for systematic variation. Variable rules incorporate into linguistic description the predicted relative frequency of a rule's application or rankings of constraints affecting rule application depending on linguistic and extralinguistic constraints. Examination of performance data is essential if one is to identify and rank the constraints on rule application.

Identification and ranking of significant constraints is, however, more complicated than has been indicated in many of the previous studies of variation. A frequently cited example of variation is final /t,d/ deletion in English, a rule whose constraints, it has been claimed, are fairly easily ranked. This study will examine the linguistic constraints on /t,d/ deletion in consonant + /t,d/ clusters in American English, present the results of a statistical analysis, compare the results with those of other studies, and demonstrate that the problems of ranking constraints may be more complex than has been previously believed.

The importance of statistical validation of the rankings will be emphasized, and the relationship between frequency of rule application and frequency of word occurrence will be discussed.

LOCATING LANGUAGE IN TIME AND SPACE

37

e Data

A modified version of the questionnaire developed by Shuy, Wolfram, and Riley (1968) was used to elicit about 10 min of natural continuous speech from each of eight men and seven women. The informants' speech was carefully transcribed and computer coded using a quasi-phonemic alphabet which included such phonological information as segment insertion, deletion, and substitution (e.g., /r/ and /ʔ/ are included), but which did not include refined phonetic information such as vowel nasalization, plosive aspiration, or narrow differences in vowel height. The computerized transcriptions used in this study did not include information concerning stress, rate of speech, and unfilled pauses. Filled pauses, such as *uh* and *um*, were transcribed and included in the data where relevant (e.g., in the data on effect of following vowels), but they were not treated as a separate factor.

The informants ranged in age from 19 to 53 years. Five speakers were between 19 and 23, eight between 27 and 35, and two were 48 and 53 years old, respectively. Major residences listed were California (five informants); Ohio, Michigan, and Baltimore (two informants from each area); Nebraska, Missouri, Massachusetts, and New York City (one informant from each area). All but one speaker had attended college, and six of them had graduate degrees (cf. Table 2.1).

Of a total of 21,219 lexical tokens in the 150 minutes of speech, 2379—or slightly over 11.2%—of these had morpheme- or word-final base form consonant + /t,d/ clusters. Of these clusters, 162 (6.8% of all consonant + /t,d/ clusters) were instances of word-final /t,d/ followed by word-initial /t,d/ (e.g., *went to, test data*). Since it is not always clear in such clusters whether both or only one of the alveolar stops is present in the realized form, the 162 instances of /t,d/ followed by a homorganic stop have been excluded from the data. The 2217 remaining words containing consonant + /t,d/ clusters represent 10.5% of the total number of lexical items in the data set.

Occasionally, alveolar flaps or glottal stops have been transcribed for word- and morpheme-final /t,d/. These variants have been tabulated as retained /t,d/. The 20 instances of word- and morpheme-final flaps (i.e., less than 1% of all consonant + /t,d/ clusters) occur in potential /nt/ clusters—9 in morpheme-final clusters (e.g., *wanted* /wanɾ#ɪd/), 11 in word-final clusters (e.g., *front of* /frʌnɾ##ə/).

Fifty-four occurrences of final /t/ and one occurrence of final /d/ (in *second and*) were transcribed as glottal stops. Eleven of these, all word-final, occur before vowels; 3 are morpheme-final, all in *-ly* adverbs. Of the 55 consonant +/ʔ/ clusters, 33 were found in negative contractions (e.g., *don't like*). Three of these were followed by word-initial /t,d/ and so have been excluded from the data.

TABLE 2.1
Informants

Speaker	Sex	Age	Principal residence(s)	Education	Birthplace	Mother's birthplace	Father's birthplace
DP	M	19	Ohio	college	Massilon, Ohio	Mississippi	Ohio
JS	M	23	So. California	college	San Diego, Ca.	Oregon	Louisiana
JH	M	27	St. Louis, Mo.	grad. degree	St. Louis, Mo.	?	?
MB	M	28	California	college	Long Beach, Ca.	Florida	Louisiana
LP	M	29	Nebraska	grad. degree	Fremont, Neb.	Nebraska	Nebraska
ME	M	35	California	grad. degree	Coos Bay, Ore.	Oregon	Montana
EH	M	35	Baltimore, Md.	grad. degree	Baltimore, Md.	New Jersey	Maryland
JB	M	53	Ohio, Los Angeles, Ca.	college	Ohio	Ohio	Ohio
NO	F	21	So. California	college	Los Angeles, Ca.	Illinois	California
CW	F	21	La Habra, Ca.	college	Lubbock, Texas	Texas	Nebraska
NT	F	22	Lexington, Ma.	college	Geneva, Ill.	Michigan	Massachusetts
LW	F	29	Michigan	high school	Michigan	Michigan	Michigan
PM	F	30	Baltimore, Md.	college	Baltimore	Maryland	Maryland
BO	F	31	S.E. Michigan; Wisconsin	grad. degree	Ann Arbor, Mi.	Phillipines	Phillipines
EJ	F	48	New York City; Calif.	grad. degree	New York, N.Y.	New York	Iowa

Preliminary Statistical Considerations

Statistical Methods

The chi-square test has been used in a previous study by Fasold (1972) to statistically justify the ranking of factors within a factor group. Guy (this volume, Chapter 1) defines a FACTOR as "any constraint on the rule that can be stated in the environmental description of the rule." A FACTOR GROUP is the complete set of mutually exclusive factors occurring at a given location in the rule; e.g., /t,d/ deletion is constrained by the manner of articulation of a following consonant. This factor group consists of the factors sibilant, stop, nasal, fricative, and liquid.

In the present study, the chi-square test will be used to validate the ranking of constraints. In addition, a confidence level of .95 was chosen to evaluate the significance of the observed percentage of final /t,d/ deletion as estimates of the true probabilities of deletion.

For each category studied, there is some number n of instances in the data where /t,d/ deletion is possible; of these, some number c of instances of actual deletion can be counted. The ratio c/n, expressed as a percentage, gives the observed frequency of deletion. At the same time, it is assumed that each category is associated with some probability p that deletion will occur. In this conceptualization, then, c/n stands as an empirical estimate of p which improves with increasing n. Either by direct calculation based on the assumption of binomial sampling or by consulting standard tables (Pearson and Hartley, 1966), it is possible to construct a CONFIDENCE INTERVAL around c/n within which p is likely to fall. Figure 2.1 shows three examples of confidence intervals constructed around sample values of $c/n \times 100 = 5\%$, 10%, and 14% with $n = 200$ in each instance. The .95 level adopted for the confidence interval in this example is the same as that used throughout this paper. This means that there is a probability of .95 that the true probability p lies within the indicated intervals. The large size of the intervals based on a sample size of 200 may appear surprising.

Looking only at the frequencies c/n, the examples in Figure 2.1 might be ranked $a < b < c$. Note, however, that the confidence intervals for a and b and for b and c overlap, whereas those for a and c share a common boundary at $p = 9\%$. In the latter case, it can be concluded immediately that $a < c$ with probability of at least .95; because $a \geq c$ only when (but not necessarily even then) the probability for case a is larger than 9% (which event has probability $(1/2)$ $(.05) = .025$) or when the probability for case c is smaller than 9% (which event also has probability .025). More precisely, $p[a > 9\%$ and $c < 9\%] = (.975)^2 = .9506$.

The ranking for the other cases is ambiguous as far as can be determined from the confidence intervals alone. Therefore, the chi-square test can be applied to see whether a and b (or b and c) are significantly different. In the

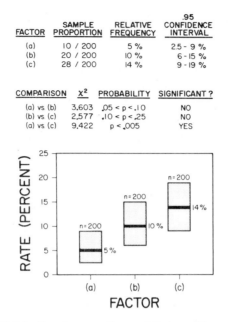

FACTOR	SAMPLE PROPORTION	RELATIVE FREQUENCY	.95 CONFIDENCE INTERVAL
(a)	10 / 200	5 %	2.5 - 9 %
(b)	20 / 200	10 %	6 - 15 %
(c)	28 / 200	14 %	9 - 19 %

COMPARISON	χ^2	PROBABILITY	SIGNIFICANT ?
(a) vs (b)	3.603	.05 < p < .10	NO
(b) vs (c)	2.577	.10 < p < .25	NO
(a) vs (c)	9.422	p < .005	YES

FIGURE 2.1   Sample proportions and their confidence intervals.

example, neither $a < b$ nor $b < c$ is found to be significant when the chi-square test is applied at the .05 level. The chi-square test applied to $a < c$ shows the ordering to be significant at even the .005 level, thus indicating that a criterion of non-overlap between .95 level confidence intervals is highly conservative. For this reason, the chi-square test was not considered necessary whenever the confidence intervals involved did not overlap.

Tests of Homogeneity across Speakers

As stated in the description of the data, the speakers studied had diverse backgrounds and could not be considered to share a common dialect. It might therefore be thought to be essential to study the results for each speaker individually, with the hope of finding some trends attributable to social or linguistic background. To test for this possibility, chi-square tests were done on the various linguistic categories of interest to check for any detectable interspeaker differences. Separate chi-square tests were performed on individual deletion rates in the entire data set as well as on different factor groups, including grammatical categories (i.e., monomorphemic, bimorphemic), following segment (i.e., consonant, vowel) and the intersection between these two groups (e.g., monomorphemic cluster followed by consonant), place of articulation of preceding consonant (i.e., [+alveolar], [−alveolar]), and deletion in the high-frequency lexical item *and*. No matter how the data set was divided into linguistic categories, the null hypothesis could not be rejected, which led to the conclusion that there was statistical justification for assuming that the population sampled was homogeneous with respect to linguistic constraints on /t,d/ deletion.

A chi-square test run to compare deletion rates among male and female speakers revealed a highly significant difference among the two groups. This difference does not invalidate the results of the chi-square tests run on the linguistic constraints affecting deletion among the total population. On the contrary, it shows that, although the entire population can be considered homogeneous, those with lower rates of deletion tend to be female, those with higher rates tend to be male, and, within each of these groups, homogeneity is even greater than within the population as a whole ($.25 < p < .5$ within each of the groups versus $p \approx .1$ within the population as a whole).

The data on final /t,d/ deletion were analyzed in two ways: (*a*) by pooling the data for all speakers, and (*b*) by treating men and women as separate populations. In the latter analysis, SIGNIFICANT rankings of constraints were never found to be reversed with respect to the rankings found in the former analysis. Occasionally, the rankings of constraints based only on observed frequencies of deletion (without reference to their statistical significance) were found to reverse as might be expected on the basis of purely random fluctuation. In some cases, rankings that were found to be significant in the total population were not significant in the separate groups due to insufficient amounts of data, even though the orderings based on frequency of deletion were the same as in the total sample. Therefore, results of the analysis of /t,d/ deletion for males and females will be presented separately only when a reversal in observed frequencies of deletion was found between the populations. Otherwise, the data from the 15 speakers have been pooled.

This study will present an analysis of those factor groups found to have the greatest influence on /t,d/ deletion in American English. These constraints include (*a*) the grammatical nature of /t,d/; (*b*) the consonantal versus vocalic nature of the following segment; (*c*) the manner of articulation of the following consonant; and (*d*) the manner and place of articulation of the preceding consonant.

Results and Discussion

Previous studies have shown that the two strongest constraints on /t,d/ deletion are (*a*) the grammatical nature of /t,d/; and (*b*) the consonantal versus vocalic nature of the following segment. Deletion is said to be favored (*a*) by the absence of a preceding morpheme boundary—that is, /t,d/ is more likely to be deleted in monomorphemic clusters than in bimorphemic clusters; and (*b*) when /t,d/ is followed by a consonant rather than a vowel.

Grammatical Constraint

The grammatical constraint is analyzed in Figure 2.2. Fasold (1972), Guy (this volume, Chapter 1), and Labov (1975) distinguish three types of clusters: MONOMORPHEMIC (e.g., *send, fast*), AMBIGUOUS (i.e., irregular past tenses such as *slept*), and PAST TENSE (i.e., clusters with a regular past tense inflection *-ed*, as in *realized*). Because previous studies analyzed only word-final /t,d/ deletion, figures for word-final and morpheme-final deletion have been listed separately. Also, because it occurs so frequently in the data, the figures for deletion in the lexical item *and* have been listed separately. Figure 2.2 shows the observed deletion rates (o.d.r.), the 95% confidence intervals, and the number of samples for each category. The figure shows that in each of word-final and morpheme-final monomorphemic clusters, roughly 32% of the final alveolar stops are deleted. Because there is no significant difference in deletion rates in these two types of clusters, they have been pooled in the rest of this study.

Deletion of final /t,d/ occurs at a significantly lower rate in bimorphemic clusters (9.3%) than in monomorphemic clusters (32.4%), with a substantial distance separating the two confidence intervals. The difference observed in this data set between ambiguous past tense clusters and regular past tense

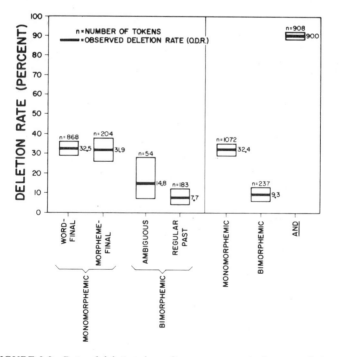

FIGURE 2.2 *Rate of deletion depending on grammatical nature of cluster.*

clusters, that is, 14.8% versus 7.7%, is shown to be not significant by the chi-square test, and the difference disappears altogether if instances of final /t,d/ followed by homorganic stops are included in the data. (A /t,d/ deletion rate of roughly 19% was observed in both ambiguous and past clusters when /t,d/ + /t,d/ clusters were included in the data.)

When the 908 instances of the lexical item *and*, which has a /d/ deletion rate of 90.9% and accounts for 41.0% of the data, are included in the monomorphemic data, the rate of deletion for monomorphemic clusters is greatly affected (deletion increases to 58.8%).

The results of this analysis are consistent with the findings of Labov (1972, 1975), Wolfram (1969), Labov *et al.* (1968), Fasold (1972), and Guy (this volume, Chapter 1), insofar as the absence of a preceding morpheme boundary (in monomorphemic clusters) is shown to favor deletion as compared to the presence of a preceding morpheme boundary (in bimorphemic clusters). However, Labov *et al.* (1968), Fasold (1972), Labov (1975), and Guy (this volume, Chapter 1) in comparing deletion rates in ambiguous and past tense clusters in their data sets, found a significantly lower deletion rate in the past tense clusters, which they attributed to the fact that when the suffix is deleted, the distinction between present and past tense is lost, whereas in ambiguous clusters the vowel change remains to indicate past tense. As was mentioned, our data did NOT show a significant difference between deletion in ambiguous clusters and past tense clusters. A possible explanation might lie in the relatively small number of tokens our data contained in these categories—a total of 237 tokens as compared to 344 in Labov *et al.* (1968), 382 in Fasold (1972), and approximately 1140 in Guy (Chapter 1). (Labov [1975] does not indicate the proportions represented by the percentages he gives in each grammatical category.) If our population size for deletion in ambiguous and past tense clusters were increased by 50% (i.e., to a total of 355 tokens) and if the same deletion rates were preserved, the distinction observed in our data would be significant at the .05 level.

Inclusion of the word *and* in the analysis of the data tends to skew the observed frequency of rule application and occasionally even the ranking of constraints, because of the extremely high frequency at which *and* occurs and at which it undergoes /d/ deletion. Therefore, it appears advisable to treat occurrences of *and* separately, since it differs so much in its behavior from the rest of the data. Except where inclusion alters the ordering of constraints (and not just frequency of rule application), further discussion of final /t,d/ deletion will be presented excluding tokens of *and* from the corpus.

Labov (1975) treats the word *just* as a special case, noting the high deletion rate of /t/ in this particular /st/ cluster. In this corpus, the difference between deletion rates in /st/ clusters in the word *just* and in all other /st/ clusters is not as large as the difference observed for /d/ deletion in the word *and* as compared to other /nd/ clusters. Even though there is a significant difference in deletion rates among these two sets of /st/ clusters, the frequency of occurrence of the second most frequent item *just* is low enough so that neither its inclusion nor exclusion would significantly alter the ordering of constraints as does the word *and*. For this reason, the 115 instances of *just* have not been isolated from the data. (A deletion rate of 49% was observed for /t/ in the word *just* as compared to a rate of 36% in other /st/ clusters. While the confidence intervals overlap, the difference in deletion rates is significant at the .025 level.)

Following Consonant versus Following Vowel

Previous studies have suggested that the presence of a following consonant promotes final /t,d/ deletion. Figure 2.3 shows the rates of deletion for a following consonant and for a following vowel. A following consonant favors deletion significantly more than does a following vowel, the difference being 35.7% deleted /t,d/ when a consonant follows versus 15.8% when a vowel follows, with no overlap in the confidence intervals. These relationships confirm the results of previous studies.

Relative Ranking of Grammatical and Following Segment Constraints

Another question that arises with respect to the two constraints examined thus far is how to rank them. That is, which is the stronger constraint

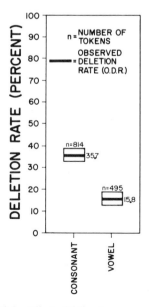

FIGURE 2.3 *Effect of following consonant–vowel.*

favoring deletion—the grammatical nature of /t,d/ or the consonantal versus vocalic nature of the following segment?

Labov (1972) has suggested that the relative ranking of these two characteristics may reflect dialect variation. He gives the following rules:

(1) $[-\text{cont}] \rightarrow \langle \emptyset \rangle \, / \, [+\text{cons}] \, \langle \beta(\emptyset) \rangle \, \_\_ \, \#\# \, \langle \alpha(\sim V) \rangle$

(2) $[-\text{cont}] \rightarrow \langle \emptyset \rangle \, / \, [+\text{cons}] \, \langle \alpha(\emptyset) \rangle \, \_\_ \, \#\# \, \langle \beta(\sim V) \rangle$

and states that "those who speak the nonstandard Negro vernacular characteristically show the pattern of (a) [=(1)], while white speakers from a wide variety of dialects show (b) [=(2)] [p. 115]." According to Labov *et al.* (1968), Labov (1972), Wolfram (1969), and Fasold (1972), in Black English the following segment is a stronger constraint on rule application than is the grammatical nature of the cluster, as in Rule (1); in Standard English, the reverse is true, as in Rule (2). In light of Labov's (1972) observations, it seemed interesting to see whether our data could be described by Rule (2).

Figure 2.4 shows the relationship between the two constraints as reflected in our data. Two sets of figures are listed for monomorphemic clusters. The first set is the rate of deletion for morpheme- and word-final clus-

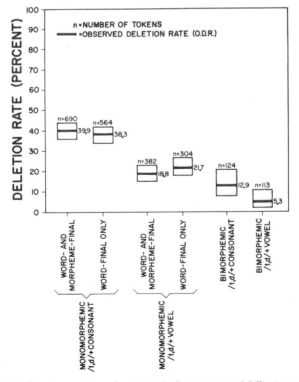

FIGURE 2.4 *Intersection of grammatical category and following segment.*

ters combined; the second set represents the rate of deletion for word-final clusters alone. This distinction has been made so that the resulting hierarchy of constraints could be compared to the results of previous studies, most of which dealt only with word-final clusters.

It is immediately apparent that monomorphemic /t,d/ followed by a consonant is more likely to be deleted than bimorphemic /t,d/ followed by either a consonant or a vowel and that monomorphemic /t,d/ is deleted more frequently than bimorphemic /t,d/ when both are followed by vowels; that is, there is no overlap in the confidence intervals for these sets of constraints. However, not all significant constraints are so easily identified, as can be seen by the overlap in the confidence intervals between monomorphemic /t,d/ + vowel and bimorphemic /t,d/ + consonant clusters and between the two types of bimorphemic clusters. The chi-square test shows the difference in /t,d/ deletion rates in the bimorphemic clusters to be significant at the .05 level; however, the difference between the observed rates in monomorphemic /t,d/ + vowel and bimorphemic /t,d/ + consonant clusters (18.8% versus 12.9%) is not significant. The 18.8% deletion rate represents the proportion of deleted /t,d/ observed both morpheme- and word-finally. Word-final /t,d/ is deleted 21.7% of the time (66/304), whereas morpheme-final deletion occurs in only 7.7% (6/78) of the clusters followed by a vowel.

It is interesting to note that all six instances of deletion of morpheme-final /t,d/ followed by a vowel are in /nt/ clusters: *fundamental* (3), *wanted* (2), *implemented* (1). This is precisely the environment in which a nasal flap might be expected. Following Fasold's (1972) example, clusters ending in nasal flaps can be tabulated as simplified clusters, whereas clusters ending in an intact alveolar stop or flap are counted as unsimplified clusters.

The chi-square test shows that the rate of deletion word-finally in monomorphemic clusters followed by a vowel is significantly higher than that in bimorphemic /t,d/ + consonant clusters—that is, the difference between 21.7% and 12.9% is significant. If only word-final clusters are examined, the grammatical nature of the cluster appears to be a stronger constraint on /t,d/ deletion than the nature of the following segment, a generality that is consistent with Labov's (1975) analysis of word-final /t,d/ deletion among 12 white speakers of various dialects of English and that is captured by his Rule (2).

A following consonant has been shown here to have a greater effect on /t,d/ deletion than a following vowel. It also appears, from previous analyses, that some consonants favor deletion more than others and that the hierarchy of factors within the following segment group can be extended to include a ranking of classes of consonants based on manner of articulation.

Manner of Articulation of Following Segment

Figure 2.5 shows the rates of deletion classified by the manner of articulation of the following segment. In Figure 2.5A (the data from which *and* has

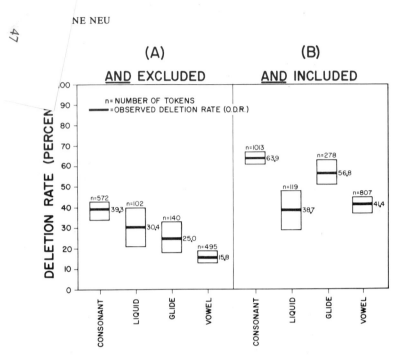

FIGURE 2.5 *Effect of manner of articulation of following segment.*

been excluded), it appears from the percentages of deletion observed in each environment, that the same ordering exists in these data as in Labov (1975) and Guy (present volume, Chapter 1)—that is, rate of deletion decreases in the order: (*a*) following consonant ($[^{+cons}_{-voc}]$); (*b*) following liquid ($[^{+cons}_{+voc}]$); (*c*) following glide ($[^{-cons}_{-voc}]$); (*d*) following vowel ($[^{-cons}_{+voc}]$). However, chi-square tests run on all of the pairs with overlapping confidence intervals showed that constraints on manner of articulation of the following consonant [i.e., (*a*)–(*c*)] cannot be significantly ranked. All the consonants are associated with significantly higher deletion rates than are following vowels, but no consonant class differs significantly from the others. Only if instances of *and* are added to the data, as in Figure 2.5B, does an ordering emerge, similar to, but not the same as, that observed by Labov and Guy, with the effect of a following consonant decreasing in the order: (*a*) consonant (i.e., $[^{+cons}_{-voc}]$), (*b*) glide, and (*c*) liquid. The difference in deletion rates observed for following liquids and vowels is not significant.

This suggests an important point—that is, that sufficiently large amounts of data are necessary to establish valid rankings. It is usually, but not necessarily, the case that the smaller the amount of data, the larger the confidence interval. Studies based on small amounts of data where proportions between different factors differ only by a few percentage points are highly questionable in their claims to establish ranking of constraints.

Manner of Articulation of Preceding Consonant

The consonant preceding /t,d/ appears to affect the ra
simplification. Manner of articulation is examined by Guy (
Chapter 1) in terms of the following factors: sibilants, nonsibilant fricatives,
stops, nasals, and laterals. The Wolfram (1969) and Fasold (1972) studies
analyze only bimorphemic clusters for this factor group. The present study
contains no separate analysis of bimorphemic clusters for manner of articulation and hence no results comparable to those obtained by Wolfram and
Fasold. Therefore my data on the effect of preceding consonants will be
presented in the framework of Guy's study.

Because the ordering of the factors sibilant, stop, and nasal, based on
observed frequencies alone, differs for male and female speakers, results for
the two groups are given separately in Figure 2.6. Among the men, the
effects of these three types of preceding consonants on final /t,d/ deletion
decreased in the order: (*a*) sibilant (44.2%), (*b*) nasal [excluding *and*]
(33.4%), and (*c*) stop (30.8%). The ordering observed among the women is
(*a*) stop (31.1%), (*b*) sibilant (29.4%), and (*c*) nasal [excluding *and*] (25.7%).
It is important to note that although the frequencies of deletion observed in
these environments do vary for the two groups, as do the respective ordering
of factors based on frequency alone, no reversal occurs in the ranking of
SIGNIFICANT constraints on deletion. Chi-square tests show that for the male
population it can be clearly established that the effect of a preceding consonant on deletion decreases in the order: (*a*) sibilant, (*b*) nasal or stop, and (*c*)

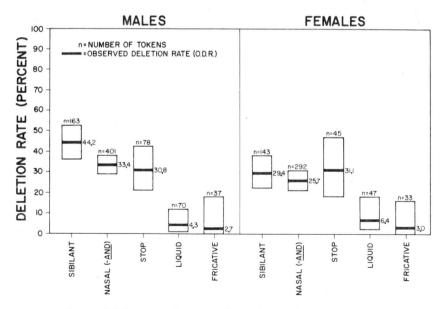

FIGURE 2.6   *Effect of manner of articulation of preceding segment.*

liquid or fricative. Among women, the effect of a preceding sibilant is not significantly different from that of nasals and stops; otherwise the ordering of constraints is the same as that observed among the men. (Obviously, if the 908 tokens of the lexical item *and* are included, a preceding nasal will have the greatest influence on deletion in both groups: 65.8% for males, 69.1% for females.)

The difficulty in ranking is due to the paucity of data on stops, fricatives, and liquids (e.g., there are only 70 potential fricative + /t,d/ clusters) and to the clustering of observed deletion rates. The hierarchy obtained basically agrees with that established by Guy, who also found considerable overlap in the rankings as a result of "insufficient data." He found that in one of his five data sets, deletion after nasals was greater than after stops and that in all other sets the reverse was true. For most of his speakers, fricatives were ordered either just before liquids or last.

Labov (1975), whose examination of the effect of manner of articulation of preceding consonants was limited to /st/ and nasal + /t,d/ clusters, found that final alveolar stops were deleted more frequently after /s/ than after nasals. My results agree with his: Of the 272 /st/ clusters, 41.2% are simplified as opposed to the 30.2% deletion observed in the 693 nasal + /t,d/ clusters, with no overlap in the confidence intervals.

Place of Articulation of Preceding Consonant

There is a definite correlation between place of articulation of the preceding consonant and the rate of final /t,d/ deletion, as is shown in Figure 2.7: final /t,d/ deletion is more likely to occur in the presence of a preceding homorganic alveolar consonant than when a nonalveolar consonant precedes (29.5% versus 21.0%, with no overlap in the confidence intervals). Only 4 of the 15 individuals delete /t,d/ more frequently in [−alveolar] contexts than in [+alveolar] contexts. Most likely, these exceptions to the regular ranking are due to the relatively small number of tokens of base form clusters consisting of a [−alveolar] consonant followed by /t,d/. Further subdivision of this class (i.e., into labials and velars) would result in so few tokens per class that no conclusions could be reached as to relative ranking of the two factors.

Other Phonological Constraints

Since a preceding alveolar consonant so strongly affects the rate at which final /t,d/ is deleted, it might be assumed that a following alveolar consonant might also promote deletion. This does not appear to be true for our data, where a /t,d/ deletion rate of 35.9% was observed with preceding [+alveolar] consonants versus a 35.7% deletion rate with preceding [−alveolar] consonants. From our data, it appears that neither place nor

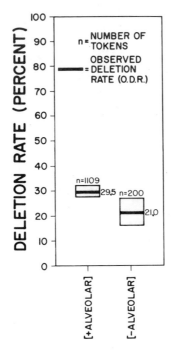

FIGURE 2.7 *Effect of place of articulation of preceding segment.*

manner of articulation of a following consonant is a significant constraint on /t,d/ deletion.

Fasold (1972) found that if the preceding and following consonants are homorganic, deletion occurs more frequently than if they are not. Since place of articulation of the following segment does not appear to be a significant constraint in our data, it cannot be said, for example, that a [+alveolar]+/t,d/+[+alveolar] sequence will be more likely to undergo cluster simplification than will a [+alveolar]+/t,d/+[−alveolar] sequence. It does appear, however, that if preceding and following consonants are identical, /t,d/ deletion is more likely to occur than if they are not. In 65 tokens in which identity occurs, 50.8% are simplified, whereas only 34.5% of the 749 clusters not composed of identical preceding and following consonants are simplified. (No overlap exists in the confidence intervals obtained.)

Sex of Speaker

As stated earlier in this paper, rate of deletion appears to vary significantly depending on the sex of the speaker. This is shown in Figure 2.8. From

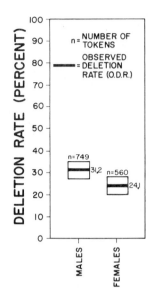

FIGURE 2.8 *Rate of deletion by sex of speaker.*

our data, it appears that for the group as a whole, men are much more likely to simplify final clusters ending in /t,d/ than are women (31.2% versus 24.1%). Although Fasold's (1972) data does not reveal a distinction, Wolfram's (1969) results show a marked difference in deletion rates based on sex, with women preserving final /t,d/ more than men.

According to Wolfram, who observed that the upper-middle-class speakers simplify clusters much less than do the working-class speakers, this would indicate that "the females seem to show a greater awareness of the consequences of cluster-final absence [p. 78]." Trudgill (1974), explaining the sex differentiation of *-ng* in his study of Norwich (e.g., *running* versus *runnin'*), gives a similar explanation for the tendency of men to lead in adoption of "changes from below [p. 95]," which are often started among the lower classes: "Women in our society are more status-conscious than men, generally speaking, and are therefore more aware of the social significance of linguistic variables [p. 94]." According to Trudgill (1974, p. 94), women are more status-conscious because their social position "in our society is less secure than that of men." He states that while men "can be rated socially by their occupation, . . . by what they do," women "have generally to be rated on how they *appear*. Since they cannot be rated socially by their occupation [if they have none], . . . other signals of status, including speech, are correspondingly more important." He further claims that because of its "connotation of masculinity," men are more likely to adopt characteristics of working-class speech. If Trudgill's explanations of the observed differences in the use of linguistic variables among men and women are correct and applicable to American society as well as British, we might expect to see a neutralization of this distinction as sex roles and attitudes toward them become more flexible in Western society.

Conclusion

In this paper, I have discussed the following points:

1. Determination of the constraints on variable rules must be based on sufficient amounts of data to yield reliable statistical results. Often in the past there has been an insufficient amount of data to establish valid rankings, a fact that is not apparent in many of the previous studies where rankings are based solely on the observed percentage of deletion. Where there are limited data, there is often no way to predict behavior that can be expected with a larger corpus.

2. High-frequency lexical items (such as the word *and*) are more likely to undergo deletion than are most other items, that is, there is a high correlation between frequency of word occurrence and frequency of rule application. This correlation is most striking when the high-frequency items are function words whose only vowel is redicible to schwa. If these items are not considered separately, one is likely to conclude that the rule applies with a much higher frequency than if these items are isolated from the body of the corpus, or else to conclude, for example, that "preceding /n/" has a much greater effect on deletion than it does.

3. The findings of the current study basically support those of Labov *et al.* (1968), Labov (1972, 1975), Wolfram (1969), Fasold (1972), and Guy (Chapter 1, this volume). In the study of deletion presented here, a fairly rigorous statistical test has been used to weigh rankings of constraints. The rankings obtained differ very little from those of previous studies and are presumably valid enough so that if the corpus were enlarged, the rankings of grammatical and phonological constraints would remain the same. Estimates of the true probabilities of deletion have been obtained and can be incorporated into the structural description of a variable rule. Thus, on the basis of these results, a variable rule could be formulated that would accurately represent performance.

Acknowledgments

I am indebted to David Broad (SCRL) for the many hours he spent teaching me the statistics necessary to write this paper and for his constant support, patience, criticism, and guidance. Grateful acknowledgment is also made to Beatrice Oshika (SCRL), who in addition to proofreading the text, offered invaluable advice and continued encouragement. June Shoup-Hummel (SCRL) and Robert Berdan (SWRL Educational Research and Development) offered helpful comments. The fine drafting of the figures was done by Ralph Fertig (SCRL).

This research was supported by the Advanced Research Projects Agency of the Department of Defense and was monitored by the Office of Naval Research under Contract Number N00014-73-C-0221.

References

Fasold, R. 1972. *Tense marking in Black English*. Arlington, Va: Center for Applied Linguistics.

Labov, W. 1969. Contraction, deletion and inherent variability of the English copula. *Language, 45*, 715–762.

Labov, W. 1972. The internal evolution of linguistic rules. In R. P. Stockwell and R. K. S. Macaulay (Eds.), *Linguistic Change and Generative Theory*. Bloomington: Indiana: University Press.

Labov, W. 1975. The quantitative study of linguistic structure. In *Pennsylvania Working Papers on Linguistic Change and Variation, I* (3).

Labov, W., Cohen, P., Robins, C., and Lewis, J. 1968. *A study of the non-standard English of Negro and Puerto Rican speakers in New York City*. Cooperative Research Report 3288, Vol. 1. New York: Columbia University. (Reprinted by U.S. Regional Survey, Philadelphia).

Pearson, E. S., and Hartley, H. O. 1966. *Biometrika Tables for Statisticians* (Vol. 1). Cambridge: University Press.

Shuy, R., Wolfram, W., and Riley, W. 1968. *Field techniques in an urban language study*. Washington, D.C.: Center for Applied Linguistics.

Trudgill, P. 1974. *The social differentiation of English in Norwich*. Cambridge: University Press.

Wolfram, W. 1969. *A sociolinguistic description of Detroit Negro speech*. Washington, D.C.: Center for Applied Linguistics.

3

Shana Poplack

THE NOTION OF THE PLURAL IN PUERTO RICAN SPANISH:[1] COMPETING CONSTRAINTS ON (s) DELETION

Introduction

The variability of syllable-final and word-final (s) in Puerto Rican Spanish is a well-documented phenomenon. Word-final (s) may appear in monomorphemes: *mes* 'month,' as the second person singular marker: *hablas* 'you speak,' and as the plural marker: *los juegos* 'the games.' Standard Spanish marks plurality redundantly across the noun phrase, so that there will be as many copies of the plural marker as there are items in a sentence modifying a plural noun, as in (1):

(1)   *Tienen muchos juegos de esos pintados en el suelo diferentes*
        'They have a lot of different games like that painted on the
        ground'   (C. T. #80)[2]

Puerto Rican Spanish (s) is variably subject to two weakening processes, aspiration and deletion, so that a phrase such as *las cosas bonitas* 'the pretty things' can also be realized [lah 'kosah bo' nitah] or [la 'kosa bo' nita]. The latter variant is apparently equivalent to the singular *la cosa bonita,* leading to potential ambiguity.

As early as 1903, Marxuach, in a description of Puerto Rican Spanish, remarked: "The only thing we have to say regarding the determiner is that it

[1] This research was supported by NSF Grant SOC-75-00245, "The Quantitative Study of Linguistic Change and Variation." Many thanks to Don Hindle for innumerable comments, suggestions, and encouragements.

[2] Initials and numbers are the code assigned to the informant and the location on tape of his or her utterance.

is very difficult to distinguish plurals from singulars in our pronunciation [p. 22]."[3] So frequent is the [∅] variant that Matluck (1961) states that "the only Puerto Rican Spanish /s/ which neither disappears nor is aspirated is initial /s/. In syllable-final position it is aspirated, in absolute final position, it is completely eliminated [p. 334]." Years before, in his monumental work, Navarro-Tomás had already recognized the inherent sociolinguistic variability of (s): "Final /s/ is generally aspirated in Puerto Rico over all social classes and regions. Educated people give this aspirated /s/ a fairly regular form, while the uneducated submit it to variants of pronunciation [1948, p. 69]." In spite of its suppression, however, "the awareness of this deleted /s/ remains entirely [p. 73]."

In other words, although the plural marker might disappear some or most of the time, the notion of the plural remains alive in Puerto Rican Spanish, and the phenomenon of deletion does not appear to impede communication among native speakers. The object of this paper is to investigate the various factors constraining deletion versus retention of the plural marker, as well as the factors responsible for disambiguation in the case of marker deletion. The understanding of processes by which languages undergo lenition and deletion of elements with a heavy functional load, as well as the mechanisms by which they compensate for these deletions, is an issue of importance to general linguistic theory.

Quantitative studies of (s) in other Caribbean dialects confirm that, in spite of potential ambiguity, the [∅] realization is the preferred variant (Cedergren, 1973; Terrell, 1976; Ma and Herasimchuk, 1968). In a study of style shifting in Puerto Rican Spanish (Poplack, 1979, ch. 3.3), undertaken in part to investigate the claim (made in Rosario, 1965, p. 36) that some (s) is reinserted in cases of ambiguity and in formal speech, 1268 tokens of (s) before a vowel—which we will see to be the most favorable environment for retention—were analyzed. The results revealed [∅] to be by far the preferred variant. What is more, (s) did not appear to be subject to style shifting for the lower-class speakers in the sample: From the most careful to the most casual speech style, (s) was consistently deleted 50% of the time. In a phonological environment more favorable to deletion, these figures would undoubtedly have been higher. As they stand, they suggest that factors other than stylistic ones are at play in constraining (s) retention.

Furthermore, results of a plural discrimination test (Poplack 1979, Appendix C) revealed, first, that less than half the informants were consistently able to identify occurrences of [s] as a plural marker, providing further testimony to its infrequency. Second, the results showed that no speaker was able to identify the [∅] realization of the plural once an NP was extracted from the larger discourse context. These results run counter to claims that vowel tensing, vowel lengthening, or lengthening of following consonant are

<hr />

[3] Translation mine, in this and following quotes.

compensatory processes for deletion (Navarro-Tomás, 1966; Matluck, 1961; Rosario, 1965; Cedergren, 1976; Milán, 1976), at least as far as Puerto Rican Spanish is concerned. Even if these phonetic processes show up instrumentally, interpretation of them does not appear to be part of these speakers' perceptive competence, or they would have no trouble disambiguating stimuli with [∅] plural realizations.

In light of the above data, we are faced with a paradox. On the one hand, we have evidence that the [∅] realization of the plural morphophoneme predominates; on the other, informants were unable to correctly interpret this [∅] realization within the context of the simple NP alone. Yet, if the potential ambiguity caused by deletion of (s) does not in fact result in ambiguity, of which we have no evidence at present, what are the disambiguating factors? If an NP string contains no morphological trace of the plural (and there are almost 1000 such strings in my corpus), the disambiguating factors must be other than morphological or elsewhere than in the NP.

Several sorts of constraints may potentially affect plural (s) deletion: the grammatical function of the token within the string, the nature of the following phonological segment and following stress, the position of the token within the string, the number of preceding plural markers, if any, and what I am here referring to as functional factors.

For the purposes of this discussion, a "functional hypothesis" will be equated to Kiparsky's "distinctness conditions": That is, there is a tendency for semantically relevant information to be retained in surface structure (1972, p. 195). Following a functional hypothesis, we would expect certain phonological processes to be blocked in those environments where their application would wipe out morphological distinctions on the surface. Conversely, in those environments where other types of disambiguating information are present, lessening the "functional load" of these distinctions, we might expect the phonological processes to apply more often. Thus Labov *et al.* (1968, p. 130) found a higher rate of /t,d/ deletion in monomorphemic types like *mist* than in past tense forms like *missed,* leading them to postulate that deletion rules would operate more frequently in monomorphemes than if the element to be deleted was itself a morpheme.

The Puerto Rican data I report on here, however, provide evidence to the contrary. As can be seen in Table 3.1, there is more (s) deletion in plural forms like *cosas* than in monomorphemic forms like *mes*. These results suggest that the constraints governing marker deletion are more complex than those that have been examined in the literature.

Other studies of functional constraints on deletion (Terrell, 1975a; Guy and Braga, 1976) have limited themselves to the examination of surface features of the sentence to explain this phenomenon. I suggest that semantic, syntactic, and morphological features, both within and outside the NP, must be taken into account in order to explicate the processes of deletion and disambiguation. In other words, if one is examining the effect of functional

TABLE 3.1
*Percentage of (s) Deletion by
Grammatical Status*

Grammatical status	Percentage of deletion
Inflection	68%
	($N = 6439$)
Monomorpheme	54%
	($N = 4028$)

factors on marker deletion, treating a token like *plantas* in (2a) as a noun with no preceding plural information (cf. Terrell, 1975a) is tantamount to classifying *plantas* in (2b) as unmodified.

(2) a. *un grupo de plantas*
'a group of plants'
b. *varias plantas*
'several plants'
c. *las plantas*
'the plants'

Although there is no possibility of plural disambiguation in the NP *plantas* in (2a) other than that of morphologically inflecting the noun, the fact that it is preceded by *un grupo de* informs the listener that the following segment will be plural. If the functional hypothesis holds true, one might expect a greater rate of deletion from a token such as this than from one with no preceding information at all. Similarly, the type of information conveyed within the NP by *varias* in (2b) is different in nature from that conveyed by *las* in (2c). Even if the marker were deleted from the former, no ambiguity could result, because *varia(s)* is understood as meaning "several." If it were deleted from the latter, the string could be interpreted as having a singular meaning.

I therefore made a distinction between morphological and nonmorphological disambiguation. In the morphological disambiguation factor group, items were coded for stem vowel change or additional information outside the NP. This factor group tests the hypothesis that there will be differential probabilities of deletion among the utterances in (3):

(3) a. *los reyes*
'the kings'
b. *las reinas*
'the queens'
c. *las reinas mandan*
'the queens command'

Even if both markers are deleted from the NP in (3a), the stem vowel changes on both the determiner and the noun adequately convey the plural information (cf. pl. [lo 'xeye] and sg. [el xey]). However, if both markers are deleted from (3b), ambiguity with the singular ([la 'xeina]) may result. If such a string is accompanied by a verb in concord with the subject, as in (3c), any realization of the morphophoneme {n} other than phonetic zero sufficiently disambiguates the number of the NP.

The nonmorphological disambiguation factor group accounts for plural information conveyed semantically or syntactically. This includes

Shared or cultural knowledge:

(4) a. *yo mi(s) hijo(s) le(s) digo*
       'I tell my kids'   (C. T. #40)
    b. *arroz con habichuela(s)*
       'rice and beans'

Lexical plurality:

    c. *un par de cosa(s)*
       'a couple of things'

Syntactic plurality:

    d. *Eran persona(s)* como que adivinaban
       'They were the people who, like, told the future   (D.F. #82)
    e. *Hablan con muerto(s)*
       'They talk to the dead'   (L. S. #41)

Instrumental in correct disambiguation of (4a) is the shared knowledge that the speaker has several children. Similarly, both speaker and hearer know that the dish in (4b) contains more than one bean. The token in (4c) is modified by semantically plural elements. A token may also obey certain syntactic rules that convey plurality: An unmodified noun immediately following a verb (4d) or certain prepositions (4e) is understood as plural. Cases of anaphoric plural referents, either in the string preceding the one in question, or within the larger context, were also included in this factor group.

The Sample

The data I will report on here consist of 6439 tokens of plural (s) collected from tape-recorded interviews of 18 adult speakers of Puerto Rican Spanish. Fourteen are residents of a single block in a predominantly Puerto Rican neighborhood in North Philadelphia. Data for these informants are part of a larger body of material I collected during a year-long study, which included informal interaction with the informants as well as interviews. The interviews were conducted in Spanish, using an interview schedule adapted to suit the needs of this community.[4] Because reading skills were not highly developed, the interview contained no formal elicitation devices such as word lists and reading texts. Instead, it concentrated on childhood games, customs, recipes, and other cultural aspects of the Puerto Rican community. The resulting speech is generally quite informal in style. All of the informants were first-generation Puerto Ricans, most of whom claimed to speak no English, although some had been in the United States for over 20 years.

The informants belonged to the poorest sector of the working class, were for the most part unemployed at the time of the interview and were largely restricted to their immediate area of residence. Many of them had never been in the downtown Philadelphia area, although it was easily accessible by public transportation. They constituted a closed and homogeneous community, quite isolated from " mainstream Philadelphia," differing in this respect from the Puerto Rican community in New York.

The remaining four informants, included here for purposes of comparison were natives of Las Piedras, Puerto Rico, who had never left the island.[5] The island Puerto Ricans were of a somewhat higher socioeconomic class than the Philadelphians, and their interviews were shorter and more formal in style than those used for the main body of the study.

The Analysis

Each occurrence of plural (s) in the data was coded for what previous studies (e.g., Ma and Herasimchuck, 1968; Cedergren, 1973; Terrell 1975a, 1976) have indicated to be relevant distinctions of grammatical category, following phonological segment, and following stress. In addition, each token was coded for the functional information discussed in relation to (3) and (4). Within each functional factor group—morphological and nonmorphological—two factors accounted for the presence of the type of disambiguating information in question as opposed to its absence. This system of coding made it possible to account for the amount, as well as the type, of disambiguating information relating to each token: Only morphological, only nonmorphological, both, or no possibility of plural disambiguation other than by inflecting some element of the NP. Following a functional hypothesis, we might expect greater probabilities of deletion in the presence of more disambiguating factors.

Each token was also coded for its position in the NP string and for the number and position of preceding plural markers, if any. Coding tokens as

---

[4] This interview schedule was adapted from the one developed for the Philadelphia community by the Project on Linguistic Change and Variation.

[5] Data for these informants were collected by Pedro Pedraza.

string members automatically assigns a different status to items that are accompanied by disambiguating information and those that are not. In (5a), a NP string with three slots, or three possibilities for plural marking, *bonitas* is coded as an adjective in third position in the string. If the realization of the string were (5b), *bonitas* would also be coded as having two preceding plural markers; if the (s) were deleted, as in (5c), *bonitas* would be coded for no preceding markers. Similarly, *cosas* is coded as a noun in second position in the string, with the appropriate preceding plural markers; and *las*, as a determiner in first position, with nothing preceding it.

(5) a. *la(s) cosa(s) bonita(s)*
   b. *la*[ˢₕ] *cosa* [ˢₕ] *bonita* ___
   c. *la*[∅] *cosa*[∅] *bonita* ___

The data were analyzed using the VARBRUL 2 program (Sankoff, 1975), which calculates probabilities for the application of a given rule. Since I am here concerned with plural marking, and since the aspirated variant of (s) cannot be said to lead to ambiguity, [s] and [h] were considered together in investigating the constraints on marker deletion. I have therefore bypassed the aspiration stage of the weakening process ([s → h]) and am examining constraints on the deletion rule [s,h → ∅].[6] Factor probabilities vary between 0 and 1, with figures higher than .5 favoring, and figures lower than .5 inhibiting rule application. The figure .5 itself has no effect on the rule. The higher the figure, the greater the contribution to rule application; thus comparisons can easily be made between various factors and factor groups.

Results

Figures for grammatical, phonological, and stress factor groups basically confirm the findings of other studies, as can be seen in Table 3.2.

TABLE 3.2
Contribution of Grammatical Category, Following Phonological Segment, and Following Stress to the Deletion of Plural (s)[a]

Grammatical category		Following phonological segment		Following stress	
Adjective	.69	Pause	.65	Weak	.56
Noun	.57	Consonant	.47	Heavy	.44
Determiner	.26	Vowel	.37		

    [a] Input probability = .65.

[6] All orthographic instances of "S" should therefore be taken to mean "marker."

Of the grammatical factors, adjectives favor marker deletion whereas determiners favor retention, an effect also found in studies of other Hispanic dialects (Cedergren, 1973, p. 46; Ma and Herasimchuk, 1968, p. 692; Terrell 1976, p. 13). Of the phonological factors, a following pause is most favorable to deletion. The results for the phonological factor group differ from those found for Panamanian Spanish, where deletion was shown to be independent of environmental constraints (Cedergren 1973, p. 46). However, following pause showed a similar effect in Terrell's study of formal Puerto Rican Spanish (1975b, p. 12), although in that same study, deletion was found to occur more in prevocalic than in preconsonantal position. The results reported here are undoubtedly somewhat skewed by the fact that [s] and [h] were treated together. When they are analyzed separately, following consonant is shown to be a favorable environment for aspiration (Cedergren, 1973; Terrell, 1975b; Poplack, 1979), which in this study was considered an instance of retention. Ma and Herasimchuk's study of vernacular Puerto Rican Spanish is not directly comparable, as they consider following consonant and pause as one category.

Following weak stress favors deletion somewhat, whereas following heavy stress favors retention of some marker. These figures could be due to the interaction of determiner and stressed vowel, in which environment (s) has been shown to be almost categorically realized [s] in Puerto Rican Spanish (Terrell 1975b, p. 30, Ma and Herasimchuk, 1968, p. 692).

When we look at the figures for the functional and position factor groups, however, the results appear somewhat less predictable. Table 3.3 indicates that functional factors have a small but regular effect on deletion, in a direction confirming a functional hypothesis. Presence of additional plural information, whether morphological or nonmorphological, favors deletion somewhat, whereas absence of additional information favors retention.

However, functional factors overall affect deletion less than any other factor group studied, except following stress. This can be seen by comparing the range of figures in Table 3.2 with the figures in Table 3.3.

The purpose of the functional group is to ascertain the effect of functional factors on the elimination of redundancy. Though the functional factors have a lesser effect than the others, the ranking of factors within the functional groups is clear. Additional plural information favors marker dele-

TABLE 3.3
Contribution of "Functional" Factors to the Deletion of Plural (s)

"Morphological" disambiguating information	None	"Nonmorphological" disambiguating information	None
.57	.43	.59	.41

tion, whereas when the only possibility for plural marking is inflectional, within the NP itself, a marker tends to be retained. This is a tendency, but it is a rather weak one. Terrell found that speakers of Cuban Spanish consistently avoided suppressing all morphological trace of the plural (1975b, p. 436). This is not the case in Puerto Rican Spanish. I have encountered almost 1000 examples of NP strings containing two to three elements, with no morphological marker at all. Moreover, the deletion rate from a given token is even higher when it is preceded by two zeros (94%) than when it is preceded by one (82%).

The purpose of the position group is to examine the phenomenon of redundancy characteristic of Standard Spanish plural marking, the effect of position of the token within the string, and presence and position of preceding markers, if any. Figures for this group indicate that there is indeed a tendency toward local redundancy, but which functions somewhat differently than the standard copying rule: Presence of a plural marker before the token favors marker retention on that token, whereas absence of a preceding marker favors deletion. The greatest effect is produced when a marker immediately precedes the token, as becomes clear when Tables 3.4A and 3.4B are compared.

TABLE 3.4A
Contribution of Position of Token in NP String and Presence of Preceding Marker to the Deletion of Plural (s)

Position of token in string	3	2	1
Marker preceding token			
Absent	.71	.58	
Present	.40	.43	
None possible			.36

TABLE 3.4B
Contribution of Position of Token in NP String and Presence of Immediately Preceding Marker to the Deletion of Plural (s). (S = [s] and [h])

Position of token in string	3	2	1
Marker(s) preceding token			
∅∅__	.73		
S∅__	.68		
∅__		.52	
S__		.44	
∅S, SS__	.40		
None possible			.24

Table 3.4A shows that markers tend to be retained when preceding markers were also retained, and when the token is in first position in the string. But the table does not show the effect of position of the preceding marker with regard to the token: When preceding S, ∅S, SS, and S∅ are treated as a single category, they appear to have the same disfavoring effect on deletion (between .40 and .43).

Table 3.4B, on the other hand, shows that the differential effect on deletion is actually due to the presence of a marker in the slot immediately preceding the token: ∅S, SS, and S continue to disfavor deletion (contributions .40 and .44, respectively), while ∅ and S∅ favor it. The most favorable context for marker deletion is precisely when the two preceding markers have already been deleted. This is exactly the opposite effect from what was found by Guy and Braga for Brazilian Portuguese, a language that marks plurality on the NP and the VP in much the same way as Spanish. It also runs counter to any functional claim.

Moreover, the results reported here are not specific to the Puerto Rican community in the continental United States, and should not be interpreted as resulting from immigrants' contact with and influence from English. This may be seen by comparing their behavior, as reported in the preceding discussion, with that of the subsample of Puerto Ricans who never left the island. Table 3.5 shows that the island group in fact has an even higher deletion rate than the Philadelphia Puerto Ricans.

TABLE 3.5
Contribution of Phonological and Grammatical Factors to the Deletion of Plural (s) for Philadelphia and Island Puerto Ricans

Grammatical category		Following phonological segment		Following stress		Place of residence	
Adjective	.64	Pause	.64	Weak	.52	Puerto Rico	.54
Noun	.56	Consonant	.44	Heavy	.48	Philadelphia	.46
Determiner	.32	Vowel	.40				

Discussion

The results point to an apparent contradiction. On the one hand, Puerto Rican speakers are tending toward elimination of redundancy, as evidenced by the figures in Table 3.3. On the other hand, redundancy is favored, or at best, not taken into account, in the data for the position group. One marker leads to more, and deletion of a marker leads to further deletions, resulting in a tendency toward concord on the string level. In other words, if a plural is going to be realized, the tendency will be for it to be realized on the first element; if it is not realized on the first element, subsequent developments will not tend to rectify this in a functional way. What follows might either be all markers or all zeros, so that a sequence like ∅∅S turns out to be virtually nonexistent. (Out of 136 cases of strings with the sequence ∅∅ preceding the token, a marker was retained on the final token in only 8 instances—6% of the time.) This would seem to tie in with Martinet's application of the theory of least effort: "Concord is redundancy, and contrary to what could be expected, redundancy results as a rule from least effort: people do not mind repeating if mental effort is thereby reduced [1962, p. 55]."

It could also point to a stage of variation in which deletion has advanced so far that Puerto Rican Spanish (s) is now seen less as a morphological marker than as a phonological entity which undergoes well-defined rules of weakening and elision in certain environments, and is retained in others (e.g., in word-initial position), and which is capable of being later reintroduced through learned channels, as by upper class speakers in formal speech.

As I have already mentioned, although there were numerous strings containing no morphological indication of the plural, there do not seem to be any instances where the NOTION of the plural is absent. There is no evidence that communication is being hindered at present. But if deletion rates increase and spread to contexts that are now comparatively conservative, a time might come when Puerto Rican Spanish will reorganize its system of morphological plural marking. Evidence I have been collecting suggests it would not be unreasonable to expect it to go the way of Modern French, and limit plural marking to the determiner alone. Recall that the first element in the string is the most highly loaded element, and that the first position seems to behave differently from the others (as shown in Tables 3.2 and 3.4B).

The determiner, which usually occurs in first position, has the lowest deletion rate of all grammatical factors. First position is also consistently the most conservative environment with regard to deletion, regardless of the grammatical category of the item in this position. For example, plural (s) is deleted far less frequently from nouns in first position (with a probability of .30) than in any other (.57).

Added to this is the fact that the masculine plural determiner undergoes a stem vowel change ($el \rightarrow los$), which indicates plurality even when (s) is deleted. Standard Spanish marks gender redundantly across the NP, as it does number, but instances of gender reassignment I have been collecting, which are now numerous enough not to be written off as performance errors, may result in the masculine plural determiner taking over as the plural marker in the NP. Occurring in such intimate environments as between determiner and noun, and between noun and adjective, we find examples of gender reassignment within the simple NP, such as

(6) a. *chorizo buena*
    'good sausage'   (P. O. #43)
  b. *unos habichuelas*
    'some beans'   (O. J. #287)
  c. *los peleas*
    'the fights'   (J. T. #565)
  d. *las castigos*
    'the punishments'   (L. T. #142)

The reassignment goes in both directions: A masculine modifier may modify a feminine noun, as in (6b), and a feminine modifier may modify a masculine noun, as in (6a), but of the examples collected so far, 70% go in the direction of masculine marking on feminine nouns.

This phenomenon parallels developments in Modern French. In a determiner system consisting of the four elements in (7), the (s) dropped from the Old French plurals *les* and *las,* and they fell together into modern [le] which does not carry a gender distinction. One would expect that some variation in gender assignment preceded such a change.

(7)   *le* (m., sg.)   *la* (f., sg.)
      les (m., pl.)   *las* (f., pl.)

Deletion of (s) is an ancient and widespread process, attested as early as Archaic Latin. There is some evidence of (s) reinsertion during the classical period, but it was subsequently lost altogether in the eastern Romance languages, although it was retained in Old French and Old Spanish.

Puerto Rican Spanish (s) is presently at a stage of variation that might also resolve itself in total deletion of this inflection. Through an examination of the factors affecting this process at a point in time at which several variants are still available, I have attempted to shed light on the mechanisms of disambiguation in the case of marker deletion. I have demonstrated that functional considerations play a small but regular role in the retention of a plural marker: There is a greater tendency toward deletion when it is possible to convey plurality other than inflectionally (Table 3.3).

However, we have also seen that, overall, functional factors affect marker deletion less than any other factor group studied, with the exception of following stress, a result that is not readily interpretable. Whether this is the case because (s) deletion in Puerto Rican Spanish has not yet advanced far enough to call functional factors into play remains to be investigated. The results of this study, moreover, indicate that the problems raised by these competing constraints on (s) deletion cannot be resolved conclusively by examining the noun phrase alone. Answers to these questions may also reside in another area of linguistic structure, such as the verb phrase. A functional study of variability in verbal marking should allow us to draw clearer conclusions about deletion and disambiguation in Puerto Rican Spanish.[7]

References

Cedergren, H. 1973. *The interplay of social and linguistic factors in Panama.* Unpublished Ph.d dissertation, Cornell University.

Cedergren, H. 1976. The disambiguation of grammatical ambiguity: Spanish /s/. Paper presented at NWAVE conference.

Elcock, W. D. 1960. *The Romance languages.* London: Faber and Faber.

Guy, G., and Braga, M. L. 1976. Number concordance in Brazilian Portuguese. Paper presented at NWAVE conference.

Kiparsky, P. 1972. Explanation in phonology. In S. Peters (Ed.), *Goals of linguistic theory.* New Jersey: Prentice Hall.

Labov, W., Cohen, P., Robins, C., and Lewis, J. 1968. *A study of the non-standard English of Negro and Puerto Rican speakers in New York City.* Report on Co-operative Research Project 3288. New York: Columbia University.

Ma, R., and Herasimchuk, E. 1968. The linguistic dimensions of a bilingual neighborhood. In Fishman *et al., Bilingualism in the barrio.* New York: Yeshiva University.

Martinet, A. 1962. Towards a Functional Syntax. In *A functional view of language.* Oxford: University Press.

Marxuach, T. 1903. *El lenguaje castellano en Puerto Rico.* San Juan, Puerto Rico: San Juan News.

Matluck, J. H. 1961. Fonemas finales en el consonantismo puertorriqueño. *Nueva revista de filología hispánica, 15,* 332–342.

Milán, W. 1976. *New York City Spanish: Myths, structure and status.* Institute for Urban and Minority Education Report Series no. 1. New York: Columbia University.

Navarro-Tomás, T. 1948. *El español de Puerto Rico: Contribución a la geografía lingüística hispanoamericana.* Río Piedras: Universidad de Puerto Rico.

Politzer, R. 1972. Final -s in the Romania. In Anderson, J. and Creore, J. (Eds.), *Readings in Romance linguistics.* The Hague: Mouton.

Poplack, S. 1979. *Function and process in a variable phonology.* Unpublished Ph.D dissertation, University of Pennsylvania.

Poplack, S. 1980. Deletion and disambiguation in Puerto Rican Spanish. *Language, 56,* 371–385.

Rosario, R. del. 1965. *La lengua de Puerto Rico: ensayos.* Río Piedras: Editorial Cultural, Inc.

Sankoff, D. 1975. VARBRUL 2. Unpublished program and documentation.

Terrell, T. 1975a. Functional constraints on deletion of word-final /s/ in Cuban Spanish. *Berkeley Linguistic Society, 1,* Berkeley: University of California, Department of Linguistics.

Terrell, T. 1975b. La interacción de la aspiración y la elisión sobre la /s/ implosiva y final en el español de Puerto Rico. Manuscript. Irvine: University of California.

Terrell, T. 1976. Sobre la aspiración y elisión de la /s/ implosiva y final en el español de Puerto Rico. Manuscript. Irvine: University of California.

---

[7] Such a study has in fact been completed (Poplack, 1979, 1980) since the analysis reported in this chapter was carried out (1977), with the result that plural marking in the NP appears to be a process that is interdependent with verbal (n) marking. The aforementioned studies also contain further analysis of the material presented here.

4

Flora Klein

A QUANTITATIVE STUDY OF SYNTACTIC AND PRAGMATIC INDICATIONS OF CHANGE IN THE SPANISH OF BILINGUALS IN THE U.S.[1]

Introduction

In the literature of Spanish–English bilingualism in the United States quantitative studies of syntactic and semantic variables are conspicuously scarce. This state of affairs is especially regrettable because contact between languages, like other factors, may bring about changes that only quantitative investigation can detect. In the area of syntax and semantics, interference effects of this kind might be expected to occur where the particular languages in contact have constructions that are parallel morphologically, and that are also similar in their conditions of use, but only partly so. In just such cases we would expect interference to occur, owing to the bilinguals' tendency to equate the two systems in function as well as in form (Weinreich, 1963, p. 39). Yet such interference may well elude impressionistic observation, to the extent that it does not give rise to utterances that, considered individually, are ungrammatical in the recipient language.

The systems of reference to present activity of English and of Spanish constitute potential sources of interference of this kind. The two languages have progressive forms that are parallel in morphology, in that they are made up of the inflected present of *be* plus the gerund of the particular main verb. In both, the progressive seems to indicate, roughly, that the activity or condition that the verb expresses is actually in progress or in force at the time of speech itself, rather than merely in a more comprehensive span of time which includes the time of speech within it (Diver, 1963, p. 173; Joos,

---

[1] An earlier version of this chapter was read at NWAVE V, Georgetown University, October 1976.

1964, p. 108). Thus, in both English and Spanish the progressive present provides a means of specifying reference to what is actually going on at the time of speaking, in contrast to what is generally the case. In both languages, the latter, more comprehensive, present is referred to by a simple form. Examples (1) and (2) illustrate the contrast between the simple and the progressive present in Spanish and in English.[2]

(1)   *El sol* sale **sale** *alrededor de las siete de la mañana*
       The sun **rises** around 7 a.m.

(2)   *Mira,* **está saliendo** *el sol*
       'Look, the sun **is coming** out

There is, however, an important difference between Spanish and English in reference to present activity. In English, in contexts where the progressive is acceptable it is often impossible to use the simple present form. So, for example, we would not say

(3)   **Look, the sun* **comes** *out*

In Spanish, however, under these same conditions either the simple or the progressive present is usually acceptable (Bull, 1965, p. 164). Thus either (4a) or (4b) would be an acceptable Spanish version of (2).

(4) a. *Mira,* **está saliendo** *el sol*
    b. *Mira,* **sale** *el sol*

This difference in usage between English and Spanish might be represented schematically as

(5)
	X	*Y*
English	*Progressive*	**Simple**
Spanish	*Progressive*	**Simple**
	Simple	

Boldface italic type stands for the possibility of using the progressive present, boldface type for the possibility of using the simple present, and *X* and *Y* for particular referential areas. It may be that, as I have suggested, *X* and *Y* differ just in their relative specificity with respect to the moment of speech,

---

[2] For the purposes of this study I considered only the present forms when used in reference to present time—that is, to time inclusive of the moment of speaking. This excludes references to intention in the future, the "historical present," etc. (see Note 7).

with X being specifically the moment of speech itself and Y merely some span of time that includes the moment of speech more or less equally among others. Yet even without a precise determination of the semantic difference between X and Y, we can observe differences between the English and the Spanish systems which suggest, in turn, plausible expectations as to interference between them in bilingual situations.

First, we note that, as far as expression is concerned, Spanish and English differ just in reference to X, where the progressive is acceptable in both languages, and not in reference to Y, where the progressive is not acceptable in either one. We further note that, because of the exact nature of this difference in possibilities of expression, from the point of view of the hearer the English system is the more precise of the two, in reference to BOTH X and Y. For in English each present form is, in effect, specific to only one of the two areas, X OR Y, to the exclusion of the other. We may therefore assume that, in English, each present form is understood as unambiguous with respect to X or Y: The progressive refers only to X, and never to Y, and the simple present refers only to Y, and never to X. In contrast to English, Spanish can be precise only in reference to X—by referring to it with the progressive form, which is specific to X alone as it is in English. But Spanish has no present form specific to Y because the form that refers to Y—the simple present—can also refer to X. In Spanish, then, the simple present does not of itself specify either X or Y.

The diagrams in (5) should also serve to illustrate our initial claim that there are potential effects of interference between languages that may not be observable at all except through quantitative means. In reference to present activity, interference from Spanish on bilinguals' English might give rise to such unacceptable utterances as (3). But interference from English on bilinguals' Spanish should not give rise to utterances which, taken individually, are unacceptable. This is of course because in Spanish it is also correct to use the progressive form in reference to X. Therefore, any influence of English on bilinguals' Spanish should manifest itself not in ungrammatical utterances, but rather in a relatively higher frequency of use of the progressive present, and a correspondingly lower frequency of use of the simple present, in reference to X.

The Study: General Hypothesis

With these considerations in mind, a study was designed to investigate the usage of Spanish–English bilinguals in New York City. The first assumption was that reference to present activity would be a likely area for interference between the two languages, given the morphological similarity and the partial similarity in usage between them. It was further assumed that, in the particular group to be studied, interference should be in the direction of

English usage and so should take the form of English influence on the bilinguals' Spanish, rather than the reverse. This expectation was based on the following interrelated considerations: First, it seemed likely that, in this country, pressure for mastering English would in general be greater than pressure for mastering Spanish. Second, given the greater prestige associated with English and/or English speakers in the larger social context, it seemed possible that bilinguals living here might tend to reinterpret the more specific English system as being not only more precise but also "more correct." Third, identification of the two systems in the direction of English would be much more likely to go unnoticed, and therefore unchecked, than would the reverse, because it would not give rise to ungrammatical utterances in either language.

In order to test the general expectation of influence of English on the Spanish of bilinguals in this country, an initial series of 19 interviews was conducted with Spanish speakers living in New York City. All the speakers were of Puerto Rican origin or descent. Each one was interviewed separately, in Spanish.[3]

Two methods of elicitation were used. The first was relatively "free" conversation, ranging from about 15 to 20 min in length, in which the speakers were encouraged to express themselves with as few interruptions as possible on subjects that seemed to interest them. Questions from the interviewer were generally directed toward eliciting references to ongoing activities, but they always were phrased in the simple present form. After this period of free conversation the speakers were shown some cartoons and photographs and were asked to describe what they saw.[4] Five of the pictures showed several persons performing different activities: for instance, a woman looking out of a window at a boy climbing a tree with another boy helping him up, and a doctor examining a patient with a nurse taking notes. Three pictures showed one person doing two things at a time: for instance, a man driving a car and turning his head to talk to the passenger in the back seat, and a woman talking on the phone while washing the dishes.

The speakers were then asked a number of questions about their background, and in particular their language background. On the basis of their answers they later were classed into two groups: A bilingual group, labeled NY, was made up of 11 speakers who either had been born in this country or had come here no later than age 8; and a nonbilingual "control" group, labeled PR, was made up of 8 speakers who had come here after age 16. All the NY speakers could speak English, whereas all but one of the PR group

[3] The interviews were conducted by the writer, a native speaker of Spanish as well as English. Two of the speakers (taxi drivers) were not aware that they were serving as informants; the relevant parts of their conversation were recorded in writing. Otherwise all interviews were taped, and the speakers were told that the object of the study was to see whether it is true that Hispanic people are more verbal and loquacious than other groups.

[4] This method of elicitation was not used with the two taxi drivers.

were virtually monolingual in Spanish.[5] Except for 2 speakers (one in each group) all were between 16 and 20 years old at the time of the interview. None had formal education beyond the high school level.

The purpose of setting up the control group PR, roughly similar to the bilingual group NY except for command of English, was of course to establish a nonbilingual norm with which to compare the usage of the bilinguals. A nonbilingual norm was needed, in turn, because the particular interference effects expected were quantitative, rather than absolute, in character.

In addition to this, because of the nature of the phenomena under consideration, and because the method of elicitation itself imposed virtually no constraints, it was necessary to distinguish between data of different kinds. In particular, it was necessary to determine just which references to present activity could be considered as potentially diagnostic of interference from English. In other words, it was necessary to determine just which of the utterances elicited fell in the area X, where English usage differs from Spanish.

For the purpose of this investigation I circumvented the problem of arriving at a precise a priori characterization of X, by applying instead after the fact a simple operational criterion: I translated the Spanish data into English, taking into account the actual context in which each utterance had occurred.[6] In this way the utterances recorded in Spanish in the simple or the progressive present forms were divided into three main classes, according to the possibilities available in English for communicating an equivalent message. The first class, labeled $S\not{P}$, consisted of Spanish utterances such as (1), which could be rendered in English in the simple present. Utterances of this kind were excluded from further consideration because in their case the two

[5] Because the PR speakers were intended to establish a norm of Spanish usage (relatively) free of the independent variable "influence from English," it was judged most important that they should have learned Spanish (a) in Puerto Rico, rather than in this country, and (b) as an only "first language"—that is, before learning English, rather than at approximately the same time. Accordingly, the PR group was made up exclusively of speakers who had come to this country after puberty, in most cases as young adults, whereas the NY group was made up of speakers who had been in this country from a much earlier age—usually from birth or early childhood. Largely as a result of these criteria, the PR speakers were clearly "Spanish dominant," both as a matter of stated language preference and of actually observed relative fluency (in fact, all but one of the PR speakers spoke little or no English at all). In contrast, none of the NY speakers expressed preference for speaking Spanish, although some actually spoke it very fluently; on the contrary, most said they preferred to use English and actually used it more than Spanish.

Each speaker's proficiency in English was tested briefly and found to correspond reasonably well with his or her own estimate of it. I should note that some speakers were interviewed whose language background, it turned out, did not place them clearly in either group. Data from such speakers was not included in the study.

[6] As mentioned in Note 3, I speak both English and Spanish natively. And, because I had conducted the interviews myself and I transcribed and classified the data shortly thereafter, it seemed that I was in the best position to judge the sense in which each utterance had been intended.

languages coincide in not admitting the progressive present at all, but only the simple form.[7] A second class, labeled SP, consisted of those Spanish utterances that could only be rendered in English in the progressive present form. Sentences (4a) and (4b) exemplify this class, as do the examples in (6), taken from the recorded data:

(6) SP: *¿Este niño **está pintándola** a ella, no? ¿O qué es lo que* **hace**?
'That boy *is drawing* her, isn't he? Or what *is he doing*?'

*Esta **está mirando** a los niños que **están jugando** en el palo . . . uno se* **trepa** *y el otro lo* **empuja**
'*She's watching* the boys who *are playing* in the tree . . . one *is climbing up* and the other *one's helping* him'

¿Ese ruido? Es el tren que **pasa**
'That noise? It's the train *that's going* by.'

*Ella **está estudiando** y yo la* **espero**
'*She's studying* [i.e., in class] and *I'm waiting* for her.'

Finally, a third class, labeled SP, consisted of those utterances that in English could admit either progressive or simple present forms. As the examples in (7) show, they seem to refer to situations that can be viewed about equally well as instances of X or of Y:[8]

(7) SP: *El **va** a la escuela*
'He **goes**/*is going* to school.'

*Bueno, yo me **gano** X pesos.*
Well, I **make**/*am making* $X.

*Ella **cuida** un muchacho.*
She **takes**/*is taking* care of a child.

Está viviendo en los proyectos de la ciudad.
She **lives**/*is living* in the city projects.

Están jugando todo el dia.
They **play**/*are playing* all day.

*Nosotros **cogemos** welfare.*
We **get**/*are getting* welfare.

[7] Also excluded from consideration were those occurrences of present forms in Spanish which could be rendered in English in still other forms, instead of or in addition to the simple and/or the progressive present. This includes so-called "historical presents" (*So he says to me*/*So he said to me*), statements of intentions for the future (*I leave*/*I'm leaving*/*I'll leave tomorrow*), etc. Finally, very frequent expressions were also excluded, on the assumption that they might tend to be "frozen" in a particular form (e.g., *¿Qué pasa?* 'What's going on?'; *¿Qué/Cómo dice?* 'What's that again?').

[8] This should not be taken as suggesting that, in these utterances or in any others, the simple present form has the same meaning as the progressive present form. On the contrary, I assume that the meaning of each form is always the same, and so that the difference between them remains the same as well. Therefore, SP utterances would refer to real-life situations which are such that either form, and its meaning, can describe them about as appropriately as the other.

Notice that both in SP and in $P utterances Spanish uses both the progressive and the simple present forms. However, the basis for classifying the data was the possibilities available in English. As a result, the two classes differ as to parallelism between the two languages in the alternatives available. In SP utterances, Spanish and English admit parallel options: either the simple or the progressive present. In $P utterances, however, whereas Spanish admits either the simple or the progressive present, English admits only the progressive.

The possibility of identifying the utterances in which English differs from Spanish in the options available for referring to present activity made it possible, in turn, to refine our expectations as to those specific differences in usage between the NY and the PR groups that might be considered to bear directly on the hypothesis. In general, I reasoned that if the Spanish of the NY bilinguals were not influenced by English, it should not exhibit a frequency of use of the simple and the progressive present forms significantly different from that of the PR controls. But more specifically, if the Spanish of the NY group were not influenced by English, it should not exhibit a significantly higher use of the progressive, as compared to the PR controls, precisely in $P utterances.

It was however just in the $P utterances that the NY speakers' usage was found to differ significantly from that of the PR controls. And the difference was in just the sense that influence of English would predict: namely, higher frequency of use of the Progressive present, and correspondingly lower frequency of use of the simple present, by the NY speakers. The results of this first series of interviews are given numerically in Figure 4.1A, with the percentages of use of the simple present form also shown graphically in Figure 4.1B.[9] Note that in SP utterances, where English usage resembles Spanish, the scores of the NY group are strikingly similar to those of the PR controls: The PR group used 57 simple present forms and 30 progressive present forms, which amounts to 65% use of the simple present; the NY group used 55 simple present forms and 25 progressive present forms, which amounts to 68.8% use of the simple present. In $P utterances however, where English differs from Spanish in not admitting the simple present, the NY speakers differed significantly from their PR counterparts, in the direction of English usage.[10] In $P utterances, the PR group used 30 simple present forms and 104 progressive present forms, which amounts to 22.4%

[9] The results for each group were combined because some of the individual speakers did not produce as much data as others. Consequently, in some cases the results for individual speakers, once subcategorized into the various classes of utterances, would have been too small to deal with meaningfully.

[10] The significance of the difference between the groups in $P utterances was established by t at $<.01$. Chi-squares were also computed for each category and are included in Figures 3.1–3.3A.

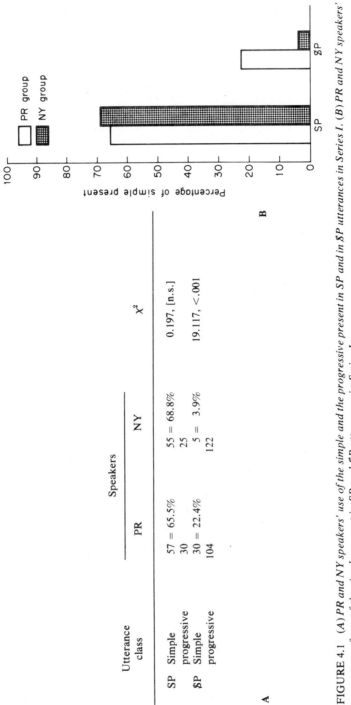

Utterance class	Speakers		χ^2
	PR	NY	
SP Simple	57 = 65.5%	55 = 68.8%	0.197, [n.s.]
progressive	30	25	
SP Simple	30 = 22.4%	5 = 3.9%	19.117, <.001
progressive	104	122	

A

B

FIGURE 4.1 (A) PR and NY speakers' use of the simple and the progressive present in SP and in SP utterances in Series I. (B) PR and NY speakers' percentage of use of the simple present in SP and SP utterances in Series I.

use of the simple present; the NY group used 5 simple present forms and 122 progressive present forms, which amounts to 3.9% use of simple present.

Specific Hypothesis

I then went on to investigate the particular assumption that the English system of present reference is more precise than the Spanish—a situation that I expected would contribute to influence from English on the Spanish of bilinguals in this country.

Turning again to the diagrams in (5), we see that, as noted above, the English system is more precise than the Spanish both in reference to X and to Y. Let us consider X. In English, references to X are unambiguous because they must be made in just that form—the progressive present—that is specific to X alone. In contrast, references to X in Spanish may be either unambiguous or potentially ambiguous. They are unambiguous when they are made in the form specific to X—the progressive—as they are in English. But they are potentially ambiguous when they are made in the simple present, since it can refer to Y as well as to X.

This difference in precision between English and Spanish usage was vividly illustrated during the interviews. The majority took place in an agency for job-training and employment of Hispanic youth, and most of the speakers interviewed were volunteers from among those waiting to see the agency personnel. A question I often asked was ¿*Qué hacen esos chicos allá afuera?* This question was intended to refer to the other young people waiting outside in the hall, and so to be interpreted as 'What are those kids out there doing?' (or 'What are those kids doing out there?'). It was thus intended to refer to X—the moment of speech itself—and it was so interpreted by Spanish monolinguals, although the question was phrased in the simple present form. Spanish–English bilinguals, however, usually interpreted this question as referring to Y (the general present), in accordance with English usage, and so as 'What do those kids out there do?' As a result it often provoked surprise, presumably because applicants at an employment agency are assumed to be unemployed. In several cases this incongruity was resolved by reinterpreting the question altogether, as referring to the agency personnel (who were themselves mostly young people). This elicited such answers as *Ellos trabajan aquí* 'They work here,' *Ayudan a los muchachos* 'They help the kids,' and the like.

In English, then, precision in reference to X is imposed by the language itself, whereas in Spanish it is not. Accordingly, it seems plausible to expect that, in Spanish, the actual choice between the more precise and the less precise alternatives for reference to X—the progressive and the simple present forms, respectively—should be determined by pragmatic strategies based on relative need for precision, and thus on such considerations as relatively greater versus lesser probability of misunderstanding. This would lead us to expect that, among *non*bilingual speakers, frequency of use of the simple present in $P utterances (i.e., in reference to X) should correlate positively with amount of contextual support. As a result, the usage of Spanish–English bilinguals should exhibit relatively greater difference from that of Spanish monolinguals in utterances that are integrated in a larger connected discourse, as compared to those occurring in brief exchanges.

In the interviews I had generally tried to elicit as much connected discourse as possible, mainly in order to avoid the need for intrusions on my part and the consequent possibility of influence from my own usage. But because I did not know most of the informants beforehand, I had little prior idea of what subjects might interest them and so might tend to elicit longer stretches of speech. As it happened, the topics that tended to elicit most interest had to do with what we might call "new developments"—new developments in the speaker's life, new governmental programs in Puerto Rico or in this country, new construction, *etc.* Therefore, the pragmatic considerations discussed in the preceding paragraph suggested that the usage of the two groups should differ most in references to new developments—that is, in references to activities or situations which the context identified as being "on the increase" at the time of speaking as compared to an earlier time—as these references occurred in the largest blocks of discourse. Utterances of this kind were therefore separated from the other $P examples and were classed in a new sub-category, labeled P_{dv}.[11] Examples from the data are given in (8):

(8) P_{dv}: (On Puerto Rico) **Progresa.**, . . . **Cambia.** . . . *Todo lo están arreglando.* . . . *Ahora* **hacen** *muchos buildings nuevos, y barriadas* . . . *las* **ponen** *nuevas.* . . . *Esos arrabales los están eliminando* . . .   '*It's progressing.* . . . *It's changing.* . . . *They're fixing* everything. . . . *they're building* a lot of new buildings now, and neighborhoods . . . *they're rebuilding* them. . . . *They're doing away* with those slums . . . *they're building* projects. . . . *They're*

[11] It should be clear that it is only the pragmatic status of the P_{dv} utterances in *this particular corpus*—specifically, their tendency to occur in relatively longer connected contexts—that should make them especially hospitable to the simple present in the speech of nonbilinguals. Outside of comparable pragmatic circumstances (which here are due to the particular real-world interests of the speakers interviewed), P_{dv} utterances in general should favor the progressive present. For it is in reference to new developments that the current situation is most clearly counterposed to the habitual one. Accordingly, it seems that the more uncommon or less stereotyped exploitations of the progressive (i.e., those generally called "impossible") are found in utterances of this type (e.g., a Spanish example from my recordings: *Yo pesaba cientas* [sic] *doce, y ahora estoy pesando cientas veinte* 'I used to weigh 112 lbs. and now I'm weighing 120 lbs.'; an English example from the MacNeil/Lehrer report, 11/11/1976: *The public is stopping watching some of those* [*violent TV*] *shows*).

están haciendo proyectos. ... **Hacen** *muchas fáb-ricas.* *Todo* *el* *mundo* **mejora.**	*building* lots of factories. Every-one *is getting* better off.'
(On the speaker's progress in English)	
No lo **aprendo** *muy ligero.*	'*I'm* not *learning* it very fast.'
(On life in New York)	
No *me* **acostumbro** *mucho.*	'*I'm* not *getting used* to it much.'

Figure 4.2A gives the results for the P_{dv} utterances, as well as those for the remaining utterances in the P class (labeled P_{non-dv}). Figure 4.2B shows in graphic form the corresponding percentages of use of the simple present. Note that, as expected, the difference in usage between the NY and the PR groups is greatest in P_{dv} utterances. Note too that, as our hypothesis predicted, the relatively greater difference between the groups in P_{dv} utter-ances is due primarily to greater frequency of use of the simple present by the PR speakers. Thus, the results show the normal pragmatic strategies for use of the Spanish system to be as expected, on the assumption that the system itself is an imprecise one.

But in addition to this, the fact that the NY speakers' use of the simple present did not increase under favorable pragmatic conditions is in itself significant. For this suggests that—presumably under the influence of English—the NY system of present reference is undergoing a semantic change. Specifically, it seems that in NY Spanish the simple present is changing in meaning, with the result that it is becoming inappropriate for reference to X regardless of the pragmatic circumstances. This assumption is further supported by the more or less persistent (mis-) interpretations that I cited, on the part of some NY speakers, of the simple present as referring to Y (habitual activity) when it was actually intended to refer to X (ongoing activity).[12] This semantic change, then, would account for both the syntactic and the pragmatic differences observed between the NY speakers' usage and that of their PR counterparts.

In order to retest the various hypotheses a second series of interviews was conducted with eighteen other speakers: ten NY bilinguals and eight PR monolinguals. A special effort was now made to concentrate on those topics that, in the first series, had elicited relatively greater interest in the form of longer stretches of connected speech—that is, "new developments." Oth-erwise the method and criteria used were essentially the same as in the first series, except that in the second both the interviewing techniques and the composition of the informant groups were even more homogeneous than in

---

[12] Owing to the relatively unstructured format of the interviews, it was not possible to measure relative degree of misunderstanding.

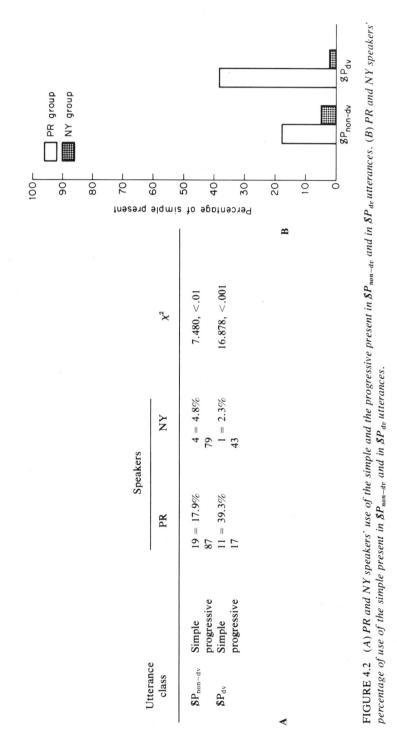

Utterance class	Speakers		χ^2
	PR	NY	
$\$P_{non-dv}$ Simple	19 = 17.9%	4 = 4.8%	7.480, <.01
progressive	87	79	
$\$P_{dv}$ Simple	11 = 39.3%	1 = 2.3%	16.878, <.001
progressive	17	43	

A

Percentage of simple present

PR group
NY group

$\$P_{non-dv}$ $\$P_{dv}$

B

FIGURE 4.2 (A) *PR and NY speakers' use of the simple and the progressive present in* $\$P_{non-dv}$ *and in* $\$P_{dv}$ *utterances.* (B) *PR and NY speakers' percentage of use of the simple present in* $\$P_{non-dv}$ *and in* $\$P_{dv}$ *utterances.*

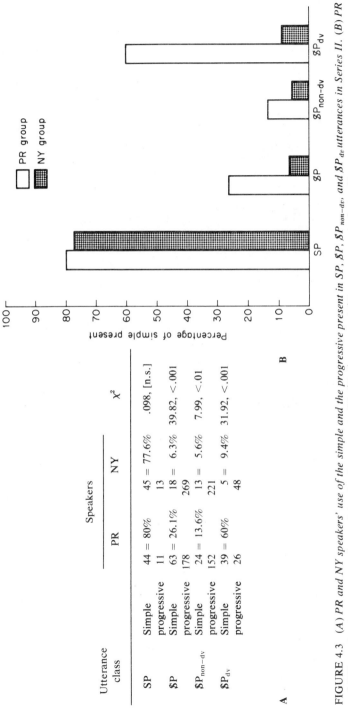

FIGURE 4.3 (A) PR and NY speakers' use of the simple and the progressive present in SP, ßP, ßP$_{non-dv}$, and ßP$_{dv}$ utterances in Series II. (B) PR and NY speakers' percentage of use of the simple present in SP, ßP, P$_{non-dv}$, and ßP$_{dv}$ utterances in Series II.

81

the first. In the second series, all speakers were between 16 and 20 years old, and none of the PR speakers could speak English.[13]

The results of the second series of interviews are given in Figure 4.3A, with the percentages of simple present also shown graphically in Figure 4.3B. Here the NY group did show somewhat higher use of the simple present in SP_{dv} utterances, as compared to the remaining utterances in the SP class (SP_{non-dv}): In SP_{dv} their percentage of simple present use was 9.4%, as compared to 5.6% in SP_{non-dv}. But the difference was still much greater among the PR speakers, whose use of the simple present was 60% in SP_{dv} utterances, compared to 13.6% in SP_{non-dv}. Thus, as the hypothesis predicted, increasing the opportunities for long stretches of connected discourse did result in even greater difference between the two groups. And as expected, the difference between them increased primarily in SP_{dv} utterances where it was mainly due to greatly increased frequency of simple present use by the PR speakers.

References

Bull, W. E. 1965. *Spanish for teachers*. New York: Ronald Press.

Diver, W. 1963. The chronological system of the English verb. *Word, 19,* 141–181.

Joos, M. 1964. *The English verb: Form and meanings*. Madison: University of Wisconsin Press.

Klein, F. 1975. Experimental verification of semantic hypotheses applied to mood in Spanish. *Georgetown Papers in Language and Linguistics* 17, Spring 1980.

Teschner, R. V., Bills, G. D., and Craddock, J. R. (Eds.) 1975. *Spanish and English of United States Hispanos: A critical, annotated, linguistic bibliography*. Arlington, Va.: Center for Applied Linguistics.

Weinreich, U. 1963. *Languages in contact*. The Hague: Mouton.

Weinreich, U., Labov, W., and Herzog, M. 1968. Empirical foundations for a theory of language change. In W. P. Lehmann and T. Malkiel (Eds.), *Directions for historical linguistics*. Austin: University of Texas Press.

[13] Also, in the second series all interviews included description of the pictures, besides "free" conversation. And all interviews were taped.

5

John Baugh

A REEXAMINATION OF THE BLACK ENGLISH COPULA[1]

Introduction

All facets of Afro-American behavioral research have obvious social implications. Undoubtedly, the catalytic impact of the civil rights movement has influenced this social orientation. In the case of linguistics, however, some of the most significant theoretical advances of our time can be linked directly with Black English Vernacular (BEV) research. In spite of the fact that scholars have typically approached BEV in a delicate and diplomatic manner, controversies rage at both professional and lay levels with regard to the viability and legitimacy of BEV research. This is not surprising because BEV is a stigmatized dialect and as such represents a highly personal and consequently an emotional topic. Though there are strong social concerns, and in some instances social consequences, involved in BEV analyses, affiliated linguistic issues also continually crop up. As a result we are forced to review the limitations, appropriateness, and social applicability of contemporary introspective linguistic theories. The present discussion, although rooted in a socially important topic, will stress linguistic concerns. This is not to suggest that the social aspects of BEV are being dismissed as unimportant, merely that they are not of primary concern here.

The present analysis reexamines the nature of copula variation in BEV and is cast in the tradition of the earlier copula research by Labov (1969) and Wolfram (1974). This analysis differs from previous examinations, however, in that more constraints have been introduced and the Cedergren–Sankoff computer program for multivariant analysis has been employed.

[1] I am grateful for comments on earlier versions of this chapter from Gillian Sankoff and William Labov.

The data are from the Cobras, an adolescent peer group that was interviewed by John Lewis ("KC") as part of Labov's earlier BEV research. Having conducted fieldwork of my own in a Los Angeles BEV community, I am aware of the stifling effect that the interview can have on the vernacular corpus. After reviewing Lewis's interview, however, I feel that the authenticity of the data is clear. At this point, let it suffice to say that Lewis showed an acute ethnosensitivity in all of the interviews that he gathered. Although these data are synchronic, the present analysis reveals some diachronic implications as well. To my knowledge, this investigation represents one of the first times that multivariant analysis has been used with regard to BEV for historical purposes.

Linguistic Variation and Linguistic Theory

When the variable rule was first introduced (Labov, 1969), the full potential of variable analysis for linguistic purposes could not be known. That its potential has been gradually maturing is seen in the works of Trudgill (1971), G. Sankoff (1974), Cedergren and Sankoff (1974), Wolfram (1974), Lavendera (1975), and others. In a sense one might view variable analysis as traditional in linguistic research; after all, what could be more natural or traditional than entering the speech community, gathering a corpus, reviewing the corpus for paradigms, and reporting the nature of linguistic systematicity wherever it is found? In spite of this traditional orientation, however, influential linguists have stressed the theoretical restrictions imposed by nonideal corpora. As a result, systematic variation—henceforth variation— has typically been viewed as free variation. In this instance it will be most beneficial to review affiliated theoretical and methodological concerns as they relate to BEV.

The research on BEV differs from the more formal research in linguistics because the latter analysis is usually inductive. Depending on one's theoretical perspective, this can be seen as a blessing or a curse. Whereas the evolution of formal linguistic research has resulted in a condition where many scholars turn to themselves as informants, there are few, if any, trained linguists whose intuitions about BEV are reliable for descriptive purposes. Another difficult choice must therefore be made. Should we strive to train speakers of Nonstandard English to become linguists so that they can then introspect about their language, or should we strive to enhance our empirical methodologies? Unquestionably, the only feasible alternative available to BEV is to continue with the empirical tradition. In training nonstandard speakers to become introspective linguists we would inevitably bombard their native intuitions with preconceptions to the point where the validity of these intuitions would be questionable.

What, then, does this have to do with linguistic theory? Quite simply, when we look at advances in linguistics, we see that the methodologies employed in introspective research are not generally applicable even in the first approach to a language. In turn, the scholar who is interested in BEV and in related social concerns finds that contemporary methodologies and theories are often not suited to the task. This is not a new point by any means; Hymes has repeatedly indicated that we must take ethnographic considerations into account when conducting linguistic investigations, simply because ethnographic factors DIRECTLY affect the language (cf. Hymes, 1962).

Returning to the special needs confronting BEV, then, there is an obvious need to enhance inductive methodologies. One could argue that these empirical needs have been in existence for many years, but in the case of BEV there seems to be a sense of urgency, a desire to rectify methodological inadequacies quickly. Unfortunately, the recognition of methodological and theoretical inadequacies does not lead immediately to rapid reassessment and revision. Nevertheless, significant strides are being made on several linguistic fronts and the resulting innovations can now be applied or reapplied as necessary. At this point in linguistic evolution, that is, with the maturation of variable research, it is safe to say that the incorporation of variable phenomena is a requisite for thorough descriptive purposes. And the greatest value lies in identifying the most significant constraints on these phenomena. A related concern must focus on what is meant by the term "Black English." In this chapter, for the sake of brevity, this issue is not treated in depth; Black English is used to refer to the vernacular dialect, namely, the dialect that is native to most working-class black Americans and that reflects the usage of "some or all of the features which are distinctive [in the colloquial dialects of these black Americans]."[2]

If we refine the accuracy of variable rules in the linguistic realm, the structural relations between Standard English (SE) and BEV will become clearer. In turn, such findings will bear directly on educational issues such as bidialectalism and linguistic–dialectal interference. Furthermore, the common concerns associated with English research in general must be considered. Given that BEV is structurally similar to SE, it stands as an important point of structural contrast and as such provides an excellent basis for comparing aspects of language change, language acquisition, and concepts of competence, both "linguistic" and "communicative" (cf. Hymes, 1974).[3] At present, linguistics is able to address these highly emotional topics with a high degree of objectivity. When valid linguistic correspondences or differ-

---

[2] I have expanded Fasold's (1969) definition in an effort to incorporate an implicit interactional dimension into the definition. It is, after all, the interactional component that Bloomfield has identified as instrumental in defining the speech community (cf. Bloomfield, 1933, p. 42).

[3] This does not imply that we should stay at the level of analyzing purely linguistic constraints. Rather, I suggest that we take full advantage of an accurate linguistic statement prior to incorporating constraints that cannot be defined with the same accuracy as linguistic phenomena.

ences can be revealed, we can hope to approach social and educational concerns with a higher level of accountability. I am suggesting that wherever systematic linguistic relationships can be identified, no matter how large or how small, those relationships should ultimately be addressed. To the extent that a given linguistic phenomenon cannot be examined or substantiated at the level of the informants within a speech community, one should question the legitimacy of the description.

The final point that I would like to make with regard to linguistic theory and variable linguistic phenomena is a personal one and closely related to BEV concerns generally. Many scholars who have little or no formal linguistic training have used the nonstandard speech of Afro-Americans as an indicator of communicative deprivation, cognitive limitation, and the like (cf. Bereiter and Engelmann, 1966). Although this is fallacious from a linguistic perspective, the nature of contemporary introspective linguistic methodology is coincidentally such that it implicitly supports the elitist perspective that assumes BEV to be an "inferior" dialect. I am not advocating as a moral obligation that we enhance empirical methods; rather, it would seem that BEV and many other stigmatized dialects throughout the world cannot be accurately described for social, educational, or other purposes until the descriptive limitations of introspective research are clearly exposed.

Field Methods

We have seen that there is a definite need to reestablish strong contacts in the speech community; it is equally important to recognize that the task of the fieldworker, especially the urban fieldworker, is difficult and often precarious, and requires an intimate ethnosensitivity to the speech community and to one's informants. This may seem to be an added burden, but in those instances where inductive evidence is the only legitimate source of data social obstacles are unavoidable.

Scanning the BEV literature written over the past decade, one is struck by the fact that much of the descriptive emphasis is focused on younger members of the community, with the data usually having been gathered by strangers (i.e. outsiders to the community) in unfamiliar surroundings. Efforts to justify these limited procedures have been based on the claim that children tend to be less formal than adults, and that, consequently, for descriptive purposes, the vernacular corpora of children represent the purest BEV forms. Such procedural limitations have been discussed before (cf. Wolfram, 1974; Mitchell-Kernan, 1971) and need not be further discussed here. However, the role of the BEV fieldworker needs to be reviewed more carefully.

The role of the fieldworker should be stressed if for no other reason than the accuracy of a final empirical analysis, but for BEV the significance of the fieldworker is critical. Ironically, there has been minimal concern—at least in the overwhelming majority of BEV research—with the importance of data gathering. It has been as if the desire to describe the language has taken precedence over the need to insure the accuracy of the corpus. Effective fieldwork can—and must—be carried out on Black English at all social levels. But the gathering of the vernacular of the city streets is fundamental for an accurate view of social, historical and educational issues.

As has been mentioned, most of the data used in this study were gathered from the Cobras by John Lewis (KC), who is an excellent fieldworker for BEV. Lewis, a black man, has lived through many of the same experiences as the Cobras, and is therefore intimately familiar with native topics of interest; he was able to argue with informants without social difficulty. These special skills were particularly useful because the Cobras lived in a situation where the ability to handle oneself in verbal confrontations was highly prized. Thus, Lewis's own verbal skill clearly increased his effectiveness as a fieldworker. Throughout these data, two factors seemed to enhance Lewis's interviews: his intimate understanding of his informants' social perspectives, and his close contacts with the Cobras in a variety of social situations—not merely in the interview.

The study of BEV has been plagued by shortcuts in the field and quiet dismissals of many adult informants for social reasons alone. Undeniably, the task of gathering BEV data is often difficult and this too is a social fact, but if we intend to address BEV in a traditionally sound manner, then we must enhance our field methods in general. Like KC, we must be able to take the time to gain the trust of several representative informants.

The BEV Copula: A Brief Review of Previous Research

Before moving on to the current analysis, let us review the implications of previous copula research. Although a variety of works on the copula have emerged in broader contexts, the present remarks are intended primarily with BEV and West Indian Creole (WIC) examinations in mind. In early statements of the creole position, Bailey (1965) and Stewart (1969) proposed that BEV had a zero copula. Although arguments for a zero copula, with emphasis on zero, have since been seen as greatly overstated, Bailey and Stewart established the importance of looking closely at the African and WIC roots of contemporary BEV.[4] Examining black–white linguistic relationships with emphasis on the creolist position, Stewart reviewed the grammatical relationship between SE and white nonstandard dialects in opposition to BEV and Gullah, and found that the auxiliary had unique and similar

---

[4] Again, we must appreciate that their remarks came at a time when the social atmosphere was such that the "awareness level," if you will, of many blacks was such that African origins were not only palatable but preferred.

markings in both Black dialects. In addition, examining another distinctive BEV feature (*be*), he questioned the possibility of European (Irish) influence:

> But if that is the origin of the Negro-dialect use of *be* (i.e., borrowed by Negroes, let us say, from Irish immigrants to North America), then why is it now so wide-spread among Negroes but so absent from the still somewhat Irish-sounding speech of many direct descendants of the Irish immigrants [1969, p. 16]?

For the purpose of the present discussion, concern necessarily concentrates on the historical influences that affect copula variation. But dialect borrowing need not be restricted to a single contact group. The Irish presence as indentured laborers and their subsequent role as slave overseers could easily explain the necessary dialectal contact. Nevertheless, the creolist position appears to be quite strong as well. It is quite possible and even likely that contemporary BEV dialects contain linguistic influences from both the Irish and the West Indians (cf. Traugott, 1972). These historical issues, although relevant to the current discussion, will be presented in greater detail at a later point in the chapter.

Labov (1969) found variation in the copula to be the result of a series of grammatical and phonological rules that were parallel to those of colloquial deletion in SE. Deletion in BEV was possible only in environments where contraction was possible in SE. Furthermore, the variable constraints on the contraction and deletion rules were parallel except for the phonological effects which opposed the deletion of a vowel to the deletion of a consonant. Labov's initial analysis has been confirmed and reduplicated in several studies (e.g., Legum *et al.*, 1971; Wolfram, 1969; Mitchell-Kernan, 1971).[5] Carrying the research further by building on the work of Labov, as well as aspects of his own research in Detroit, Wolfram (1974) examined the nature of copula variation in a comparison of white and black Southern speech.

But, although these studies have led to a synchronic understanding of copula variation, numerous historical questions still remain unanswered. Recognizing the complexity of the diachronic issues that surround this particular problem, Fasold (1976) proposes an alternative historical solution that takes both the creole and SE origins into account. Citing evidence from Botkin's narratives (1945) as a structural point for historical reference, as well as the contemporary works of Labov, Stewart, and his own previous discussion of the phenomena (1972); Fasold posits that the copula may have originally been omitted as a grammatical feature because of BEV's African and creole origins, but that this deletion was later transformed into a phonological rule. Furthermore, his argument suggests that the transition from initial grammatical constraints to more current phonological condition-

---

[5] A number of other works centering on the copula have treated it in broader linguistic and social contexts, for example, Day's work on Hawaiian Creole (1972) and Ferguson's multilingual comparative survey on the absence of the copula (1971).

ings could have taken place with minimal changes in the surface forms. We will return to Fasold's position shortly, but for the moment, let us say that his argument seems quite plausible given the strength of the arguments that have been presented from both sides of the diachronic debate.

The Present Analysis

The Cobra data are excellent from a synchronic standpoint owing to the handling of the data and the Cobra's collective command of BEV. But significant strides have also been made beyond the realm of field procedures: It is, appropriately, the advanced analytic techniques that have been developed by Cedergren and Sankoff, (1974) that now provide the necessary tools to look at these variable phenomena in more detail (cf. Griffin, Guy, and Sag, 1973; Guy, this volume, Chapter 1).

The Sample

These data were gathered in the mid-1960s. Since that time, some of the Cobras have ended up in jail or been killed or wounded in urban disputes. Most of the members are now in their mid to late twenties and, as far as I know, are still living in and around Harlem. I should also point out that KC did not record all of the 26 taped conversations of which the analyzed corpus is composed. Some of the interviews were conducted by Clarence Robins,[6] and some of the group interviews were successfully conducted by combinations of black and white investigators. For the most part, however, it was KC and the Cobras.

During the mid-1960s the primary concern of the Cobras was the defense of their "turf" against rivals, most notably the "Jets."[7] There came about a noteworthy philosophical change in the Cobras, however, with the members of the group striving to become more aware of their plight as Afro-Americans; consequently, they began to spout the rhetoric of black awareness and cultural taboos.[8] More generally, these transitions in attitude caused the Cobras to question their outlook on society and several of the interviews contain the theme of "the plight of black America(ns)." In all, the data contained 578 tokens (i.e., environments where we would anticipate the presence of a copula in other dialects). Table 5.1 shows the breakdown of the totals in relation to the following grammatical constraints.

---

[6] Clarence Robins worked closely with John Lewis in gathering BEV data. Robins was also one of the co-authors of Labov et al., 1968.

[7] The Jets were also studied in Labov's original work and a detailed description of the peer group can be found in Labov et al., 1968.

[8] I am using "black rhetoric" here because the Cobras were obviously imitating popular rhetorical styles and as a result would often contradict themselves on a variety of ideological points.

TABLE 5.1
*Sample Totals for the Cobras: Based on Following
Grammatical Constraints*

gon(na)	Verb + ing	Loc/Adj	NP	Misc.
108	122	134	162	53

locative   adjective   NP   Det. # NP

48   86   126   36

Total = 578

The Analytic Procedure

The first version of the Cedergren–Sankoff program for multivariant analyses was run on the Cobra data in two series of calculations: (*a*) calculations that measured the same constraints as were measured by Labov and Wolfram; (*b*) a series of calculations that introduced new and subdivided constraints. Since Labov's original analysis employed an additive model, and Wolfram's analysis concentrated on white informants, it was felt that the synchronic clarification of BEV copula variation would be enhanced at this time by employing the Cedergren–Sankoff program.[9]

Once having conducted an initial series of calculations on the familiar constraints, it was necessary to repeat the calculations incorporating the following adaptations:

1. Question/non-question: Each token was identified as either a question or non-question and was submitted under this new factor group.
2. Miscellaneous factor for following grammatical constraints: It was necessary to introduce a miscellaneous category for those instances where the arbitrary factors were insufficient. For the most part these were adverbs of manner.
3. The subdivision of __ NP: Previously, following NP had been calculated as a single factor. The secondary calculations dividing this factor into:
   (*a*) __ NP
   (*b*) __ Det. # NP (i.e., *a* and *the*)
4. The separation of __ Loc/Adj: Heretofore, the analysis of __ Loc/Adj. appeared as a single constraint owing to quantitative confines. The Cedergren–Sankoff program, however, allowed the present separation of these features.

[9] At the 1976 NWAVE conference at Georgetown University, Pascale Rousseau presented advances in the computer program that have not been included in this analysis; however, the revised program is available for general use at this time. She and David Sankoff are most responsible for the many technical improvements in variable rule research.

The Comparable Calculations

At first blush, the need for a comparable series of calculations might seem dubious, and cumbersome, but it was felt that a parallel series of calculations would substantiate and/or clarify previous synchronic assessments and show whether the original relations were preserved in a multivariant analysis with extended (i.e., finely divided) constraints. Thus, the first series of calculations was purposely designed to mesh with the previous analyses of Wolfram and Labov, in that identical factors were analyzed. Parenthetically, Cedergren and Sankoff developed their computer methods—at least in part—by reexamining Labov's 1969 data, and they found that their fit of prediction with observation reliably identified those environments that favored both contraction and deletion.

Table 5.2 shows that, as in Labov, 1969, a preceding pronoun subject heavily favors contraction and somewhat less strongly favors deletion. The phonological effects do not show the reversal for contraction and deletion, but preceding vowels still tend to favor both rules. However, the differential effect on both rules will emerge as the analysis proceeds. The following phonological consonant appears to have an increased effect, but this will diminish in later analyses as well (see Table 5.3). The significant revisions of the original examination concentrate on the following grammatical constraints; these will therefore be of primary concern here.

The percentages from Labov's original research for the Cobras, of full, contracted, and deleted forms of *is* according to the preceding and following grammatical environments are given in Figure 5.1.

TABLE 5.2
Feature Weights for the Comparable Series of Calculations for All Measured Constraints

	Contraction	Deletion
-C__	0.000	0.000
-V__	.396	.239
__C-	.465	.525
__V-	0.000	0.000
NP__	0.000	0.000
Pro__	.919	.622
__gon(na)	1.000	.567
__Vb + ing	1.000	.375
__PA/Loc	.336	.868
__NP	.430	0.000

TABLE 5.3
Feature Weights for Phonological Constraints

		Contraction	Deletion
Labov	-C__	.410	.800
	-V__	.900	.410
Present analysis	-C__	0.000	.061
	-V__	.408	0.000
	__C-	.522	.322
	__V-	0.000	0.000

The current contours, based on feature weights from the nonapplications probability model, appear in Figure 5.2. (Labov's illustrated contours are separated with regard to preceding grammatical constraints, whereas the present multivariant analysis does not need to make this kind of separation since all groups are considered simultaneously.) With the exception of the PA/Loc,[10] the orderings from the multivariant analysis are substantially the same with regard to the relative impact of following grammatical constraints

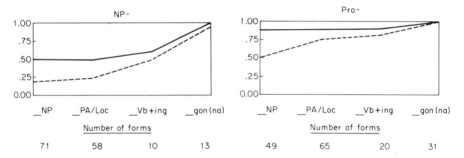

FIGURE 5.1 *Percentage of full, contracted, and deleted forms of* is *according to preceding and following environments for the Cobras:* ——, *percentage contracted;* – – – –, *percentage deleted.* (*From Labov, 1972, p. 92.*)

---

[10] Those who are familiar with previous analyses will immediately recognize that the new implications of the PA/Loc. reversal are not a trivial matter. The situation has changed, or rather, the assessment of the situation has changed, because of a complete analysis. Please recall that previous analyses for the Cobras did not account for all of the available data: ". . . the data presented here do not exhaust all the material which is available for the Jets and Cobras . . . [Labov, 1972, p. 91]." The present analysis does exhaust the Cobra data in a multivariant analysis, and the difference that has emerged results from the thorough analysis. It is important, therefore, that the difference illustrated in Figure 5.2 is not construed as a conflict with earlier research.

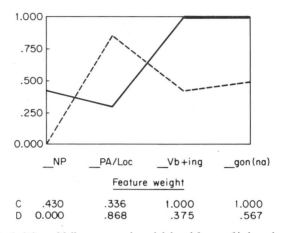

	__NP	__PA/Loc	__Vb+ing	__gon(na)
		Feature weight		
C	.430	.336	1.000	1.000
D	0.000	.868	.375	.567

FIGURE 5.2 *Probability of full, contracted, and deleted forms of* is *based on feature weights according to following grammatical constraints for the Cobras:* ———, φ *contracted;* – – – –, φ *deleted.*

on the contraction and deletion rules. Wolfram's analysis of white Southern speakers reflects similar patterns as well:

> The patterning of *is* -deletion, although restricted in terms of the proportion of informants who realize the rule and the frequency with which it occurs for these informants, does appear to be a process found among some white Southern dialects. From a qualitative viewpoint, it appears to be a process quite similar to the one observed for VBE [Wolfram, 1974, p. 514].

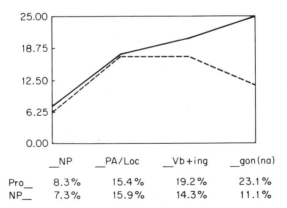

	__NP	__PA/Loc	__Vb+ing	__gon(na)
Pro__	8.3%	15.4%	19.2%	23.1%
NP__	7.3%	15.9%	14.3%	11.1%

FIGURE 5.3 *Percentage of* is *absence in Pro—and NP—by following* environments for white southern speakers: ———, *Pro——;* – – – –, *NP——.* (*From Wolfram, 1974, p. 514.*)

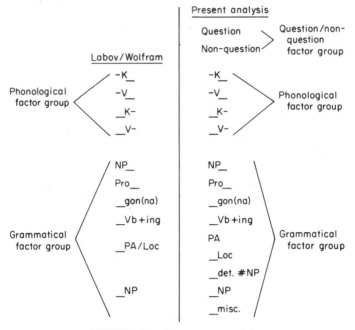

FIGURE 5.4 *Factor group revision.*

Before shifting the focus to the second series of calculations we might ask ourselves about the structural similarities and what they mean. First of all, given the increased potential and analytic accountability of the Cedergren–Sankoff program, we see that, by and large, previous assessments were legitimate in their rule orderings. But, additionally, the present confirmation now allows us to look at the nature of each constraint more closely. Thus, leaving aside the factor revisions that we mentioned, the remaining constraints in the second series of calculations were the same. (see Figure 5.4).

The Phonological Constraints

Beginning with preceding phonological constraints, we find the following (see Table 5.3).

In the earlier analysis, the following phonological environment was significant only for adults; here it appears that both contraction and deletion are favored by a following consonant, which indicates the likelihood that an underlying copula is present.

It is important to recall that $-C\_$ factors appear less frequently than do $-V\_$ factors since all relevant pronouns end in vowels. Nevertheless, the comparative findings clearly indicate consistencies with regard to implications for the preceding phonological conditionings: namely, $-V\_$ favors contraction over deletion, whereas the reverse is true for $-C\_$. The difference that is illustrated here, however, would indicate that the phonological constraints are not the strongest constraints with regard to either rule. At the same time, the weighting for $-V\_$ (.408 contraction) is the stronger phonological constraint and this accentuates the comparability with previous assessments.

The preceding phonological factors, in spite of the vocalic appearance as a "slight" constraint are significant because they confirm the preference of a CVC pattern (cf. Labov *et al.*, 1968; Labov, 1969). The maintenance of a CVC pattern is further supported when we consider that much of the evidence of pidgins and creoles has suggested that CVC contours are generally present in contact vernaculars (cf. Hall, 1966). From the standpoint of a more general picture of the phonological conditioning for BEV, consider the case as stated by Labov, 1972 (see Table 5.3): "In any case, the way in which contraction and deletion are opposed with respect to the preceding vowel clearly demonstrates that both contraction and deletion are phonological processes . . [p. 106]." The present research, although still upholding this position, does not emphasize phonological conditioning in a PRIMARY sense. The point will be examined further when the independence of phonological and grammatical constraints is reviewed, but for the moment it is significant to note that the phonological conditioning is maintained although it does not receive primary emphasis.

The Question of Weightings

The situation with regard to questions is fairly complex, owing to the phonological, morphological, and syntactic issues that relate to the general class of questions proper and the issues that relate specifically to those questions occurring in copula constructions. From the standpoint of phonology, final *ts* clusters have been shown to have a unique effect on rule application; consequently, *it's, that's,* and *what's* are generally omitted in this type of analysis (cf. Labov, 1969; Wolfram, 1974), as they have been here. But given the importance of *what* in the broader context of questions, its omission necessarily limits the extent to which the impact of questions can accurately be assessed with regard to contraction and deletion. Also, considering the exclusive focus on *is* here, the scope of the question factor is further restricted (see Table 5.4).

The Grammatical Constraints

The grammatical arguments surrounding copula variation are by far the most interesting. In the past, it has primarily been the grammatical con-

TABLE 5.4
Feature Weights for Question Constraints

	Question	Nonquestion
Contradiction	1.000	0.000
Deletion	1.000	0.000

straints, and, more specifically, the explanations surrounding various grammatical conditionings, that have lent viable support to both the creole and the English diachronic perspectives. Although the historical alternatives are not of primary importance at this point in the discussion, it is significant to note that the grammatical issues cover a tremendously wide range of diachronic and synchronic territory. This is clearly the case because scholars have been able to construct feasible, yet different, explanations from similar synchronic evidence. With the complexity of grammatical features having been noted, the nature of their conditionings may now be described.

Preceding Grammatical Constraints

Table 5.5 shows that a preceding pronoun favors both rules, with contraction receiving primary emphasis. This is not surprising given the discussion surrounding pro__:

> it is plain that contraction is heavily favored when the subject is a pronoun. But the effect is much stronger than for other noun phrases ending in vowels. In the case of deletion, it can be seen that the rule operates much more often when a pronoun precedes . . . [Labov, 1972, pp. 106–107].

A further significant finding here that confirms previous analyses is the replication of the powerful constraint exerted by preceding NP. And, whereas Wolfram and Labov examined the nature of following grammatical

TABLE 5.5
Effect of Preceding NP or Pro on Contraction and Deletion as Shown by Feature Weights

	NP __	Pro __
Contraction	0.000	.856
Deletion	0.000	.714

conditionings based on separate analyses of the preceding factors, the present analysis has the advantage of being able to identify the overall conditioning. We can therefore see the relative impact of preceding grammatical elements without sacrificing other facets of the analysis.

Following Grammatical Constraints

UNCHANGED FACTORS

The only factors to remain the same in the following grammatical factor group were (a) _gon(na) and (b) _ verb + ing. Both of these factors reflect the same conditioning and rule orderings that have been identified in the past: Following gon(na) strongly favors contraction and has a significant effect on deletion; verb + ing also favors contraction with a somewhat lesser effect on deletion (see Table 5.6). Stated simply, in the final analysis the relation of _ gon(na) and _ verb + ing to other constraints remains unchanged when all analyses are considered.

THE SUBDIVISION OF FOLLOWING NP

With the complementary factors indicating similar rule orderings, we can now review the implications of the adjusted factors beginning with the following NP. Previous analyses have examined _ NP as a single constraint. The present analysis, however, has subdivided _ NP into two factors.

Labov/Wolfram   The present analysis

                                              —→-- _ a NP
                    ————→ _ Det. # NP ————→-- _ the NP
_ NP ——→——————————→ _ NP

Thus, the implications that have been posited with regard to a following NP can now be reviewed more closely. Consider the rule conditionings that have been suggested thus far (see Figures 5.1, 5.2, and 5.3). As these findings stand, their impact would suggest _ NP as the least favored environment—within the realm of the following grammatical factors—for the

TABLE 5.6
Effect of Following Gon(na) *and Verb* + ing *on Contraction and Deletion Feature Weights*

	_ Gon(na)	_ Verb + ing
Contraction	1.000	1.000
Deletion	.601	.402

TABLE 5.7
Effect of a Following NP or Det. # NP on Contraction and Deletion as Shown by Feature Weights

	__ NP	__ Det. # NP
Contraction	0.000	1.000
Deletion	0.000	.741

application of either rule. With the division of the factor, however, another picture emerges (Table 5.7). We can see, therefore, that it is necessary to subdivide __ NP in the preceding manner because the true nature of the conditioning is camouflaged until this is done. The significance of this separation is further amplified because __ Det. # NP now emerges as a primary factor in the application of both rules. The other side of the coin finds residual __ NP as a low level constraint; in fact, __ NP is the least favored following grammatical factor.

FURTHER CONFIRMATION OF THE INDEPENDENCE OF
PHONOLOGICAL AND GRAMMATICAL CONDITIONING

At this stage of the discussion, it is beneficial to look back at some of the concerns that have been raised with regard to the independence of phonological and grammatical constraints (cf. Fraser, 1972). In spite of the importance of the various historical options that have been aired, there still remains some confusion—and some justifiable concern—as to the independence of analyzed constraints. We find grammatical criteria and phonological criteria, and numerous questions as to their mutual dependence or independence. The subdivision of our __ NP constraint, however, clearly emphasizes the independence of previously discussed phonological factors, namely, the preference for CVC sequences. The phonological conditioning is clear, but, more than that, the present analysis suggest that grammatical and phonological factors are independent. Turning our attention to grammatical concerns, then, we are again faced with the prospect of an either/or hypothesis: grammar or phonology. The reweighting of the subdivided __ NP constraint, however, would suggest that an either/or approach is insufficient;[11] consider the phonological relations as illustrated here:

```
                        ┌───→ a NP    ___ Obligatory vocalic status
__ Det. # NP →──┘
                        └───→ the NP  ___ Obligatory consonantal status
```

[11] Traugott (1972, p. 5) has discussed the limits of an either/or perspective with regard to the historical issues before. The new findings presented here tend to reinforce her position.

Given the rule-favoring strength of the __ Det. # NP factors (i.e., contraction [1.000], deletion [.741]), we clearly see the overriding impact of the grammatical conditioning. This being the case, the obvious questions shifts to what might be perceived as a conflict between the preference for CVC contours and the grammatical conditioning. The point that is being emphasized here is that NO SUCH CONFLICT EXISTS; rather, these findings suggest that both grammatical and phonological conditionings are operating simultaneously. Undoubtedly, this simultaneity is selectively conditioned and therefore should not be generalized. Thus, the present analysis, while providing additional insights into the synchronic nature of copula variation, has also confirmed that phonological conditionings and grammatical conditionings are operating simultaneously. It will be necessary to return to this point with regard to Fasold's historical discussion, but for the moment it is significant to note the independence of grammar and phonology—that is, the reconfirmation of their independence and, more importantly, the fact that both condition rule application in selective ways.

The Separation of Locatives and Adjectives

The final grammatical features that must be reviewed are the following locatives and adjectives. Heretofore, PA/Loc. has been measured as a single constraint. The limitation in the past was simply a quantitative barrier. "Because the total number of forms is considerably reduced for each group (even when single and group styles are combined), the following predicate adjectives and locatives are given together [Labov, 1972, p. 92]." Wolfram (1974) also measured locatives and adjectives as a single constraint, stating:

> Although there may be justification for categorizing this set on a different basis (e.g., considering adjectives as verbs, treating locatives as a separate category, etc.), it (i.e., the classification of factors) is considered here in the more traditional classification for the sake of comparability with previous studies [p. 505].

Whereas previous samples may have been considered too small, they are not so rare that their isolated conditionings cannot be accurately assessed at this time.

In the case of locatives, the conditioning is similar to the combined conditionings that have been reported in the past (see Table 5.8). The contraction rule is strong and is also favored over deletion. In addition, the ordering of these rules would strongly suggest an underlying copula, at least in this environment. With adjectives, an unexpected result appears. The rule orderings are emphatically reversed. Reflecting momentarily on the implications of the combined constraints, we see that the true nature of the conditioning was previously obscured. It is of course important to note that previous efforts combined these factors out of procedural necessity; however,

TABLE 5.8
*Impact of Following Locative and Adjective on
Contraction and Deletion as Shown by
Feature Weights*

	_Locative	_Adjective
Contraction	1.000	.116
Deletion	.682	1.000

with the difference now revealed, we must turn to the more complicated questions of how and why.

For the sake of discussion, let us assume for the moment that the unexpected did not occur: that locatives and adjectives reported similar weightings and by extension, indicated rule orderings as suggested in previous analyses. The situation would merely be one of synchronic clarification. Since the rules are emphatically reversed, however, the historical question of an underlying copula in BEV becomes more complicated and, by extension, requires further diachronic perusal. Now that adjectives have been shown to favor deletion in a rather convincing manner (deletion = 1.000; contraction = .116), the crossover pattern of the rule orderings suggests dialectal influence from at least two sources (see Table 5.8). The implication for adjectives is that deletion must have predated "the emergence of contracted forms for this environment.

Based on the illustrated examples, we can see that previous assessments suggest consistent rule orderings with regard to all of the following grammatical constraints (Figures 5.1 and 5.3). Moreover, the historical implications that such an ordering supports would lead one to the conclusion that an underlying copula was a general feature of BEV at an earlier point in history. However, with adjectives favoring deletion over contraction, it is quite possible that a ZERO COPULA did exist in protoforms. This possibility is further reinforced by the relatively slight influence that adjectives have on the contraction rule. This does not imply that we should posit a zero copula in all environments any more than that we should assume an underlying copula was automatically present. Rather, the new locative and adjectival findings would again suggest that phonological and grammatical conditionings are operating independently yet simultaneously, with emphasis, of course, on environmental—and possibly historical—selectivity. The diachronic implications of these findings are unavoidable given the rule reversals that have been identified. It is important to maintain caution in this diachronic regard, and to recognize the limits that such speculation has previously brought to bear. Wolfram (1974) states the case concisely:

This is the historical question of how VBE and Southern white speech arose, and how the relationship between black and white speech has developed since the settlement of the United States. In spite of the polemic with which the various historical options have been aired, evidence at this point still tends to be fragmented and anecdotal [p. 522].

Some Historical Implications

In this instance, my proposed historical explanation is not based on speculation alone. Recalling the orientation of Fasold's recent discussion, namely, that both grammatical and phonological influences can account for fluctuations in the BEV copula, we can see that his position receives further confirmation based on the final analysis presented here. Let us now consider aspects of Fasold's discussion:

Proponents of the Creole history of Vernacular Black English often disagree with linguists who have studied the dialect synchronically over the degree to which decreolization has progressed. . . Accepting Labov's analysis of the modern dialect is not tantamount to a denial of the Creole origin hypothesis, but simply to recognize that VBE has reached a late post-Creole stage.

Fasold goes on to outline a "hypothesized development of present tense *be* deletion in Black English." For the purpose of the discussion at hand, his concluding remarks are illuminating:

It is interesting to notice, if I am correct in the historical analysis of *be* forms, that while substantial changes in rules are going on in the background, the surface forms change little. From Stage 3 on, once *da* is relexified as *is,* there continues to be variation between *is* and deletion up to the present day.

As the situation stands now, with Fasold's position reinforced by the present analysis, we would posit that European versus African perspectives on the diachronic origins of BEV are far too simplistic. What is needed is evidence that substantiates a position that further considers both the African and European influence; but for the moment let us consider the linguistic consequence of West Indian contact.

Based on a comparison of two Creole varieties, Holm (1975) examined the grammatical hierarchy of following grammatical constraints. Concentrating on Jamaican (Le Page and De Camp, 1960) and Turner's description of Gullah (1949), Holm found that the syntactic environments where copula deletion were favored differed from the orderings initially identified by Labov. Holm's analysis is illuminating, and the constraint orderings that he has identified are given in Table 5.9.

Holm's research is quite similar to the present analysis because of his quantitative methodology. But more immediately relevant to my purpose is Holm's demonstration of the importance of separating locatives and adjec-

TABLE 5.9
*Grammatical Hierarchy Based on Percentage of
Deletion for Jamaican and Gullah*

Jamaican	Percentage	Gullah	Percentage
—Adj.	66	—*gonna*	88
—*gonna*	32	—Adj.	52
—NP	22	—V	52
—V	17	—Loc.	22
—Loc.	17	—NP	11

tives. The orderings that Holm has identified tend to confirm the altered grammatical conditionings that have been identified in the present analysis.

In an effort to further resolve the issue, let us turn out attention to Bailey's (1966) description of Jamaican Creole English (JCE). Bailey has identified the nature of locatives and adjectives in JCE as follows:

1. Locatives: "the locating verb (V_L) de, 'be' . . . MUST be followed by a locative complement or modifier [emphasis my own]."

   (a) *im de a yaad*
   'She is at home.'

   (b) *jan no de ya nou*
   'John is not here now.'

   (c) *wan trii de batamsaid me hous*
   'There is a tree below my house.'

2. Adjectives: The adjectives in JCE operate similarly to those used by the Cobras, that is, the *be* form is absent.

   (a) *di kaafi kuol*
   'The coffee is cold.'

   (b) *di tiicha gud*
   'The teacher is good.'

   (c) *di bos faas*
   'The bus is fast' [pp. 43, 64].

If we keep in mind the inverse relationship observed in Table 5.9 and how the present assessment differs from the implicit historical perspective presented by Labov (see Figure 5.1), the diachronic aspect of this variation becomes clearer. In the case of locatives, the *—de* + loc. constructions that Bailey has outlined in JCE are structurally similar to the overriding number of full and contracted forms that have been used by the Cobras. One would necessarily attribute this to an underlying copula, as seen in JCE. Thus, this particular environment in BEV unquestionably reflects structural similarities to JCE (see the relationships presented in Figure 5.5).

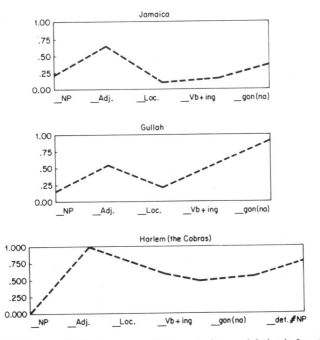

FIGURE 5.5 The impact of following grammatical constraints on deletion in Jamaica, Gollah, and Harlem (the Cobras).

The argument is further strengthened when applied to adjectives because, with the strength of the deletion rule now revealed, related historical concerns must come to the fore. This being the case, the adjectival evidence from JCE, which is structurally similar to the corresponding evidence from the Cobras, lends additional support to the position that there was no copula before adjectives. This also reinforces the creole origin hypothesis. When we consider the overall implications of the preceding investigations, the quantitative confirmation that emerges from the present analysis establishes the creole ancestry of contemporary BEV beyond any doubt.

At this point, however, it is wise to look at the historical implications a little more closely. Although it is necessary to recognize that creole origins have been posited before, it is equally important to recognize that many of these positions were presented prior to concise verification of the historical, empirical, or quantitative facts. The present confirmation, then, stresses the need for this type of validation, especially given the social importance of these historical questions and the availability of new analytic techniques.

Conclusion

The historical perspective that is revealed here can be simply stated in spite of the rather elaborate steps that have brought us to this point. It appears that the synchronic status of BEV copula variation has been influenced by West Indian creoles, as well as by SE. Based on the evidence presented, this seems to be the only feasible alternative. Moreover, when all of the structural and phonological facts are weighed, arguments for African versus European origins must again be seen as overly simplistic.

There are unavoidable limitations to the diachronic scope of research on stigmatized languages. This is simply because many of today's stigmatized dialects and languages were the languages of the poor and uneducated classes of yesteryear. The present analysis and discussion attempts to take a step forward with the recognition that new diachronic tools must continually be forged for stigmatized languages. We have justifiably been distracted by the linguistic machinery that seems to operate so quickly, cleanly, and efficiently in more prestigious languages. The question is, are we to let the efficiency of prestigious linguistics dictate the focus, direction, and overall development of these new and special tools?

The fact that BEV should not be viewed in a monogenetic fashion is not surprising considering the wide range of embryonic explanations which have been debated at such length. The difference that I wish to stress focuses on accountability. Based on the needs of linguistics, and for that matter those of all the behavioral sciences, as well as the needs of those who are the object of our scientific investigations, we must continue to strive to maximize the level of accountability before we neglect available data from real world contexts.

It is easy to see how linguists, influenced by a desire to pursue theory, have in large part tried to avoid the descriptive limitations imposed by inductive corpora. However, we must focus our efforts on thorough linguistic descriptions. As long as scholars are willing to dismiss empirical evidence under the banner of "performance" our descriptions will never reflect the complete structure of *langue*. As long as systematic variation exists, and as long as these phenomena are beyond the introspective grasp of the analyst, we must be willing to reestablish the empirical traditions that will expose such phenomena; otherwise, our descriptions cannot possibly represent *langue* in an actual sense.

In the case of BEV, however, the situation is even more complex. The social inequities and problems that were responsible for the initial hubbub about Afro-American research, or lack of it, are still with us today. In fact, these concerns are more vital than ever because many Afro-Americans still suffer from poverty and, by extension, from its social and cultural side effects. The unemployment figures from any urban city in the United States will substantiate my point. Those of us who are concerned with the social consequences of linguistic research are confronted with several decisions. Even when confined to the realm of obligatory empirical research, these decisions cannot be taken lightly. The need to enhance methodologies and theories is clearly desirable whenever and wherever possible, especially considering the subjective tradition within the field.

When one considers the extraneous factors that can influence the impetus and direction of future BEV research, it is important to recognize the unique position in which linguistics finds itself. In the case of BEV, we should make every effort to capitalize on strict linguistic principles to insure that our socially relevant concerns are not distorted by preconceived notions. We have a rare opportunity to make precise statements about an aspect of human behavior. Furthermore, we can hope that such information will benefit native members of the speech community.

References

Anshen, F. 1969. *Speech variation among Negroes in a small Southern community.* Unpublished doctoral dissertation, New York University.

Bailey, B. L. 1965. Toward a new perspective in Negro English dialectology. *American Speech, 40,* 171–77.

Bailey, B. L. 1966. *Jamaican creole syntax.* London: Cambridge University Press.

Bereiter, C., and Engelmann, S. 1966. *Teaching disadvantaged children in the pre-school.* Englewood Cliffs, N.J.: Prentice-Hall.

Bloomfield, L. 1933. *Language.* London: George Allen & Unwin.

Botkin, B. A. 1945. *Lay my burden down: A folk history of slavery.* Chicago: University of Chicago Press.

Cedergren, H. J., and Sankoff, D. 1974. Variable rules: Performance as a statistical reflection of competence. *Language, 50,* 333–355.

Day, R. 1972. *Patterns of variation in the use of tense, aspect and diathesis in the Hawaiian Creole continuum.* Unpublished doctoral dissertation, University of Hawaii.

Fasold, R. W. 1969. Tense and the form *be* in Black English. *Language, 45,* 763–776.

Fasold, R. W. 1972. Decreolization and autonomous language change. *Florida FL Reporter, 10:* 9–12, 51.

Fasold, R. W. 1976. One hundred years from syntax to phonology. Chicago Linguistic Society, University of Chicago.

Ferguson, C. A. 1971. Absence of copula and the notion of simplicity: A study of normal speech, baby talk, foreigner talk and pidgins. In D. Hymes (Ed.), *Pidginization and creolization of languages.* Cambridge: University Press.

Fraser, B. 1972. Optional rules in grammar. *Monograph Series on Languages and Linguistics, Georgetown University, 25,* 1–16.

Griffin, P., Guy, G., and Sag, I. 1973. Variable analysis of variable data. *University of Michigan Papers in Linguistics, 1.*

Hall, R. A., Jr. 1966. *Pidgin and creole languages.* Ithaca, N.Y.: Cornell University Press.

Harris, Z. 1951. *Methods in structural linguistics.* Chicago: University of Chicago Press.

Holm, J. 1975. Variability of the copula in Black English and its creole kin. Unpublished manuscript.

Hymes, D. 1962. The ethnography of speaking. In T. Gladwin and W. C. Sturtevant (Eds.), *Anthropology and human behavior.* Washington, D.C.: Anthropological Society of Washington.

Hymes, D. 1974. *Foundations in sociolinguistics.* Philadelphia: University of Pennsylvania Press.

Labov, W. 1969. Contraction, deletion and inherent variability of the English copula. *Language, 45,* 715–762.

Labov, W. 1972. *Language in the inner city.* Philadelphia: University of Pennsylvania Press.

Labov, W., Cohen, P., Robins, C., Lewis, J. 1968. *A study of the non-standard English of Negro and Puerto Rican speakers in New York City.* USOE Final Report, Research Project No. 3288.

Lavendera, B. 1975. *Linguistic structure and sociolinguistic conditioning in the use of verbal endings in si-clauses (Buenos Aires Spanish).* Unpublished doctoral dissertation, University of Pennsylvania.

Legum, S. E., Pfaff, C., Tinnie, G., and Nicholas, M. 1971. *The speech of young black children in Los Angeles.* Technical report 33. Inglewood, California: Southwest Regional Laboratory.

LePage, R. and DeCamp, D. 1960. *Jamaican creole (creole language studies I).* London: Macmillan.

Mitchell-Kernan, C. 1971. *Language behavior in a black urban community.* Language-Behavior Research Laboratory Monographs, 2. Berkeley: University of California.

Sankoff, G. 1974. A quantitative paradigm for the study of communicative competence. In R. Baumann and J. Sherzer (Eds.), *Explorations in the ethnography of speaking.* London: Cambridge University Press.

Stewart, W. A. 1967. Sociolinguistic factors in the history of American Negro dialects. *Florida FL Reporter, 5:* 2, 11, 22, 24, 26.

Stewart, W. A. 1969. Historical and structural bases for the recognition of Negro dialect. *Monograph Series on Languages and Linguistics, Georgetown University, 22,* 515–524.

Traugott, E. C. 1972. Principles in the history of American English—a reply. *Florida FL Reporter, 10:* 5–6, 56.

Trudgill, P. J. 1971. The social differentiation of English in Norwich. Unpublished doctoral dissertation, University of Edinburgh.

Turner, L. 1949. *Africanisms in the Gullah dialect.* Chicago: University of Chicago Press.

Wolfram, W. 1969. *A sociolinguistic description of Detroit Negro speech.* Washington, D.C.: Center for Applied Linguistics.

Wolfram, W. 1974. The relationship of white southern speech to vernacular Black English. *Language, 50,* 498–527.

6

Walt Wolfram

a-PREFIXING IN APPALACHIAN ENGLISH[1]

Introduction

Of the variety of forms that characterizes what we may loosely refer to as Appalachian English (AE), perhaps the form that holds the most linguistic interest is the *a*- prefix occurring with -ing participial.[2] Thus, in Appalachian English we encounter sentences like the following:

(1) a. . . . *and John boy, he come **a-runnin'** out there and got shot*   44:6
 b. *It was a dreadful sight, fire was **a-flamin'** everything.*   16:(434)
 c. *He just kept **a-beggin'** and **a-cryin'** and **a-wantin'** to go out*   83:18

Although forms such as those given in (1) have been found to occur in a number of varieties of American English, they are apparently most frequent in AE (Atwood, 1953, p. 35), so that a survey of AE provides an ideal data

[1] Donna Christian, Peg Griffin, Roger W. Shuy, Ralph W. Fasold, Corky Crawford Feagin, and Becky Michael are among those who have made significant comments on an earlier version of this paper. In several cases, they rescued me from my own lack of insight by suggesting alternative analyses.

[2] There are occasional occurrences of *a*-prefixed forms on items other than -*ing* participial forms [e.g., *I went through a house that's supposed to be a-haunted.* 17:(1194).] These include participial -*ed* forms and even nonparticipial adjectives and adverbs. In this account, we shall not be considering these infrequent occurrences of *a*-prefixing on non-*ing* participial forms.

[3] Sentences taken from our corpus are referenced by the informant number preceding the colon and the page on our typescript where the example is found following the colon. In the case of informants for which we have no typescript, the counter number on the tape recorder is included within parentheses.

Due to the regular realization of the -*ing* participial forms as [ɪn] or [ɨn] phonetically, we have adopted the popular convention in which these forms are indicated as *in'* orthographically.

LOCATING LANGUAGE IN TIME AND SPACE

base for the analysis of this form. A-prefixing is, of course, a linguistic phenomenon that has solid historical roots in the history of the English language. Krapp is just one of the many writers on the history of the English language who notes the occurrence of this form.

> A very frequent syntactical form of contemporary popular speech is that which puts an *a* before every present participle, especially after *go,* as in *to go a-fishing, bye baby bunting, daddy's gone a-hunting,* etc. In phrases like these, the construction is historical, the *a-* being a weakened form of the Old English preposition *on* in unstressed position, and *fishing, hunting,* etc., being originally verbal nouns which have been assimilated in form and, to a considerable extent, in feeling, to present participles. Starting with these phrases, however, the *a-* has been prefixed to genuine present participles, after forms of *to be* and other verbs, with the result that in popular speech almost every word ending in *-ing* has a sort of prefix, *a-* [1925, p. 268].

Most sources consider *a*-prefixing to be derived historically from prepositions, notably *on.* Jespersen, for example, notes:

> we start from the old phrase *he was on hunting,* which meant 'he was in the course of hunting, engaged in hunting, busy with hunting'; he was, as it were, in the middle of something, some protracted action or state, denoted by the substantive *hunting.* Here *on* became phonetically *a,* as in other cases, and *a* was eventually dropped, exactly as in other phrases: *burst out on laughing, a-laughing, laughing; fall on thinking, a-thinking, thinking; set the clock on going, a-going, going,* etc. [1933, p. 53].

Although the status of *a*-prefixing as an archaism is relatively secure and its historical source seems to be fairly well documented, its current use in AE and other varieties of English where it is found generally has been overlooked. In most cases, it is simply considered to be a nonsignificant alternant of its nonprefixed counterpart, an older form which has now become socially stigmatized. As we shall see, aspects of *a*-prefixing are relevant to several different levels of language organization, showing in particular how phonological constraints may interact with syntactic constraints to account for the ultimate realization of this form. The purpose of this discussion, then, is to consider how we may account for the realization of *a*-prefixing, including both categorical and variable parameters of its occurrence.

The Sample

In order to provide an adequate data base for this analysis of *a*-prefixing in AE, a fairly extensive collection of tape-recorded samples has been obtained from Mercer and Monroe Counties, located in the southeastern part of West Virginia (Wolfram and Christian, 1976). This area is in the heartland of Appalachia and therefore should be representative of an area considerably broader than these particular counties. Furthermore, the two counties represent the two types of lifestyles most typically associated with rural Appalachia. Monroe County is largely an agricultural county, whereas the economy and lifestyle of Mercer County center around the mining industry. This, however, is not to say that the counties as a whole are radically different. The rural sections of Mercer County are much like Monroe County, and appear to be much like rural Appalachia in general, consisting of a number of small communities and relatively isolated groups living in the mountains.

In the setting of these two counties, over 100 tape-recorded interviews were made. The subjects were divided into five different age levels: 7–11 years, 12–14 years, 15–18 years, 20–40 years, and over 40 years. Although there is some representation of the entire social range of the population in the area, according to current indices, the majority of the informants would be considered of the lower socioeconomic level. Our sample is thus somewhat out of proportion with the entire population since recent figures indicate that approximately 25% of the population fall below the federally defined poverty level. Our concentration on the lower socioeconomic classes was motivated by the fact that we were initially concerned with the language variety that might be considered most divergent from some of the more mainstream varieties of English.

The subjects in this study were all interviewed by fieldworkers from the area, nonlinguists who were trained specifically to do sociolinguistic interviews. Typically, males were interviewed by males and females by females. Conversations were flexible but usually related to local interests. Themes found frequently in our tapes include childhood games, hunting, fishing and ghost stories, the mining industry, and local farming customs. These spontaneous conversations served as a basis for our analysis.

In the analysis that follows, I have concentrated my efforts on the tape-recorded samples of the 49 informants from our total sample of over 100 informants who realized some incidence of *a*-prefixing in their interviews. Over 300 examples of *a*-prefixing found in this corpus comprise the basis for the discussion. In addition, the corpora of Hackenberg (1972) and Feagin (1979) have been checked as secondary data sources. In most cases, the examples cited here are quite similar to the types of *a*-prefixing examples found in these other sources, even though their studies were done in different regions of Appalachia. It is assumed that a lack of unity in the phenomenon would have surfaced in this comparison, particularly with respect to Feagin's study, which was conducted in the southernmost part of Appalachia extending into Alabama. It would appear, then, that the observations concerning *a*-prefixing that come from this study have much greater applicability than to the specific counties where the data were collected.

Syntactic Properties of *a*-Prefixed Forms

The common viewpoint on the syntactic privileges of *a*-prefixed participles unfortunately seems to have been represented by Krapp (1925) when he noted that "in popular speech, almost every word ending in *-ing* has a sort of prefix *a* [p. 266]." Such a broad claim is currently unwarranted, as will become obvious from the examples that we will present, and there is probably good reason to believe that such was never, in fact, the case. There are clear-cut instances where *a*-prefixing is permissible, some where it is clearly ungrammatical, and some that appear to fall on a continuum between these extremes. We will now present a summary of the grammatical and ungrammatical cases, which will provide the basis for a precise specification of the syntactic privileges of this form.

To begin with, we must note that the most common cases of *a*-prefixing occur with progressives, including past tense, nonpast tense, and *be* + *ing* not marked for tense.

(2) a. *I knew he was **a-tellin'** the truth but still I was **a-comin'** home*   83:1
    b. *My cousin had a little brown pony and we was **a-ridin'** it one day*   124:19
    c. *Well, she's **a-gettin'** the black lung now, ain't she?*   83:25
    d. *. . . and he says, "Who's **a-stompin'** on my bridge?"*   16:(610)
    e. *This man'd catch 'em behind the neck and they'd just be **a-rattlin'***   28:25
    f. *He'll forget to spit and he'll cut and it'll just be **a-runnin'**, **a-drippin'** off his chin when he gets to catch them*   146:25

In addition to its common occurrence with progressives in which the auxiliary *be* is overtly realized, *a*-prefixing is also found with those forms that have undergone WHIZ deletion. That is, *a*-Verb-*ing* may occur in embedded sentences that have had the *wh* relative pronoun + *be* removed. We thus get examples such as those found in (3).

(3) a. *I had twelve children and I got two dead and ten **a-livin'***   153:3
    b. *Well, let's say you had a little headache or somethin', or maybe a bone **a-hurtin'**, your leg **a-hurtin'**, mother would get you up some kind of a sassafras tea*   30:13

A-prefixed forms without an overt form of *be* are most common with verbs of perception, such as *see* and *hear*.

(4) a. *. . . and I heard something **a-snortin'** coming up the hill and I said "Aw heck!"*   29:17
    b. *. . . and I turned around and I seen that old snake **a-layin'** there all coiled up, his mouth was open like this, getting ready to bite me*   44:22

With respect to the occurrence of *-ing* forms with verbs of perception, however, it is wrong to conclude that all the participial *-ing* forms are the result of WHIZ deletion. There are cases of post-nominal -*ing* forms that must be considered as verb complements rather than reduced relative clauses. Kirsner and Thompson (1974, p. 11) point out that there are two possible readings for Sentence (5) which point to the distinction between verb complement or adverbial function on post-nominal -*ing* and WHIZ deletion.

(5)   *I saw the girls playing handball*

The different readings are brought out by *but* clause continuations.[4]

(6) a. *I saw the girls playing handball, but I didn't see them playing tennis*   (sensory verb complement)
   b. *I saw the girls playing handball, but I didn't see those who were playing tennis*   (reduced relative clause)

In Sentence (6a) we have a description of what the girls were seen doing (the identity of the girls being presupposed), whereas in (6b) we have a description of which girls were seen (namely those girls who were playing handball). A close inspection of the context of participial -*ing* with verbs of perception indicates that many of them appear to be adverbial in nature rather than reduced relative clauses. One of the common contexts for *a*-prefixing, then, is the verbal complement of verbs of perception.

In addition to its occurrence on complements of perception verbs, there are cases of *a*-prefixing with other types of adverbial constructions, as indicated by the sentences in (7).

(7) a. . . . *you was pretty weak by the tenth day,* **a-layin'** *in there in bed*   37:(177)
   b. . . . *one night my sister, she woke up* **a-screamin'**—*crying, hollering, and so we jumped up*   156:(1044)
   c. . . . *say Chuck would comé by and want to spend a hour* **a-talkin'***, I always figure I'm not too busy to stop*   30:4
   d. . . . *course a lotta times you can't, and grow up* **a-huntin'** *with them instead of hunting for them*   31:22

The essential adverbial nature of the participial -*ing* forms in (7) is indicated by the fact that they are questioned by *how* or *why*, so that appropriate questions for (7a) and (7b) would be (8a) and (8b), respectively.

(8) a. *Why were you pretty weak by the tenth day? (From lying in bed.)*
   b. *How did my sister wake up? (She woke up screaming.)*

A further environment in which *a*-prefixed forms can be found is that of movement verbs such as *come, go,* and *take off,* as illustrated in (9):

[4] See Kirsner and Thompson (1974) for other motivations for this distinction.

(9) a. *All of a sudden a bear come **a-runnin'** and it come **a-runnin'** towards him and he shot it between the eyes*   44:18
   b. *. . . and then I took off **a-ridin'** on the minibike*   4:(888)
   c. *they wasn't in there no more and I went down there **a-huntin'** for em*   44:20

There is also *a*-prefixing that occurs with verbs of continuing or starting. Most predominantly, this involves the form *keep,* but there are also some instances of forms like *start, stay, get to,* and so forth.

(10) a. *He just kep **a-beggin'**, and **a-cryin'** and **a-wantin'** to go out*   83:18
   b. *Then send the rope back down, just keep **a-pullin'** it up till we got it built*   124:2
   c. *You just look at him and he starts **a-bustin'** out laughing at you*   80:(683)
   d. *. . . and we'd get plowed, and we'd get to laughing and **a-gigglin'!***   85:15

All the examples given thus far represent *a*-prefixing on the morpheme to which *-ing* is also attached, but the prefixing may be extended to compound forms as well, as in the following examples.

(11) a. *I went **a-deer huntin'** twice last year*   31:31
   b. *I told her I was going **a-pheasant huntin'***   31:30
   c. *We was going up there **a-squirrel huntin'***   159:(1007)

In the preceding paragraphs, we have presented the main types of syntactic structures in which *a*-prefixing is found. In order to understand the systematic nature of its syntactic properties, it is also instructive to note the types of structures in which it is NOT found. For the most part, our presentation of ungrammatical structures with *a*-prefixing is extracted from those structures that are never found in our own corpus, with confirming evidence from Hackenberg's (1972) and Feagin's (1979) corpora. There is also some informal intuitional evidence from indigenous fieldworkers to support these cases.[5]

In the first place, we find that *a*-prefixing is never found in nominals that occur with determiners or in possessive *-ing* constructions. We therefore do not get sentences such as the following:

(12) a. **He watched their **a-shootin'***
   b. **He heard every **a-shootin'***
   c. **He saw the **a-shootin'***

[5] More formal evidence on intuitions about *a*-prefixing (cf. Wolfram, forthcoming) also supports the distinctions cited here.

The ungrammaticality of these constructions is obviously due to the nominalization of these *-ing* forms, which is most apparent with a determiner of some type. But it is also true of other nominalized *-ing* forms as well. The following types of sentences are therefore not found:

(13) a. * *A-sailin' is fun*
     b. * *He likes a-sailin*

Although these sentences appear to fit the classifical definition of a gerund construction, we have deliberately avoided this classification since the traditional designation would also include as gerunds some of the sentences previously given as acceptable in AE. We shall have more to say about this matter shortly.

Just as we do not get *a*-prefixing with the nominal constructions in (12) and (13), we do not find cases of *a*-prefixing with adjectival *-ing*, whether they occur in predicate adjectives constructions or have undergone modifier preposing. We therefore do not find sentences like the following:

(14) a. * *The man was a-charmin'*
     b. * *The movie was a-shockin'*
     c. * *The a-shootin' hunters didn't hit the bear*
     d. * *The hunters shot the a-runnin' bear*

A further type of syntactic environment in which *a*-prefixed forms are apparently not found involves adverbial *-ing* in a prepositional phrase. Note the ungrammaticality of the following sentences:

(15) a. * *He got sick from a-workin' so hard*
     b. * *John hit his dog for a-breakin' the dish*
     c. * *John built a turkey blind before a-huntin' turkey*
     d. * *He nearly died from a-laughin' so hard*
     e. * *He makes money by a-buildin' houses*

Although *a*-prefixing cannot follow a preposition as such in (15), it should be noted that it may occur attributively with respect to a prepositional phrase. We therefore do get sentences like the following:

(16) a. *No, that's something I hadn't ever got into, with dogs **a-fightin'*** 22:34
     b. *I know you might have heard of peppermint **a-growin'** along the streams of the water*   157:(506)

An examination of the differences between (15) and (16) suggests that it is the occurrence following a preposition that results in the ungrammaticality of (15). This becomes more clear when we consider those sentences given in (15) that may occur without the overt realization of a preposition. When the sentences given in (15) occur with the same adverbial function (i.e., manner, reason, *etc.*) but without the preposition, the *a*-prefixed forms are acceptable, as indicated in (17):[6]

(17) a. *He got sick **a-workin'** so hard*
     b. *He nearly died **a-laughin'** so hard*
     c. *He makes money **a-buildin'** houses*

We therefore conclude that it is something about the overt appearance of prepositions in these cases that causes the sentences to be unacceptable.

Given the types of constructions in which we find *a*-prefixing and those where we do not find it, we may now ask how we can account for its occurrence. As a first restriction, we shall claim that *a*-prefixing is restricted to verbal and adverbial categories. For progressives, such as those given in (2) and (3), this restriction is obvious, as it is in the case of adverbial participles illustrated in (7). But its occurrence in constructions such as (9) and (10) is in need of some explanation.

The traditional view has often considered the *-ing* suffixed forms like *I went fishing* and *He keeps working* to be nominals which function similarly to the gerund in a sentence such as *I like hunting.* A closer inspection, however, suggests that there are important differences between these types of *-ing* suffixed forms and that the former examples are not nomianls at all.

Let us first look at the *-ing* forms occurring with verbs of movement such as *go, come,* and *take off.* Silva (1973, p. 91) has pointed out that the *-ing* participial forms with verbs of movement do not function as nouns; instead, they function as adverbs. The syntactic categorization of these forms as adverbs rather than nouns is based on the fact that *-ing* forms with verbs of movement fail to function as nouns insofar as they cannot be questioned by *what* or *which* (18), they cannot be pronominalized with *it, that,* or *one* (19), and they cannot be qualified by a nominal modifier (20):

(18)   * $\left\{ \begin{array}{l} What \\ Which \end{array} \right\}$ *(hunting) are you going tomorrow?*

(19)   * *We want to go hunting, but John doesn't want*

        to go $\left\{ \begin{array}{l} it \\ that \\ one \end{array} \right\}$

---

[6] The structures where the overt preposition need not occur are, of course, identical to those where it need not occur in standard varieties of English. That is, we get:
   (i) a. *He got sick working so hard*
      b. *He nearly died laughing so hard*
      c. *He makes money building fences*
These are all cases that Williams (1971) refers to as adverbial *-ing,* as opposed to adjectival and nominal *-ing* participles.

(20) * We're going $\begin{cases} our\ fishing \\ some\ fishing \\ good\ fishing \\ fishing\ that\ lasts\ all\ day \end{cases}$

The non-nominal function of *-ing* with the movement verbs is readily contrasted with *-ing* participles that function as true gerunds, as in the construction *I like fishing*. None of the restrictions exemplified by (18)–(20) are found for these *-ing* participles (21)–(24):

(21) $\begin{cases} What \\ Which \end{cases}$ *fishing do you like?*

(22) *We like fishing, but John doesn't like it*

(23) We like $\begin{cases} our\ fishing \\ some\ fishing \\ good\ fishing \\ fishing\ that\ lasts\ all\ day \end{cases}$

Positive evidence for the adverbial function of *-ing* forms with verbs of movement is provided by the type of forms used in response to the question *where* (24) and in adverbial phrases headed by *from* (25):

(24) *Where are you going? I'm going* $\begin{cases} downtown \\ to\ the\ circus \\ fishing \\ hunting \end{cases}$

(25) *She just came from* $\begin{cases} the\ university \\ the\ woods \\ hunting \\ fishing \end{cases}$

Thus, the evidence that *-ing* participles with verbs of movement are adverbs appears to be fairly clear-cut. And, as *a*-prefixing occurs with these *-ing* forms, but not with the ones that appear to be gerunds, this supports the claim that only adverbial and verbal participles are eligible for *a*-prefixing.

Verb forms like *start* and *keep,* particularly the latter, which is very frequent with *a*-prefixing, also appear to be specialized cases where the following *-ing* form cannot be considered a nominal, but must be considered verbal or adverbial in nature. Forms like *keep* + *-ing* participles have sometimes been considered to be part of the so-called "catenative" verbs, because they indicate relations that are most adequately treated as verb clustering rather than verb + gerund.

The clustering nature of *keep* + -ing participle is revealed in questions, where the sequence cannot be broken up as it is with other verb + *-ing* participles. Consider the contrast between (26b) and (27b, c):

(26) a. *He loves talking*
     b. *What does he love?*

(27) a. *He keeps talking*
     b. *What does he keep doing?*
     c. **What does he keep?*

Further differences between constructions like those cited in (26) and (27) are found with respect to noun phrase complementation. Whereas an infinitive complement is an alternate for the gerundive complement of *love* (28), it is clearly not a possibility with *keep* (29):

(28) a. *John loves hunting*
     b. *John loves to hunt.*
     c. *John loves for his wife to hunt*

(29) a. *John keep hunting*
     b. **John keeps to hunt*
     c. **John keeps for his wife to hunt*

Although there are other arguments that could be raised here to support the basic distinction between *keep* + *-ing* participles and other types of verb + *-ing* participles, such as the failure of *keep* + *-ing* participles to take pre-nominal modifiers as in

(30)   **We keep* $\begin{Bmatrix} \textit{our hunting} \\ \textit{some fishing} \end{Bmatrix}$

it is reasonable to conclude that *keep* functions quite differently from the true verb + gerund participial constructions. There is, in fact, reason to suspect that *keep* here functions as a "quasi-progressive," due to the semantic compatibility of *keep* and other habitual functions of the progressive.

There are several observations that support the treatment of *keep* as a quasi-progressive. It is noted that *keep* does not take the progressive with a following *-ing* participle (31), although it does when followed by an adjective (32):

(31)   **He is keeping hunting for snakes*

(32)   *He is keeping quiet at the moment*

There are also specialized contexts in which *be* may be used as the proform for a *keep* + *-ing* participle, whereas the potential substitutibility of *be* with a verb + gerund participle is clearly unacceptable. This contrast is indicated in the difference between (33) and (34):

(33) *Even though I told him not to fish there, he kept fishing at the creek, and he probably still is*

(34) **Even though I told him not to fish there, he loved fishing at the creek and he probably still is*

Whether or not one prefers to go so far as to consider *keep* a quasi-progressive, the treatment of the following *-ing* form as nongerundive in nature still seems to be the only reasonable conclusion. The establishment of this following *-ing* participle as adverbial or verbal, then, fits in with our claims concerning the syntactic privileges of *a*-prefixing.

The Underlying Source of *a*-Prefixing

In the preceding paragraphs, we have tried to establish that *a*-prefixing is restricted to those *-ing* participles that are part of the verb or its complement (i.e., the adverb); it does not occur in other types of contexts such as true gerunds. We now are ready to focus more specifically on the restrictions for *a*-prefixing and suggest its underlying source. What we shall claim here is that all *a*-prefixed participial forms are derived from prepositional phrases, and that *a*- itself comes from a preposition. This includes *a*-prefixing on progressives, verbs of movement, and adverbs such as those we cited previously. Although this source has been cited as an historical explanation for present-day *a*-prefixing, this analysis can be motivated entirely apart from the consideration of the historical evidence.

The postulation of an adverbial prepositional phrase as the basis for all *a*-prefixed forms necessarily involves interpreting progressives as derived from prepositional phrases, since this is one of the main constructions where *a*-prefixed forms are found. Bolinger (1971) has provided such an analysis which we can use as a starting point in developing our argument. We shall not cite all of the different motivations that are included in Bolinger's argument; however, it may be helpful to summarize some of his main points that are relevant to this discussion.

To begin with, it is observed that the preposition *at* is used when progressive action is nominalized, giving us (35):

(35) *He was working an hour ago and I guess he's still **at it***

Bolinger (1971, p. 247) further observes that a preposition (usually *at* or *on*) is used in questions answered by a progressive:

(36) *What are you **at** now? I'm getting these reports ready*

Prepositions are also used in cleaving progressives, giving us sentences like (37):

(37) *Is it studying he's **at** or making love?*

Action nominalization is also observed which parallels progressive constructions, as seen in (38a) and (38b).

(38) a. *She is **at prayer***
b. *She is **praying***

A number of-*ing* complements also parallel other prepositional complements and are found with the construction *to be busy*.

(39) a. *I'm busy **working***
b. *I'm busy **at work***

Finally, we should notice Bolinger's observation (1971, p. 248) that *where* questions that are normally answered by an adverb of location may also be answered by a progressive.

(40) *Where's Joe? He's reading*

On the basis of the type of evidence that has been presented (and some additional arguments given in Bolinger, 1971a, b), it is suggested that the progressive may be derived from a locative-type prepositional phrase. Once it has been established that progressives are related to locational complements in this way, it is a relatively small step to observe that the underlying prepositional phrase which can be motivated for most varieties of English may simply be realized as *a*-prefixing in AE.

Just as progressives can be shown to be related to prepositional phrases, a quasi-progressive such as *keep* can be shown to have a similar type of relationship. Although there is not complete isomorphy in the type of constructions that reveal the locational nature of *be* + *ing* progressives and a quasi-progressive like *keep*, a number of the same relationships do exist. For example, we observe that action pronominalization reveals a preposition for *keep*, just as it does for the progressives [cf. (35)].

(41) *He just kept fishing in the river and I betcha he's still **at it***

Similarly, we find that cleaving with *keep* + *ing* participle surfaces a preposition.

(42)   *Is it studying he keeps* **at,** *or making love?*

And we further find that action nominalization requires a preposition in its parallel form for *keep,* just as it did for "true progressives."

(43) a. *They* **kept at their quarreling** *all day*
     b. *They* **kept quarreling** *all day*

(44) a. *They* **keep busy working**
     b. *They* **keep busy at work**

We likewise find that there are constructions used with verbs of movement that also suggest a relationship between certain prepositional phrases and the verbs of movement + *ing.*[7] While action nominalization does not seem quite as natural for *go* + *ing* participle, it still seems acceptable in some contexts.

(45)   *We went fishing this morning and he's probably still* **at it**

Action nominals clearly parallel verbs of movement and their alternant participial forms.

(46) a. *He went* **on a hike**
     b. *He went* **hiking**

The locational nature of the construction is also revealed by the types of questions appropriate for these constructions [cf. Sentence (24) discussed earlier as well as (47)]:

(47)   *Where's John* (**at**)? *He went fishing*

Once we have demonstrated the relationship between locational and progressives, *keep,* and movement verbs, adverbial phrases as we have done, it is a reasonalble step (to be discussed in further detail in what follows) to conclude that these prepositional phrases serve as the basis for deriving *a*-prefixing from a preposition.

The constructions that we previously labeled adverbials [e.g., (7a)–(7d)] simply appear to be more transparent cases of prepositional phrases than the *be* + *ing* progressives, *keep* + *ing,* or movement verbs + *ing.* With the

---

[7] The compatibility of *keep* + *ing* participle and movement verbs + *ing* participle with *be* + *ing* progressives seems to reveal a "squishy" category for progressives. Although we shall not develop arguments for this interpretation here, it appears that *keep* + *ing* is more compatible with *be* + *ing* than movement verbs + *ing* although both of them share certain properties of the category "progressive."

traditionally labeled adverbials, question forms (48) and cleaving (49) also surface a preposition.

(48)   *What did he die from? Working so hard*

(49)   *What he died from was working so hard*

The transparency is found in the cases where an alternant form of the construction can occur with the prepositional phrase overtly realized [(50a), (50b); (51a), (51b)]. In these cases, we see that the AE *a*-prefixed form alternates with these constructions [(50c), (51c)].

(50) a. *He died **working** so hard*
      b. *He died **from working** so hard*
      c. *He died **a-workin'** so hard*

(51) a. *You was pretty weak by the tenth day **laying** there*
      b. *You was pretty weak by the tenth day **from laying** there*
      c. *You was pretty weak by the tenth day **a-layin'** there*

Additional evidence can also be cited to support the relationships between these prepositional phrases and *a*-prefixed forms. For one, we note that there is a pattern of overt prepositional retention in AE which is somewhat broader than it apparently is in some other varieties of English.[8] There are, for example, occasional cases of *on* or *at* prepositions that are retained in constructions such as those given in (52).

(52) a. *How do you avoid [drugs] if you were a parent **at rearin'** a child in an environment that had a lot of that sort of thing?*   Fieldworker 61:20
      b. *I'm trying to get him back **on huntin'** again*   159:(668)
      c. *. . . 'cause there's some things that, just really no use **on fussin'** about*   148:7

This broader range of alternant realization for *-ing* participles and prepositions + *ing* participle in AE is simply an extended version of the argument that was given concerning the overt realization of prepositions in alternant forms.[9]

---

[8] Many varieties of English do, of course, have a limited aspect of *on* ~ *a*- alternation relating to nonparticipial forms. Note, for example, the relationships between sentences like *He set the house on fire* ~ *He set the house afire* or *He got on board* ~ *He got aboard*.

[9] Since several of these "extended *on* or *at* alternants are found in the speech of the fieldworkers who use *a*-prefixed forms relatively rarely, it might be suggested that this is actually a type of hypercorrection away from *a*-prefixed forms. If this is, in fact, the case, this simply adds confirmation to the basic argument for the underlying prepositional base from a different source.

Finally, we should mention the constraint that prohibits *a*-prefixing from co-occurring with an overtly realized preposition as its head in a prepositional phrase, as previously noted in (15). This type of restriction is readily understood if *a*-prefixing is originally derived from a preposition and only one preposition may introduce a prepositional phrase.[10] That is, there is a prohibition on preposition clustering with respect to locational prepositions.

In the preceding paragraphs, we have cited several different overt prepositions that are realized as the alternant of *a*-prefixed forms. At this point, we shall not concern ourselves with this divergence, but we will return to the overt realization of what we consider to be the underlying locational preposition when we discuss the semantics of *a*-prefixing. It is sufficient here to establish the need for positing a preposition as the source from which *a*-prefixing is ultimately derived.

Variability and Grammatical Category

The previous discussion has focused on the syntactic contexts in which *a*-prefixing is permissible, suggesting a source for its derivation. It is important, however, to note that *a*-prefixing is a variable phenomenon; that is, all the forms eligible for *a*-prefixing do not necessarily realize it in every instance. We now turn to the variable parameter of *a*-prefixing in order to determine the extent of its usage and possible grammatical constraints that may favor or inhibit its realization. In this aspect of our study, we follow other studies of structured variability in language (e.g., Labov, 1969; Fasold, 1972; Wolfram, 1974a, 1974b). In order to look at possible grammatical constraints on variability, we have tabulated the actual realization of *a*-prefixing in terms of the potential cases where it might have occurred, following the analysis presented earlier as a basis for determining what constitutes a potential environment for *a*-prefixing. In line with the different types of grammatical contexts where *a*-prefixing might occur, we have broken down our count in terms of four different categories which are related to the surface grammatical constructions: (*a*) *be* + *ing* progressives, including those that have undergone WHIZ deletion; (*b*) the quasi-progressive *keep* + *ing;* (*c*) movement verbs + *ing* participle complements; (*d*) adverbial phrases with alternate surface realizations of a preposition + *ing* participle. Tabulations in terms of these four categories are given in Table 6.1. The figures in Table 6.1 are based on the 13 informants in our corpus who reveal the most frequent instances of *a*-prefixing so that we might have adequate numbers of *a*-prefixed items for investigating the possible variable constraints. The table is arranged in terms of the rank frequency of *a*-prefixed forms.

[10] Some apparent exceptions that occur seem explainable through lexicalizations which have lead to changes in the categories of overtly realized forms. For example, although we do get forms like *He kept on a-huntin'* the *on* in this case functions as an adverbial particle rather than a preposition.

Several observations can be made on the basis of Table 6.1. To begin with, we note that the frequency levels of *a*-prefixing are below 50% of all cases in which it might have been realized, the range typically falling between 10% and 40%. In terms of the grammatical constructions we have isolated as possible constraints, it is instructive to note that the verbs of movement and the quasi-progressive *keep* are actually realized at higher frequency levels than either the progressive *be* + *ing* or the surface adverbial phrases. Although there are certainly more actual instances of *a*-prefixing with *be* + *ing* progressives than with the other categories, it is important to note that this high number is due to the fact that many more potential occurrences of *a*-prefixing occur for *be* + *ing* progressives. The observation that *be* + *ing* progressives are realized at lower relative frequency levels than *keep* + *ing* or movement verbs + *ing* is in conflict with some observations concerning *a*-prefixing which imply that *be* + *ing* is a constraint favoring the incidence of *a*-prefixing over *keep* + *ing*. Hackenberg, for example, comes to this conclusion, based on two different types of data. First of all, Hackenberg (1972, p. 123) observes that there are only 3 instances of *a*-prefixing with *keep* out of his total of 51 instances. Given the vast proportional differences in the potential occurrences of these two constructions, it is not surprising that it should actually occur that rarely. In the corpus of examples we have examined here, there are almost 17 times as many potential occurrences of *be* + *ing* eligible for *a*-prefixing as there are cases of *keep* + *ing*. The low frequency levels of *a*-prefixing with *keep* turn out to be an artifact of disproportionate potential instances rather than a real constraint inhibiting *a*-prefixing. On this point, Hackenberg's conclusion suffers from the fact that he did tabulate actual cases of *a*-prefixing in relation to potential cases.

Hackenberg also used results from a forced choice test as a basis for suggesting that *be* + *ing* was favored over *keep* + *ing*. Informants were simply given sentence pairs containing *keep* + *ing* and *be* + *ing* and asked to select which of the forms was preferred. Although there was some discrepancy, Hackenberg suggests that the results indicate a preference for *be* + *ing* over *keep* + *ing*. It is important to note, however, that Hackenberg makes no mention of whether the subjects for this forced choice test were actual users of *a*-prefixing, and his own corpus for descriptive analysis indicates the limited usage of *a*-prefixing.) (Only 12 out of 39 speakers indicated any incidence of *a*-prefixing.) Hackenberg's conclusion must therefore be viewed with considerable suspicion.[11] One would expect that informants who do not typically use *a*-prefixing would favor forms with higher raw numbers

[11] It is curious that Hackenberg gives no background information on the 130 subjects who responded to his forced choice questionnaire other than to say that they were residents of the county where his study took place. Some of them were, however, apparently school children as indicated by his remarks concerning the elicitation of background information (Hackenberg, 1972, p. 80). If a substantial number of these are, in fact, school children, the likelihood of their being regular users of *a*-prefixing is even more suspect.

TABLE 6.1
A-Prefixing; by Several Surface Categories

Tape no.	Inf. age	Inf. sex	Progressives		Keep		Movement verbs		Adverb		Total	
31	67	M	13/28	53.6	0/2	0.0	2/3	66.7	2/7	28.6	17/40	42.5
83	93	F	16/37	43.2	3/6	50.0	0/1	0.0	0/2	0.0	19/46	41.3
85	78	F	18/57	31.6	4/4	100.0	—	—	3/12	25.0	25/73	34.2
153	83	F	9/35	25.7	0/1	0.0	2/2	100.0	1/4	25.0	12/42	28.6
22	60	M	18/64	28.1	—	—	0/4	0.0	3/11	27.3	21/79	26.6
152	64	F	11/43	25.6	1/4	25.0	1/1	100.0	1/10	10.0	14/58	24.1
157	52	F	14/52	26.9	—	—	0/3	0.0	1/8	12.5	15/63	23.8
30	50	M	7/52	13.5	1/5	20.0	2/5	40.0	4/16	25.0	14/78	17.9
44	14	M	4/41	9.7	1/2	50.0	4/7	57.1	0/3	0.0	9/53	17.0
124	11	M	1/45	2.2	1/2	50.0	8/16	50.0	0/10	0.0	10/74	13.5
146	52	M	9/59	15.3	—	—	0/10	0.0	0/9	0.0	9/78	11.5
2	13	M	3/54	5.6	5/13	38.5	1/12	8.3	0/5	0.0	9/84	10.7
29	33	F	7/79	8.9	—	—	1/10	10.0	1/4	25.0	9/93	9.7
Totals			130/646	20.1	16/39	41.0	21/74	28.4	16/101	15.8	183/860	21.3

h lower raw figures but higher proportional realizations. That
l not be expected to show sensitivity to linguistic constraints
lalized cases in relation to potential instances.

of interest to observe in Table 6.1 that *a*-prefixing is apparently
favored in the intermediate constructions in the continuum ranging from
surface adverbs to *be + ing* progressives. That is, the quasi-progressive *keep*
+ ing and movement verb + complement *-ing* are favored over "true progressives" and adverbial phrases. It may well be that the indeterminacy of the
categories is compensated for by favoring the overt specification of temporal
locative marker, but this must be viewed as a speculation rather than conclusion in the absence of additional evidence. We may, however, cautiously
conclude that these intermediate constructions favor the retention of
a-prefixing (without distinguishing the quasi-progressive *keep* from movement verbs in terms of their constraining effect). Our caution is due to the
low number of potential cases for some of the categories and some seeming
inconsistencies as speakers are compared with each other.

Although our concern here is primarily with the linguistic aspects of
a-prefixing, it may be noted that Table 6.1 presents clear-cut support for the
contention that *a*-prefixing is a phenomenon which is dying out rather rapidly
in Appalachia. It is noteworthy that the eight speakers with the highest
relative frequency levels for *a*-prefixing are all 50 years of age or older. All
speakers who reveal *a*-prefixing above the 20% level of incidence in terms of
its potential realization are in this category.

Phonological Constraints on *a*-Prefixing

In the previous section, we attempted to examine the syntactic privileges of *a*-prefixing. We have also suggested that all *a*-prefixed forms are
ultimately derived from an underlying preposition. In order to understand
the full range of *a*-prefixing, however, we must now consider certain aspects
of phonology which may strongly affect its realization.

If we conclude that *a*-prefixing is ultimately derived from an underlying
preposition, as we have done, then there is at least one rule that operates on
prepositions to reduce them to *a*- ([ə]). If we maintain that a temporal locative such as ON underlies all *a*-prefixing, we need a rule that will reduce it in
unstressed environments. This may be represented approximately as:

(53)   ON → (ə)/ ## _____ ## Verb + *ing*
$$\text{[-stress]}$$

Although we have not specified it here, a more detailed version of this
rule would be needed to specify exactly where such a process is obligatory
(e.g., with surface progressives) and where it may be optional (e.g., with
surface adverbs). Further detail would also make preposition reduction a

more general process which can affect other unstressed VC prepositions with non-*ing* forms in the casual speech of most English speakers (e.g., *of* as in *I'm tired a (of) him.*).

If we view this resultant *a*- form as having a different relationship to the following verb + *ing* form than the original preposition, we also need a rule that changes the boundary status. We may, for example, change the boundary status following ON from that of an external word boundary to an internal word boundary (i.e., $\#\# \rightarrow \# / \partial$ ___ Verb + *ing*). The above operation(s) is preliminary to a variable phonological rule of schwa deletion that eliminates the phonological vestige of the underlying preposition completely.

In considering the rule that eliminates the initial prefix *a*-, it is important to observe several different constraints on its operation. To begin with, we must notice two types of phonological environments where *a*-prefix deletion is categorical, or at least semicategorical. First, we observe that *a*-prefixing is never observed to be realized when the following morpheme begins with a vowel. That is, we have no instances in our corpus such as the following:

(54) a. **John was **a-eatin'** his food*
    b. **He kept **a-askin'** him the question*

On the basis of our previous discussion of syntactic privileges for *a*-prefixing, there is no reason why sentences such as (54) should not be permissible unless we consider the canonical shape of the verb. Although there are considerably fewer cases in English of verbs beginning with vowels than consonants, there still appear to be a sufficient number for some *a*-prefixing to be realized. We thus consider vowel-initial forms to have categorical deletion of the *a*-prefixed form where the syntactic considerations have permitted the forms to occur.[12] The explanation of the nonexistence of sentences like (54) is reasonable in terms of the general phonotactic restrictions against words that begin with initial vowel clusters in English, particularly those where the first vowel is a schwa. There are very few sequences of vowel clusters word initially in English (e.g., *oasis, aorta*) and there is some question as to whether these can be considered vowel clusters phonologically. I am not, however, aware of any cases where an initial [ə] (the phonetic form of the *a*- prefix) is followed by another vowel. What we have, then, is certain of the grammatically permissible structures being filtered out because of a general phonological restriction on the English language.

Another type of phonological restriction on *a*-prefixing involves the realization of *a*- on forms where the initial syllable of the form is not stressed.

---

[12] Although there are no examples of *a*-prefixing that are realized on -*ing* forms beginning with a vowel in this corpus, Feagin (personal communication) has brought one such item to our attention from her corpus. Hackenberg (1972) has no examples in his corpus. It is possible that the constraint may be semi-categorical for some speakers.

If the initial syllable of verb base is stressed, then *a*-prefixing may be variably realized, as in the following:

(55) a. *She was just standing quietly **a-hollerin'***   28:26
     b. *. . . so he kept **a-follerin'** me around for a week*   77:10

Although *a*-prefixing can occur on such forms when the initial syllable is stressed, we have no instances in which they occur when the initial syllable is not stressed. That is, we do not get examples such as those in (56):

(56) a. **He was **a-discoverin'** a bear in the woods*
     b. **He was **a-returnin'** from his house*
     c. **He was **a-retirin'** to his cage*

The absence of such items does not appear to be accidental; it seems to be an environment where deletion of the initial unstressed *a-* of the item simply takes place categorically.[13]

In addition to these categorical phonological restrictions, there are several variable constraints which can be seen to affect the deletion of the *a*-prefix. One of the factors increasing the deletion of *a-* is a preceding vowel. If the word preceding an *a*-prefixed form ends in a vowel, the deletion of *a-* is favored. This is demonstrated in Table 6.2, where a preceding vowel is differentiated from a preceding consonant. Figures are given for the 13 informants that were used in Table 6.1.

The pattern seen in Table 6.2 appears to be fairly regular, although there are two individual exceptions (Subjects 85 and 22) to the pattern that might be attributed to the low potential numbers of examples found when a potential *a*-prefixed form follows a vowel. This deletion appears to be natural in terms of the nonpreference for syllables beginning with a vowel following a syllable that ends in one.

At this point, it is instructive to see how unstressed initial [ə] deletion in *a*-prefixing relates to a more general process in which other unstressed initial syllables are deleted. It is a well-known fact that many varieties of English can delete the initial syllable of a polysyllabic word when it is unstressed (Wolfram and Fasold, 1974, p. 147). This process affects all varieties of English to some extent, although the class of items affected in non-mainstream varieties is somewhat more extensive than their mainstream counterparts (e.g., mainstream varieties may reveal this process in items like *'cause, 'round, 'cept*, whereas some nonmainstream varieties would reveal it additionally in items like *'rithmetic, 'member,* and *'lectricity*). To determine the relationship between the form being discussed here and the more general

---

[13] An examination of the data reported by Hackenberg (1972) and Feagin (1979) reveals no counterexamples to this claim.

TABLE 6.2
Unstressed Initial Syllable Deletion in a-*Prefixed Forms*

Informant tape no.	C##__		V##__			
	No. D/T	Percentage D	No. D/T	Percentage D	Total	Percentage
31	23/40	57.5	—	—	23/40	57.5
83	21/40	52.5	6/6	100.0	27/46	58.7
85	45/64	61.3	3/9	33.3	48/73	65.8
153	28/40	70.0	2/2	100.0	30/42	71.4
22	56/75	74.7	2/4	50.0	58/79	73.4
152	44/58	75.9	—	—	44/58	75.9
157	44/59	74.6	4/4	100.0	48/63	76.2
30	53/67	79.1	11/11	100.0	64/78	82.1
44	40/49	81.6	4/4	100.0	44/53	83.0
124	62/72	86.2	1/1	100.0	63/73	86.3
146	54/62	87.1	15/16	93.7	69/78	88.5
2	69/78	88.8	6/6	100.0	75/84	89.3
29	76/85	89.4	8/8	100.0	84/93	90.3
Totals	615/789	77.9	62/71	87.3	677/860	78.7

deletion process, it is instructive to examine the deletion of unstressed initial syllables in non-*a*-prefixed forms. In Table 6.3, we have tabulated the extent of deletion for unstressed initial syllables in non-*a*-prefixed forms for the same 13 speakers that were used in Tables 6.1 and 6.2. Syllables are differentiated according to two factors. First, they are distinguished on the basis of syllable type; namely, initial V syllables as opposed to CV syllables. Second, they are differentiated according to preceding environment; namely, a preceding word ending in a vowel as opposed to a consonant. This distinction matches the distinction made for the deletion of *a*-prefixed forms. Whereas Tables 6.1 and 6.2 were arranged according to rank frequency, Table 6.3 is arranged following the rank frequency of the previous two tables rather than in terms of its own rank frequency, although the rank frequency is given as a part of the table. This arrangement will be useful in comparing Tables 6.2 and 6.3.

There are several important observations that must be made on the basis of Table 6.3. To begin with, we note that the effect of a preceding vowel favoring deletion is very regular, especially with respect to an initial V syllable. In fact, there are no exceptions to this pattern among our 13 speakers. We note that there is a general constraint where a preceding vowel favors the deletion of all unstressed initial syllables. It therefore seems reasonable to consider the deletion of the prefix [ə] to be part of this general process.

TABLE 6.3
Unstressed Initial Syllable Deletion in Non-a-Prefixed Forms

Informant tape no.	Initial V						Initial CV							Rank frequency
	C##__		V##__		Total		C##__		V##__		Total			
	No. D/T	Percentage	No. D/T	Percentage	Number	Percentage	No. D/T	Percentage	No. D/T	Percentage	Number	Percentage	Total	Percentage	
31	6/36	16.7	4/13	30.8	10/49	20.4	2/6	33.3	2/6	33.3	4/12	33.3	14/61	22.9	1
83	6/21	28.6	4/5	80.0	10/26	38.5	0/6	0.0	0/3	0.0	0/9	0.0	10/35	28.6	3
85	6/17	35.3	8/14	57.1	14/31	45.2	5/18	27.8	0/2	0.0	5/20	25.0	19/51	37.3	6
153	14/37	37.8	10/13	76.9	24/50	48.0	3/10	30.0	1/1	100.0	4/11	36.4	28/61	45.9	10
22	17/48	36.4	8/11	72.7	25/59	42.2	6/13	46.1	3/5	60.0	9/18	50.0	34/77	44.2	9
152	11/44	25.0	5/8	62.5	16/52	30.8	2/15	6.7	1/3	33.3	3/18	16.7	19/70	27.1	2
157	9/33	27.3	8/15	53.3	17/48	35.4	0/14	0.0	3/8	37.5	3/22	13.6	20/70	28.6	4
30	7/27	25.9	8/10	80.0	15/37	40.5	2/21	9.5	3/10	30.0	5/31	16.1	20/68	29.4	5
44	12/25	48.0	5/5	100.0	17/30	56.7	9/16	56.3	2/2	100.0	11/18	61.1	28/48	58.3	13
124	11/24	45.8	6/6	100.0	17/30	56.7	3/6	50.0	—	—	3/6	50.0	20/36	55.6	11
146	14/35	40.0	5/7	71.4	19/42	45.2	3/12	25.0	0/2	0.0	3/14	21.4	22/56	39.3	7
2	15/31	48.4	3/6	50.0	18/37	48.6	8/11	72.7	3/4	75.0	11/15	73.3	29/52	55.7	12
29	23/51	45.1	6/12	50.0	29/63	46.0	5/20	25.0	1/3	33.3	6/23	26.0	35/86	40.7	8
Totals	151/429	35.2	80/125	64.0	231/554	41.7	48/168	28.6	19/49	38.8	67/217	30.9	298/771	38.7	

It is also of considerable interest to compare the figures of deletion in Table 6.3 with the figures of Table 6.2 to see how the more general process of initial-syllable deletion relates to *a*-prefixed forms. Although the rank frequency of deletion for non-*a*-prefixed forms and *a*-prefixed forms is by no means isomorphic, a general pattern does emerge in which the lower frequencies of non-*a*-prefix initial-syllable deletion tend to correlate with the lower frequencies of *a*-prefix deletion. The correlation coefficient for these two tables is .58 (Spearman *rho*), suggesting a moderate to substantial correlation between general unstressed initial-syllable deletion and *a*-prefixing deletion. Six of the first 8 informants with the lowest frequency for general initial-syllable deletion are also among the lowest 8 in terms of the frequency levels of deletion with respect to *a*-prefixing. This observation is additional evidence for considering *a*-prefixing deletion to be part of the more general unstressed initial-syllable deletion process. Speakers who delete *a*-prefixed forms the least will also be least likely to delete other unstressed initial syllables.[14]

At this point, we can summarize the various constraints on the deletion of unstressed initial syllables, following the conventions established for incorporating variable constraints set forth in previous studies of structured variability (cf. Labov, 1969; Fasold, 1972; Wolfram, 1974a,b; Wolfram and Fasold, 1974). Capital Greek letters are assigned in order of rank to indicate the ranking of constraints on the operation of the rule, and $\sim$ is used to refer to "the absence of."

$$(57) \qquad \Delta \sim [+\text{cons}] \begin{bmatrix} +\text{syll} \\ -\text{cons} \end{bmatrix}$$

$$\rightarrow (\emptyset) \ / \ B \begin{bmatrix} +\text{syll} \\ -\text{cons} \end{bmatrix} \# \# \underset{[-\text{stress}]}{\underline{\qquad}} A \begin{bmatrix} \text{Verb} + ing \\ \Gamma \sim \begin{bmatrix} -\text{PROG} \\ -\text{ADV} \end{bmatrix} \end{bmatrix}$$
$$*[+\text{syll}]$$
$$C_0 \ *[-\text{stress}]$$

In (57) the asterisk (*) indicates that the constraint is categorical (i.e., a "knockout constraint"); in this case, the deletion rule must take place when a syllable is followed by a vowel or an unstressed syllable. The major variable constraints on deletion are the *a*-prefixed form (first order constraint) and the preceding word ending in a vowel (second order constraint). Lower order constraints are an unstressed syllable beginning with a vowel

---

[14] This conclusion does not match the stereotype that AE speakers who use *a*-prefixing will also tend to delete unstressed initial syllables with relatively high frequency. The impression may have arisen from the fact that, although initial syllable deletion is not that frequent overall for these speakers, there are lexical items affected by this process that are not typically affected in mainstream varieties (e.g., *'taters* for *potatoes* and *'maters* for *tomatoes*).

TABLE 6.4
Nonapplication Probabilities, Multiplicative Model (Cedergren and Sankoff, 1974)

Grammatical category	*-ING*				NON-*ING*
	ADV	PROG	MOV	KEEP	
Effect	.778	.720	.553	.442	.000
		NON-*ING*			*-ING*
Syllable type		V		CV	
Effect		.130		.000	.000
Preceding environment		V##__			C##__
Effect		.350			.000

Input probability $p_0 = .265$

as opposed to a consonant (i.e., V as opposed to CV syllables) and the surface grammatical category of the quasi-progressives (indicated here formally as $[{-PROG \atop -ADV}]$).

Support for the ranking of constraints as we have done in (57) comes from an application of the mathematical model for computing probabilities for variable constraints set forth in Cedergren and Sankoff, 1974.[15] In Table 6.4, we present the probabilities associated with each constraint for the multiplicative, nonapplication probabilities model presented by Cedergren and Sankoff as calculated by the computer program they developed (1974, p. 337). The formula for computing probabilities associated with an entire environment from those of the individual constraints for this model is:

(58) $(1 - p) = (1 - p_0) \times (1 - p_i) \times (1 - p_j) \times \cdots \times (1 - p_n)$

[15] I am indebted to Donna Christian and Peg Griffin for providing me with the data presented in Tables 6.4 and 6.5.

The symbol $(1 - p)$ is the probability that the rule does not apply in the environment, p_0 is the input probability, and p_i, p_j, etc., are the probabilities for each of the constraints in the environment.

In Table 6.5, we present the hierarchy of environment probabilities based on feature weightings from Cedergren and Sankoff's nonapplications model, with an adaptation from Griffin (1974, pp. 4–6) which allows us to hierarchize the features in a way that is comparable to "classical" variable rule formulations as in Labov, 1969 (i.e., it allows us to look at necessary cross-products to establish geometric ordering of constraints). Table 6.5 does indicate that the lower order constraints (that is, the different categories of Verb + *ing*) may be more finely ordered than we have formulated in Rule (57), but more investigation concerning the linguistic categorization of these constructions is required before taking a strong position concerning these constraints. We conclude that a variable phonological rule with several different types of constraints on its structured variability most adequately accounts for the deletion of the *a*-prefix. There is undoubtedly a parallel process to the one we have formulated for AE which ultimately led to the complete deletion of this form in some varieties of English.

A Special Alliterative Constraint

In the previous section, we have examined several different types of constraints on the phonological rule that deletes *a*-prefixed forms as a part of the general unstressed initial-syllable deletion process. Our discussion of

TABLE 6.5
Hierarchy of String Probabilities Based on Feature
Weightings from Nonapplications Model

String			Nonapplication probability
+ING	V##__	+ADV	.896
+ING	V##__	+PROG	.869
+ING	C##__	+ADV	.837
+ING	C##__	+PROG	.795
+ING	V##__	+MOV	.790
+ING	V##__	+KEEP	.738
+ING	C##__	+MOV	.671
+ING	C##__	+KEEP	.590
−ING	V##__	V	.591
−ING	V##__	CV	.530
−ING	C##__	V	.361
−ING	C##__	CV	.265

phonological aspects of *a*-prefixing, however, would not be complete without mentioning an apparent constraint which disfavors the deletion of *a*-prefixed forms. This is what we may call the "coordination constraint." It is observed that coordinate participial constructions separated by a simple coordinate such as *and* or *or* show a strong tendency to retain *a*-prefixing on both *-ing* forms in the construction. We thus get constructions such as:

(59) a. . . . *they'll be all bushed up **a-struttin'** and **a-draggin'***   146:17
    b. *He just kept **a-beggin'** and **a-cryin'** and **a-wantin'** to go out*   83:18
    c. . . . *just keep **a-rockin'** and **a-rollin'** rock the car and you finally can rock you a way to get out*   24:(218)

We have only 16 potential instances of coordination where an *a*-prefixed form is found, but of these 12 have *a*-prefixing on both *-ing* forms in the coordination.[16] One way of explaining this would be to observe that some degree of code-specificity can be found with respect to *a*-prefixing (cf. Feagin, 1979) and that code-switching would not typically be expected to occur between close coordinate constructions of this type. It may also be suggested, however, that we have here a type of alliterative affect, in which we have an intervening syllable of the conjunction between the repetition of the *a*-. Certain literary writers have been known to use *a*-prefixing as an alliterative device in their dialect representations (McKay, 1973, p. 210). Additional evidence may come from the fact that *a*-prefixed forms, if they are going to occur on only some of the forms of a coordinate, will tend to occur on the second (and successive *-ing* forms in the series) rather than simply the first. That is, we are more likely to get forms like:

(60)   *I heared her **barking**, and **a-barkin'** and **a-barkin'***   22:26

than:

(61)   *? I heared her **a-barkin'** and **barking** and **barking***

Although we do not have sufficient examples to formally propose this apparent preference as a constraint, informal reactions of speakers from *a*-prefixing areas tend to support the claim that forms such as (59) are preferred over (60) and (60) over (61). The upshot of this preference is, of course, that AE speakers do have rhythm in their use of *a*-prefixed forms.[17]

[16] It is interesting to note that the dialect geographers who cite *a*-prefixing as a part of their descriptive inventories often cite the coordinate form of this construction (cf. Atwood 1953, p. 34).

[17] Wolfgang Wölck, in a personal communication, has noted a similar constraint in the Scottish use of *a*-prefixing and suggested that it may be accounted for as a type of anepestic rhythm.

Semantic Aspects of *a*-Prefixing

Whereas the syntactic and phonological considerations discussed in the previous sections have been virtually ignored in recent descriptions of *a*-prefixing, the few recent attempts to describe the semantic properties of this phenomenon have been the focus of interest. Treatments of *a*-prefixing by Stewart (1967), Hackenberg (1972), and Feagin (1979) have all focused on the potential semantic distinctiveness of *a*-prefixing as part of the verbal system of English. Because of the attention that *a*-prefixing has been given in this regard, our own consideration of its semantic properties can be interwoven with the discussion of the recent proposals that have been offered.

Stewart (1967) initially suggested that *a*-prefixing involves an aspectual relationship that is related to indefiniteness and/or remoteness of the verbal activity of the *a*-prefixed forms. He observes:

> The prefix shows that the action of the verb is indefinite in space and time while its absence implies that the action is immediate in space or time. Thus, *he's a-workin'* in Mountain Speech means either that the subject has a steady job, or he is away (out of sight, for example) working somewhere. On the other hand, *he's workin'* in Mountain Speech means that the subject is doing a specific task, close by. A similar (though not identical) grammatical distinction is indicated in Negro Dialect by the verbal auxiliary *be* [p. 10].[18]

Stewart gives no formal motivation for his conclusion, but does qualify his interpretation by noting that it is intended only to be approximative. There are, however, fairly clear-cut counterexamples that suggest that even an approximative version of Stewart's proposal cannot be justified. The following counterexamples to Stewart's claim, which are not atypical, cause us to question the interpretation that restricts *a*-prefixing to idefiniteness and/or remoteness.

(62) a. *I's **a-washin** one day and to go under the door I had to go under that spider*   28:21
    b. *I's **a-cannin** chicken one time . . .*   156:(229)
    c. *. . . all of a sudden, a bear come **a-runnin'** towards him and he shot it between the eyes*   44:18
    d. *"Who's **a-stompin** on my bridge?" . . . and the second one come by and says, "Who's **a-stompin'** on my bridge?"*   16:(610)
    e. *Count to about 10 or 15 so we can see if this machine's **a-workin***   FW:13:1

---

[18] It seems apparent that the discovery of a unique contrast for distributive *be* in Vernacular Black English (cf. Fasold 1969) has inspired the search for a unique semantic aspect of *a*-prefixing in AE. In fact, this investigation started out with such a bias. Hopefully, however, the ensuing discussion will reveal that our eventual conclusion is not subject to a self-fulfilling prophecy.

In cases such as (62a)–(62c), adverbial modifiers such as *one day, one time,* and *all of a sudden* refer to a particular activity in terms of space and/or time. Each relates an incident in which the speaker·is located at a specific time or place, such as the location of the speaker in a particular room engaged in a specific activity (62a). Even more specific is the sentence used by one of our indigenous fieldworkers (an authentic *a*-prefixing speaker) in (62e). The directions given in (62e) refer to the tape recorder located at the point of the interview at that particular time. The example of (62d) comes from a recounting of the story of "Billy Goat Gruff" where a goat stomps immediately overhead on the bridge. Examples such as these are not difficult to find, and Feagin (1979) also gives a number of examples which could not be accounted for in Stewart's proposal. It must thus be concluded that Stewart's proposal concerning the semantic distinctiveness of *a*-prefixing simply cannot be justified. This conclusion should not be interpreted to mean that *a*-prefixing cannot occur in indefinite and/or remote contexts. It can occur in such contexts but is in no way restricted to them. There is actually a fairly wide range of temporal and aspectual contexts in which *a*-prefixing can be found. We already mentioned the past and nonpast contexts of *a*-prefixing [cf. Sentences (2a)–(2d)] and we showed in (62) that it can be found in single occurrence events. We find further that it can be found in regularly occurring activities, whether they involve an activity which occurs at intermittent periods of time (63) or an activity of continuing duration (64):

(63) a. *They always told me when I was **a-drivin'** to always watch the other feller and not myself*   83:25
   b. *This man said, "We're gonna have to try to kill the ghost one way or another" Well now, it keeps **a-comin'** back*   77:2
   c. *He said, "Now Sherry, stay out of the refrigerator if you want to go on a diet" Sherry wouldn't, she kept **a-gettin'** in the refrigerator*   77:19

(64) a. *Every Sunday morning he used to, whenever Earl was **a-livin'**, they'd always go somewhere every Sunday*   83:3
   b. *Well, it brings back memory to me, when I was a child **a-growin'** up, just about the same way that they played*   157:(108)
   c. *I had twelve children and I got two dead and ten **a-livin'***   153:3

The breadth of semantic contexts in which *a*-prefixing can be found is indicated by its co-occurrence with various types of time adverbs. Feagin (1979), utilizing Crystal's (1966) taxonomy of time adverbs, shows the wide range of temporal and aspectual contexts in which *a*-prefixing can occur. An examination of co-occurring time adverbs for the data in this corpus indicates a similar pattern. Perhaps more important is the fact that there appears to be no systematic formal restriction in terms of the categories of time adverbs found in Crystal. This is quite unlike the pattern found for a form such as distributive *be* in Vernacular Black English, where its apparent restriction in terms of co-occurring time adverbs is an essential motivation in arguing for its semantic distinctiveness (cf. Fasold, 1969).

Hackenberg (1972), like Stewart, views *a*-prefixing as representing a semantic aspect different from non-*a*-prefixed forms ("the addition of the prefix seems to be a syntactic manifestation of semantic conditioning [p. 116]"), although his argument takes a somewhat different form. Hackenberg starts by accepting an analysis of English progressives that delimits them into three types: (*a*) CONTINUOUS aspect, in which an activity is currently viewed in progress (e.g., *They're playing bridge right now*); (*b*) INTERMITTENT aspect, in which an activity is viewed as recurring or habitual (e.g., *They're playing bridge this year*); and (*c*) PLANNED aspect, in which the progressive expresses an activity to take place in the future (e.g., *Tomorrow they're playing cards*). In terms of these different aspects of progressive, Hackenburg then observes that *a*-prefixing tends to occur most frequently with intermittent aspect and least frequently with planned aspect. The preference for *a*-prefixing with intermittent aspect is further confirmed by a preference test Hackenberg administered to Nicholas County residents (cf. Note 11). In his test, subjects were given sentence pairs contrasting the various combinations of progressive aspect with *a*-prefixing. For example, subjects were asked to express a preference between sentences considered to be reflective of intermittent aspect (e.g., *He's been a-jumpin' from one job to another for years*) vis-à-vis continuous aspect (e.g., *I see him a-jumpin' the fence right now*). Given such choices, subjects tended to show a preference for *a*-prefixing with intermittent aspect over continuous and planned aspect. On the basis of these data, Hackenburg then concludes that *a*-prefixing is systematically favored with intermittent aspect. A variable rule inserting the *a*-prefix is then written in which *a*-prefixing is formally shown to be favored by this semantic aspect.[19]

If we assume the validity of distinctions such as "planned," "intermittent," and "continuous" aspect for progressives, we must ask if the preference for intermittency is a unique function of *a*-prefixing. In other words, is this preference a function of the category progressive with or without *a*-prefixing or is this a preference that uniquely correlates with *a*-prefixing? From all available evidence, the preference for intermittency appears to be a function of the category progressive and is not unique to *a*-prefixing at all. One argument for this conclusion comes from studies of the progressive which show that intermittent aspect is more common to progressives than continuous and planned aspect. For example, Sag (1973) shows that there is a progressive squish, in which HABITUAL aspect (roughly equivalent to Hackenberg's "intermittent") is more inherent to the category progressive

---

[19] Hackenberg (1972, p. 132) eventually ends up calling the semantic aspect favoring *a*-prefixing "durative" rather than intermittent, for reasons that do not appear to be motivated on any formal basis.

than PROCESS (roughly equivalent to Hackenberg's "continuous") and FUTURATE (roughly equivalent to Hackenberg's "planned"). We shall not detail Sag's formal arguments here; however, it is instructive to note his conclusion:

> I know of no verbs, however, which occur only in the FUTURATE, only in the PROCESS, only in the FUTURATE and HABITUAL, or only in the FUTURATE and the PROCESS. Consequently, if we represent graphically the observation . . . , we see that it is possible to formulate the implicational hierarchy given in (21):
>
> (21) FUTURATE   ⊃ PROCESS   ⊃ HABITUAL
>   PROGRESSIVE   PROGRESSIVE   PROGRESSIVE

[Sag, 1973, pp. 86–87]

Sag's conclusions clearly match the preference that Hackenberg found for progressives with *a*-prefixing. This type of evidence suggests that the observed preference for "habitual" and "intermittent" activity is related to the category progressive and is not unique to *a*-prefixing at all.

In order to confirm the preferences shown in Hackenberg's test as a function of progressivity rather than *a*-prefixing as such, Hackenberg's preference test was replicated in this study with two major changes (cf. Hackenberg, 1972, pp. 358–369). One change involved the items in the test and another the subjects to which it was administered. Instead of giving Hackenberg's test with the *a*-prefixed forms, identical sentences were given without the *a*-prefixing. Thus, for example, instead of Hackenberg's original preference choice such as (65), the item was given in its non-*a*-prefixed form as in (66)

(65) a. *I see him **a-jumpin** the fence right now*
   b. *He's been **a-jumpin** from one job to another for years*

(66) a. *I see him **jumping** the fence right now*
   b. *He's been **jumping** from one job to another for years*

The test was given to 39 university students in Washington, D.C., who were not *a*-prefixing speakers. Of the 19 items found in Hackenberg's study, 15 of them showed identical preferences without the *a*-prefixed forms, and the 4 that showed different preferences did not differ in any systematic way in terms of the three aspects of progressive.[20] Quite clearly, then, the results from Hackenberg's test must be seen to be at best a reflection of preferences for the category progressive and not uniquely correlated to *a*-prefixing.

[20] It became apparent that many of the 39 subjects who took this test were responding on the basis of facts totally unrelated to progressive contrasts in some of the items. It seems that the same would hold true for the subjects in Hackenberg's study due to the nature of the test. This observation causes us to question the validity of any of the conclusions drawn from this test with respect to progressives or *a*-prefixed forms.

There are other facts observed with respect to a-prefixing that can be seen to be a reflection of the surface category progressive rather than a function of a-prefixing. For example, Feagin's (1979) breakdown of verbs with a-prefixing indicates that there are many more active verbs occurring with a-prefixing than statives or quasi-stative verbs. This, however, is a function of the permissibility of progressives with active verbs rather than any unique reflection of distributional privileges for a-prefixing. It is a well-known fact that stative and quasi-stative verbs are much less likely to pro-gressiveize than active verbs (Sag, 1973). We thus do not get forms such as (67) because of this restriction.

(67) a. *John is **knowing** the answers
     b. *John is **believing** the remark

Similarly, we do not get forms like (68) with a-prefixing:

(68) a. *John is **a-knowin'** the answer
     b. *John is **a-believin'** the remark

The higher frequency of active verbs with a-prefixing is obviously due to their greater potential incidence with progressives. All of the semantic re-strictions we find for a-prefixing with progressives are obviously general to the category progressive.

The observations made above are primarily concerned with a-prefixing on surface progressives. It might also be noted that there appear to be some general semantic restrictions on a-prefixed participles occurring as comple-ments of the movement verbs. Consider, for example, the list of a-prefixed participles occurring with the movement verbs in our corpus:

(69)

a-runnin'	*a-swimmin'*
a-rollin'	*a-birch-sappin'*
a-walkin'	*a-beatin'*
a-huntin'	*a-squirrel-huntin'*
a-crawlin'	*a-deer-huntin'*
a-jumpin'	*a-shootin'*
a-hollerin'	*a-ridin'*
	a-pheasant-huntin'

The activities represented in the list in (69) tend to be physical in nature and involve relatively unstructured activities as far as game-like rules are concerned. In most instances, there may be some continued motion from one undetermined location to another. The physical restriction is seen in the acceptability of sentences like (70) vis-à-vis the unacceptability of sentences like (71):

(70) a. *John went* **a-runnin'** *through the field*
  b. *John went* **a-pheasant-huntin'**

(71) a. *John went **a-dreamin'**
  b. *John went **a-puzzle-solvin'**

The contrast between semantic activities that are relatively unstructured as opposed to those that are structured in a game-like manner is seen in comparing sentences like (70) and (72):

(72) a. *He went **a-baseballin'**
  b. *He went **a-polo playin'**

These types of restriction are not, however, unique to *a*-prefixed participles. Silva (1973) has, in fact, shown that these are the restrictions that must be placed on all participial complements to the movement verbs.[21] We thus conclude that any semantic restrictions found for *a*-prefixing with movement verbs can be shown to involve a similar sort of restriction for the non-*a*-prefixed counterpart.

Not only does *a*-prefixing occur in all the semantic contexts allowable for non-*a*-prefixed surface progressives, the quasi-progressive *keep,* and movement verbs, but the overall semantic domain covered by *a*-prefixed forms can actually be shown to be somewhat broader when its usage with certain adverbial phrases is considered. In sentences like (17) (e.g., *He got sick* **a-workin'** *so hard*), it was shown that phrases denoting time could also involve causal relationships with the temporal and causal relationships being interrelated. In these cases, the occasion of the activity in the *a*-prefixed form resulted in the activity of the main verb. Again, however, we see that this is not something unique to *a*-prefixed forms, but a function of the underlying temporal locative ON or AT. Similar relationships have been noted for the surface realizations of prepositional phrases introduced by *on* or *at.*

> *On* is used with miscellaneous abstract head-words to indicate a point of time, though there is nearly always a short lapse of time between this point and the action expressed by the verb in the sentence and the action is conceived of as ensuing as the immediate and logical consequence of that which the prepositional phrase denotes, a causal relationship thereby being established. For similar cases with contemporaneity, see *at . . .* [Sandhagen, 1956, p. 82].

Although such causal relationships have largely been taken over by the propositions *from* and *by* in current usage [cf. Sentence (50b)] the temporal

---

[21] This is not to say that I am in complete agreement with all the semantic restrictions on these complements set forth by Silva. There are qualifications that need to be made on her semantic properties. The point we are emphasizing here, however, is that there is nothing about the verbal complements with movement verbs that can be seen to be unique to *a*-prefixed forms as opposed to their non-*a*-prefixed counterparts.

locative *on* still may carry this function in some specialized contexts, as in sentences like (73):

(73) a. **On investigating** *the accident, he changed his mind about their guilt*
      b. *He changed the structure of the program* **on assuming** *the chairman-ship*

Nonetheless, the present use of temporal locatives such as *on* and *at* with this causal relationship is now quite restricted, and most varieties of English would not allow the realization of *on* as the surface preposition for the sentences given in (17). That is, we do not get sentences like (74):

(74) a. **He got a sick* **on working** *so hard*
      b. **He nearly died* **on laughing** *so hard*
      c. **He makes money* **on building** *houses*

Although we previously noted [cf. the sentences in (52)] that *on* and *at* have a somewhat broader surface range in AE than that found in some other varieties of English, it is unclear whether *on* would be allowed in sentences like (74). From our limited evidence, however, it appears that they would not be permissible for most AE speakers, and the surface realizations would also have to be *from* or *by* for this variety. If this is indeed the case, then we have here a slightly broader surface range for *a*-prefixed forms than that of the alternant surface *on* or *at* forms. This is not, however, related to any inherent semantic distinction, but a general manifestation of the fact that underlying temporal locatives are realized in a number of different ways. The more widespread use of the temporal locatives *on* or *at* during earlier periods in the English language seems to be fairly well-documented (cf. Jespersen, 1933, p. 53).

Finally, we should mention Feagin's proposal concerning the meaning of *a*-prefixing. Although Feagin is somewhat more cautious in her interpretation than Stewart or Hackenberg, she ends up suggesting that *a*-prefixing has the meaning of INTENSIFIED ACTION or IMMEDIACY OR DRAMATIC VIVIDNESS.

> In conclusion, the prefixed present participle has the meaning of 'intensified action' or 'immediacy or dramatic vividness' which Leech suggests is an offshoot of the progressive in general. . . . The prefixed participle tends to occur in emotional contexts such as narration of stories about ghosts, accidents, murders, tornadoes, fires, juicy gossip, hunting, or childhood games and escapades. This could lead to opposite interpretations. First, that it occurs as a stylistic device to add color and immediacy to the story. Second, that it occurs here because the speaker is caught up in his own thoughts and has let slip older, more rural forms, which he normally edits out, especially in front of strangers like me. I believe the first interpretation to be the correct one, since 24 of the examples in the data as a whole occur with the intensifier *just*, 16 with *keep* (which has an intensifying meaning of "persevere"). Of these 16, 7 of the examples occurred with *just* as well, as in *just kept on a-churning*. Thus, the action described was triply intensified: *just* + *kept on* + *a-churning* [1979, pp. 114–115].

It is unclear whether Feagin is proposing a formal semantic distinction of INTENSIFICATION or VIVIDNESS, but if so, such a claim seems difficult to motivate. While intensifying *just* is the most frequently co-occurring adverb in both Feagin's data and the data considered here (34 of the 89 co-occurring adverbs with *a*-prefixing are *just*), intensifying *just* also occurs with non-*a*-prefixed forms for the same speakers who reveal it with *a*-prefixing. A formal distinction between an intensifying adverb like *just* or *really* as compared with a minimizing one such as *hardly* [(75) and (76)] apparently does not obtain.

(75)   *He was really* **a-runnin'**

(76)   *He was hardly* **a-runnin'**

Although there is no clear-cut evidence for a formal distinction on the basis of the sort of semantic distinctions suggested by Feagin, our evidence does indicate that AE speakers would at least stylistically prefer a sentence like (75) over (76), since intensifying *just* is more likely to co-occur with *a*-prefixed forms than with non-*a*-prefixed ones.

Feagin's argument for intensification on the basis of its co-occurrence with *keep* is subject to the same types of considerations that we have raised with respect to intensifying *just*. In addition, we may mention that *keep* is most often used in the same way as habitual progressives, the category which appears to be most inherent to the notion progressive. Although this may indicate a stylistic preference, no formal semantic distinction can be motivated on this basis.

Another argument raised by Feagin comes from the observation that *a*-prefixing tends to occur in emotional contexts in narratives. While it is very difficult to specify precisely the degree of emotion that would qualify as "emotional," there is evidence that *a*-prefixing occurs more in narratives than in other discourse styles. Our breakdown in terms of the category "narrative" indicates that 67.2% of all *a*-prefixed forms in our corpus are found in narratives. Here again, though, we are talking about a stylistic preference rather than a qualitative formal distinction.

Although Feagin eventually ends up her discussion with a choice between two interpretations for *a*-prefixing (namely a stylistic device to add color or a narrative shift into older, more rural forms), these need not be viewed as mutually exclusive choices. We would expect that the emotional narration of stories with dramatic vividness would certainly give rise to older, more rural forms, which it obviously does in this case. That an older, more rural form should be used as a stylistic device in dramatic narratives certainly stands to reason. This is especially true in the case of forms that may not carry any apparent formal distinction, which is what appears to be the case with *a*-prefixing.

The upshot of this discussion of semantic aspects of a-prefixing is that we have found no formal evidence for positing a distinct semantic category for a-prefixing. Investigation of several different proposals for a semantic distinction carried by a-prefixing has shown that these cannot be motivated. This, of course, is not to say that no formal distinction can be found since we are always limited by the finiteness of our investigation. We are, however, reinforced in our conclusion concerning the lack of formal semantic distinction by the fact that a-prefixing shows such sensitivity to phonological constraints. It seems reasonable to conclude that we would not expect to find semantic conditioning when we have already found evidence that the variation is taking place at a level influenced strongly by phonological factors. Although further investigation might prove our conclusion to be unwarranted, some of the possible interpretations have been eliminated and further examination of this phenomenon can start at this point.

References

Atwood, E. B. 1953. *A survey of verb forms in the Eastern United States*. Ann Arbor: University of Michigan Press.

Bolinger, D. 1971a. The nominal in the progressive. *Linguistic Inquiry, 2,* 246–250.

Bolinger, D. 1971b. A further note on the nominal in the progressive. *Linguistic Inquiry, 2,* 584–587.

Cedergren, H. J., and Sankoff, D. 1974. *Variable rules: Performance as a statistical reflection of competence. Language, 50,* 333–355.

Crystal, D. 1966. Specification and English tenses. *Journal of Linguistics, 2,* 1–33.

Fasold, R. W. 1969. Tense and the form *be* in Black English. *Language, 45,* 763–776.

Fasold, R. W. 1972. *Tense marking in Black English: A linguistic and social analysis*. Arlington, Va.: Center for Applied Linguistics.

Feagin, C. 1979. *Variation and Change in Alabama English: A Sociolinguistic Study of the White Community*. Washington, D.C.: Georgetown University Press.

Griffin, P. 1974. Notes on reading the output of VARBRUL. Unpublished paper. Georgetown University.

Hackenberg, R. 1972. *A sociolinguistic description of Appalachian English*. Unpublished doctoral dissertation, Georgetown University.

Jespersen, O. 1933. *Essentials of English grammar*. University, Ala.: University of Alabama Press.

Kirsner, R. S., and Thompson, S. A. 1974. The role of pragmatic inference in semantics: A study of verb complements in English. Unpublished manuscript, University of California, Los Angeles.

Krapp, G. P. 1925. *The English language in America*. New York: Frederick Ungar Publishing Company.

Labov, W. 1969. Contraction, deletion, and inherent variability of the English copula. *Language, 45,* 715–762.

McKay, J. 1974. *A linguistic study of Samuel Clemens' style*. Unpublished doctoral dissertation, Princeton University.

Sag, I. 1973. On the state of progress on progressives and statives. In C. -J. N. Bailey and R. W. Shuy (Eds.), *New ways of analyzing variation in English*. Washington, D.C.: Georgetown University Press.

Sandhagen, H. 1956. *Studies on the temporal senses of the prepositions* **at, on, in, by** *and* **for** *in present-day English*. Uppsala: Almqvist and Wiksells.

Silva, C. M. 1973. Adverbial *-ing. Ohio State Working Papers in Linguistics, 16,* 90–94.

Stewart, W. A. 1967. *Language and communication problems in Southern Appalachia*. Washington, D.C.: Center for Applied Linguistics.

Williams, E. S. 1971. Small clauses in English. Unpublished manuscript, MIT.

Wolfram, W. 1974a. The relationship of White Southern speech to Vernacular Black English. *Language, 50,* 498–527.

Wolfram, W. 1974b. *Sociolinguistic aspects of assimilation: Puerto Rican English in New York City*. Arlington, Va.: Center for Applied Linguistics.

Wolfram, W. Forthcoming. "Speaker-Hearer Knowledge and other Lects: A Sample Case. *New Ways of Analyzing Variation in English*. Washington, D. C.: Georgetown University Press.

Wolfram, W. and Fasold, R. W. 1974. *The study of social dialects in American English*. Englewood Cliffs, N.J.: Prentice-Hall.

Wolfram, W., and Christian, D. 1976. *Appalachian speech*. Arlington, Va.: Center for Applied Linguistics.

7

Arvilla C. Payne

FACTORS CONTROLLING THE ACQUISITION OF THE PHILADELPHIA DIALECT BY OUT-OF-STATE CHILDREN[1]

Introduction

In recent years, linguists have returned to the study of the acquisition of language with a greater appreciation of the complexity of the task and the ability of the children who learn to speak. Most models of language acquisition are based upon the parent–child relationship; that is, on the process of the transmission of the basic input of speech patterns from parent to child (Brown and Bellugi, 1964; Bloom, 1970). These models have been useful, particularly in describing the earliest years of acquisition. However, they have not dealt with the broader social context of language learning.

The study immediately addresses the problem of determining the extent to which children of various ages acquire the phonological system of a second dialect after moving from one dialect region to a new one, as a way of exploring the general mechanism of language acquisition. These data suggest the answer to two further questions: first, whether a child freely reorganizes and/or restructures his grammar up to the age of 14; and second, whether a child will learn to speak like his peers or retain the system learned from his parents.

[1] This work was supported by the National Science Foundation under contracts GS-3287 and GS-36382X, A Quantitative Study of Linguistic Variation and Change, during the years 1972–1974. I owe to my associate Bruce Lee Johnson many thanks for the hours of discussion of the issues and problems encountered during the development of this work. I would also like to express my appreciation to the other members of the research project for their encouragement of my work.

One of the major concerns of linguists is the writing of grammars that represent the underlying forms and rules that produce the structures used in speech. The approach most common today assumes that phonological syntactic rules are freely added to a child's grammar and are continually reorganized in his grammar up to the age of 13 or 14 (Halle, 1962). However, there is another possibility that might have to be considered: that grammar is based upon forms acquired EARLY in the process of language acquisition, say up to about age 6–8, and different rules are required for those forms which are acquired after the period of initial learning has stopped.

If a grammar is acquired in layers and sections at various ages, then a theory of grammar that stresses simplification from a single data base will not have the explanatory force that a grammar embodying the various levels of acquisition would have. If there are various stages and levels in acquisition, then linguists may find themselves writing grammars in which simple structures which are learned early are produced by one set of rules, and complex structures which are learned later, are produced by a different set of rules. This study provides an opportunity to examine what ability children have to reorganize, or add to, or to restructure their linguistic rules as new data are encountered. In particular, this study is concerned with a specific class of facts about the successful acquisition and development of the phonological and phonetic representations of the speech of children who have moved from one dialect region to another. The question is, how does one represent such change in underlying forms? In this study the term RESTRUCTURING will be applied to any change in the dictionary representation of a morpheme; REORGANIZATION will be applied to indicate (a) "FREE INSERTION" of rules in the grammar; or (b) RULE ADDITION, that is, the addition of rules at the end of the grammar.

Sample Selection

The community selected for this study was a middle-class suburb of Philadelphia, Pennsylvania—King of Prussia. The community was selected because it provided the requisite independent variables; the study required (a) an area where there was one dominant dialect and many families from other dialect areas; (b) an area where children moving in had the opportunity of learning new dialect forms; and (c) a situation in which the parents' dialect had a maximal opportunity of influencing a child's linguistic acquisition. In King of Prussia (a) the local dialect details were well known; (b) at least 50% of the population was local; and (c) the nonlocal dialects were known to have high or neutral prestige.

King of Prussia is a bedroom community which has developed from a farming town into an industrial center since World War II. Many major companies such as General Electric, Western Electric, ITT, and General Motors are located in the area and are largely responsible for the influx of people. Exploratory methods indicated that 45% of the population was transient. The exploratory interviews also revealed that the local people in King of Prussia used a phonology and grammar indistinguishable from those of the central areas of Philadelphia and also that they were familiar with most of the local Philadelphia children's games and lexical items.

During the course of the fieldwork a block-study method was used. Three types of blocks were selected, reflecting the different residential patterns of neighborhoods. The first type of block was called MOBILE, since the majority of families living on it were transient, out-of-state families, the parents having been born and raised in another dialect area and the children usually having spent at least part of their lives in another dialect area. The second type of block pattern, the MIXED block, was defined as consisting of approximately half out-of-state families and half local families, where local meant that the parents and children had been born and raised within the Philadelphia dialect area. The third type was the LOCAL block, which consisted of primarily local families. At least 4 families on each block were interviewed. In order to assure a more accurate view of the influence of the residential composition of a block on acquisitional patterns, two of each type of block were located; that is, six blocks in all. In the mobile block, 3 out-of-state families and 1 local family were interviewed; in the mixed block, 2 of each type of family were interviewed; and in the local block, 3 local families and 1 out-of-state family were interviewed. Further control was introduced by selecting three types of families: (a) families with local-born parents and children; (b) families with local-born children and out-of-state parents; and (c) families with out-of-state-born children and parents. The second group provided a controlling factor for the comparison of parental influence versus peer group influence as the children in that group had spent their entire lives in the Philadelphia dialect area. A total of 24 families, half local and half out-of-state, with a total of 108 children, were interviewed. Over 450 hours of speech were recorded.

Initial contacts with families were made by approaching the children playing in the yards or streets. A number of scout and church leaders in the community gave generous cooperation and helped to identify and then contact families in blocks that met the requirements. In some cases the church supplied lists of names. The leaders of the Catholic church located all the families on one local and one mixed block.

Each child was asked to bring his best friend to his interview. This strategy was used in order to create a situation in which there would be close peer interaction (cf. John Lewis's interviews of peer pairs in Labov *et al.*, 1968). This in turn would result in the long periods of spontaneous speech needed for the analysis of the vernacular (Labov 1966, 1972a). The development of this strategy lengthened the average interview from about 40 minutes to about 2 hours of spontaneous speech. When the parents were interviewed together the interview lasted from 3 to 4 hours.

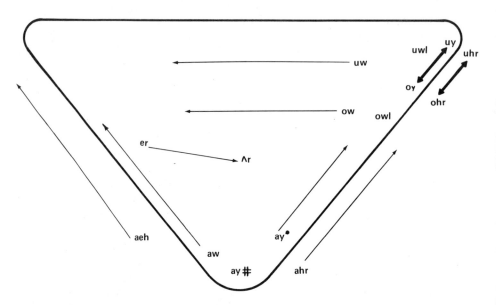

FIGURE 7.1 *The phonetic and phonological variables in the King of Prussia study.*

Linguistic Variables

Figure 7.1 identifies the Philadelphia vowel system, against which a speaker's conformity to a local pattern can be measured. Some of the variables have been recognized in earlier studies on Philadelphia speech. Trager and Smith (1951) pointed out the merger of the *merry–Murray* word class. Ferguson (1968) is particularly concerned with the sound change occurring in the short-*a* class in Philadelphia. Kurath and McDavid (1961) in synopsis 72, Philadelphia, located in the educated speech the following phonetic values: (*a*) slight fronting of (ow)— [oʽuˆ]; (*b*) slight fronting of (uw)— [uʽ]; (*c*) some rounding of (ahr)—[ɒˆəˆ]; (*d*) beginning raising of (ohr)—[ɔˆəˆ]; (*e*) beginning raising of (aw)— [aˆu]; and (*f*) some lengthening. In 1970, the project on linguistic change and variation (LCV)[2] began an investigation of linguistic change in Philadelphia, and provided the detailed data on the Philadelphia dialect needed as a base for this study. The data used in this report were gathered as an integral part of the project: The vowel system was studied by spectrographic methods and later by the more accurate techniques of spectral analysis and linear prediction. Phonological patterns were traced by sociolinguistic techniques which take into account stylistic and social variation.

In addition to tracing the further progress of the variables that have been mentioned, the research project located several new developments in sound

[2] The project LCV was a sociolinguistic research project sponsored by the National Science Foundation at the University of Pennsylvania.

changes taking place in Philadelphia in the following vowels: (aw), (ay⁰), (ahr), (ohr), and (oy). Spectrographic studies contributed toward understanding the linguistic processes responsible for the changes now in progress.

The profile of the Philadelphia/King of Prussia dialect that follows is drawn from the most advanced features of the changes occurring in the dialect. The profile is a framework in which each variable is rated according to whether the child has acquired the Philadelphia norm, shows correction toward it, or does not have the Philadelphia norm. The following variables are considered as diagnostic of the Philadelphia/King of Prussia pattern.

1a. (æ): The class of short *a* is split into a tense and a lax set under a complex series of conditions which will be further discussed.

1b. (æh): The tense set of (æh) is raised to the level of [eˆ·ə] or higher.

2. (aw): The nucleus of (aw) is fronted at least to [æ] and in younger speakers is raised to the level of [ɛ] and even [e]. Further, the direction of the glide is phonetically towards [ǫ] or even [ɒ] instead of [ʊ].

3. (ay): The nucleus of (ay) is centralized before voiceless obstruents and then often backed to [ˆ] or fronted to [əˆ].

4. (ohr): (ohr) is raised to the level of (uhr), with which it merges.

5. (oy): The nucleus of (oy) is raised to [u].

6. (uw) and 7. (ow): The nuclei of (uw) and (ow) are in the process of extreme fronting and centralization except before /l/ with greater advances in free position.

8. (er): Finally, in pairs such as *merry–Murray* and *ferry–furry* the nuclei of the *er* class are merging with those of the class [ər].

Three to eight tokens of each of the vowels discussed above were taken, except for the membership classes of short *a* for which all words were transcribed. Spectographic studies were made where there appeared to be a continuum in the short-*a* pattern.

The two basic questions considered were:

1. What are the types of rules out-of-state children are capable of learning when they move to Philadelphia?

2. What are the social factors that might hinder or contribute to a child's acquisition of the new dialect?

First, both of these questions are examined in relation to the acquisition of the five phonetic variables—(aw), (ay⁰), (uw), (ow), and (oy).

Figure 7.2 shows the basic pattern for social influence on acquisition of language in terms of age moved and current age, and it displays the three main areas of experience that are significant to a study of this nature. The horizontal axis shows the age at which a child entered the community; the vertical axis shows the age of the child at the time of the interview. Area 1 is the period of early acquisition under parental influence, the age during which the child is beginning to learn language, and the primary stage of language acquisition. Some parental influence on specific dialect rules is assumed;

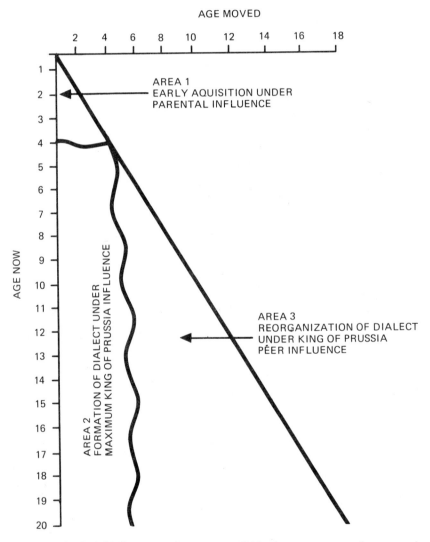

FIGURE 7.2 *Social influences on language acquisition by current age and age moved.*

however, the extent and period of this influence has not been determined conclusively. This uncertainty is indicated by the wavy lines in Figure 7.2. Area 2 is the formulation of a dialect under maximum King of Prussia influence. This area includes children born in King of Prussia and raised there during the period of consolidation of their dialects under peer influence. Area 3 includes children reorganizing their dialects under King of Prussia influence. It is here that the children who have moved in from another dialect area and who have spent only part of their lives in King of Prussia are found. This area is the one of most interest for this study, as it is here that one can examine what happens to children who first learn to speak in a different dialect area and then apparently begin to speak differently when exposed to the influence of new peers.

Phonetic Variables

In this study there are 12 out-of-state families[3] from various dialect regions: 3 families from New York City (Morgan, Baker, and Miller); 3 families from Massachusetts (Martin, Kelly, and Douglas); 1 family from upstate New York (Hunter); 1 family from upstate Pennsylvania (Jackson); 1 family from Western Pennsylvania (Burk); 1 family from Cleveland (Cameron); and 1 family from Kansas (Barnes). With the diversity of the dialect backgrounds represented in the data, it is necessary to determine if any of the phonetic and phonological variables of the Philadelphia dialect are phonetically realized in the same manner in any of the out-of-state dialects. Table 7.1 displays the relevant patterns (Johnson, 1971; Kurath and McDavid, 1961; Labov, 1974; Labov, Yaeger, and Steiner, 1972). The five phonetic and three phonological variables are located on the vertical axis. If a given variable is phonetically realized in the same manner in the Philadelphia and the out-of-state dialect a plus (+) is used, if the variable is not the same a minus (−) is used; if there is insufficient information available a question mark (?) is used. Evidence for these decisions is given in the references cited.

As not all of the dialects are totally different from the Philadelphia dialect for all of the variables, a rating of overall success in acquisition for each variable is based upon the total number of children whose original dialect did not realize the Philadelphia variable in the same way. For example, children from New York City realize (aw) as [æɒ], which is the same as the base position of Philadelphia (aw). Children from Western Pennsylvania front and raise the nucleus of (aw) as high [e] and often lower the glide. As this overlaps with the pattern of many Philadelphia speakers, these out-of-state children are not included in the count of how many children have

---

[3] The names of the families have been changed to respect confidentiality.

TABLE 7.1

The Presence (+) and Absence (−) of the Same Phonetic Realizations of the Philadelphia Variables in the OOS[a] Dialects

	Phonetic variables					Phonological variables		
	(aw)	(ay°)	(uw)	(ow)	(oy)	(uhr) ‾(ohr)	(er) ‾(ʌr)	(æh) ‾(æ)
New York City	+	−	−	−	+	+	−	−
Massachusetts	−	−	−	−	−	+	−	−
Cleveland	−	−	−	−	−	−	−	−
Binghampton	−	−	−	−	−	−	−	−
Scranton	−	−	+	+	−	−	−	−
Western Penn.	+	−	+	+	+	+	−	−
Upstate Penn.	−	−	?	?	−	+	−	−
Kansas	−	−	?	?	−	−	−	−

[a] Out-of-state.

acquired that Philadelphia variable. The same situation holds true for children from Scranton and Western Pennsylvania in the fronting of the nuclei of (ow) and (uw). As moderate to extreme fronting is already present in their dialects for the nuclei of these two variables, they are not included in the tabulations on acquisitions of (ow) and (uw).

The overall results of the investigation of learning of the five phonetic variables are given in Table 7.2 for natural speech.[4] The variables are listed across the top of the tables and the three rows show categories for degree of learning:

1. ACQUIRED—The child has acquired the Philadelphia variable in a way that matches local patterns.
2. PARTIALLY ACQUIRED—This indicates that although the child uses the Philadelphia variable part of time, he also uses the non-Philadelphia variable part of time. For example, for the variable (ay°), a child who has partially acquired the Philadelphia norm may pronounce the word *fight* as [fəit] part of the time and [fait] the rest of the time.
3. NOT ACQUIRED—The child has not acquired the variable at all.

The overall percentages of acquisition were determined by taking the total number of children who could acquire a given variable and dividing that

[4] Although the results for word lists are very interesting, they will not be considered here. For details see Payne, 1976.

TABLE 7.2

Acquisition Pattern for the Percentage Acquired for Phonetic Variables for Natural Speech

Pattern	Variables				
	ay°	aw	oy	uw	ow
Acquired (%)	50	40	60	52	68
Partially acquired (%)	44.1	40	30	48	32
Not acquired (%)	5.9	20	10	0	0
Number of children who needed to learn variable	34	20	20	25	25

into the total number of children who acquired, partially acquired, and did not acquire that given variable.

Looking at Table 7.2 one of the most striking results is the high percentages in the categories "acquired" and "partially acquired" compared to the very low percentages in the category "not acquired." With the exception of (aw), each variable has been completely acquired by 50% or more of the children, and very few children have failed to acquire the pattern at all. The variable (aw) alone shows a moderate percentage for nonacquisition.

One question that arises immediately is why the out-of-state children show less success in learning (aw) than (uw), (ow), (oy), and (ay°). To answer this question, it is first necessary to understand the relationship of the various variables to each other and the changes they have undergone.

In the case of (uw) and (ow), there are various reasons, both linguistic and social, why these variables are easily acquired. The extreme fronting and centralization of (uw) and (ow) except before /l/ in Philadelphia goes far beyond the subtle distinction found among the allophones in other dialects. Yet, other studies (Kurath and McDavid, 1961; Labov, 1972; LYS 1972; Johnson, 1971) show that there is a slight to moderate fronting tendency already present in many dialects. Thus, there is available in many speakers' dialects a rudimentary distinction, however slight, between the fully backed allophones of /uw/ and /ow/ before /l/ and their allophones in other environments. In this way the acquisition of the precise Philadelphia norms is a relatively easy task. In view of these facts, (uw) and (ow) are probably not as likely to be stigmatized by nonlocal speakers.

A similar situation exists for (ay°). In the pronunciation of such pairs of words as *right* and *ride* and *sight* and *side,* there is, in almost all dialects, a subtle distinction between the allophone that occurs before voiceless consonants and the allophone that occurs before voiced consonants. In Canada, the Upper South, and Martha's Vineyard it is a very marked distinction. In Philadelphia this distinction is even more exaggerated among younger speakers producing the centralized nucleus [əi]. This shifts back for some speakers to [ʌi] and front for others. Again, if the distinction is present in other dialects, the basis for the formation of the rule is greatly facilitated.

A slightly different situation obtains for (oy). There are at least two main factors involved. First, there are very few words in the (uy) word class; if functional factors are effective as an out-of-state child begins to raise the nucleus of (oy) to the height of (uy), there are few words with which the (oy) words would become homophonous and cause confusion. Second, the chain shift that is merging (oy) and (uy) in Philadelphia is taking place in other dialects, and it seems reasonable to assume that unless there is strong negative stigmatization in the first dialect, speakers would not show a quick acquisition of the new forms.

The conditions under which /aw/ becomes [æ̞] have deeper historical roots than those of the other phonetic changes discussed. First of all, the fronting of the nucleus of /aw/ in Philadelphia and in other dialects clearly represents a continuation of the nucleus glide differentiation begun in the Great Vowel Shift, during which Middle English /ū/ became [a̞], which in the majority of Standard English dialects is represented by [a̞]. It does not seem unreasonable to assume that independent developments elsewhere in the vowel system are necessary in order for the fronting of /aw/ to proceed. Specifically, it would seem, first, that this is a response to the fronting of the nuclei of /uw/ and /ow/ and, second, that there would also be a tendency for the nucleus of /aw/ to be identified with the tensing and raising of short *a*. Assuming /uw, ow, aw/ are an integrated subsystem, changes affecting the first two members of this class might be expected to operate eventually on /aw/. In this way, the fronting of the nucleus of /aw/ can be interpreted as a generalization of the environment in which the fronting operates:

RULE 1

$$[-\text{low}] \rightarrow [-\text{back}] \: / \underline{} \begin{bmatrix} -\text{voc} \\ -\text{cons} \\ +\text{back} \end{bmatrix}$$

RULE 1′

$$\begin{bmatrix} +\text{voc} \\ -\text{cons} \end{bmatrix} \rightarrow [-\text{back}] \: / \underline{} \begin{bmatrix} -\text{voc} \\ -\text{cons} \\ +\text{back} \end{bmatrix}$$

In any case, although these may be necessary conditions for the fronting of the nucleus of /aw/ to take place, they are probably not sufficient for it. There are dialects that have fronted variants of both /uw/ and /ow/, [e:ᵊ] for some of the allophones of /æ/, and still do not have [æ̞].

Moreover, the broad phonetic transcriptions used here do not reveal the fact, as found by the research project, that the glide segment of /aw/ is shifting to a low or lower-mid back glide; that is, to [ɔ̯]. This unusual phonetic character of /aw/ may make acquisition more difficult.

Another factor that may affect the success of acquisition of (aw) and (ay⁰) is that both of these variables are new changes in progress which are not complete. Subjective reaction tests administered to native Philadelphians by the research project reveal that the speakers are less sensitive to the newer changes and show little correction.

The notable success of the out-of-state children in acquiring the Philadelphia phonetic variables is consistent with the observation that these variants can be added to the grammar by simple rule addition. Labov (1974, pp. 41–42) gives three rules for adding (uw), (ow), and (aw), and (ay⁰) to the grammar of a New York City speaker.[5] Rule 2 insures that all diphthongs with lax vowels and upgliding back glides will be fronted. This separates (uw) and (ow) from the category of back vowels. When (uw) and (ow) occur before /l/, they are ingliding with a central glide and are not affected by Rule 2.

RULE 2

$$[-\text{low}] \rightarrow [-\text{back}] \: / \: \underline{\quad} \begin{bmatrix} -\text{cons} \\ +\text{back} \end{bmatrix}$$

Rule 3 is an extension of Rule 1. If fronts /aw/ to approximately the same position as [æ].

RULE 3

$$[+\text{low}] \rightarrow [-\text{back}] \: / \: \underline{\quad} \begin{bmatrix} -\text{cons} \\ +\text{back} \end{bmatrix}$$

Rule 4 centralizes any nucleus of a diphthong and removes it from the category of low vowels when it occurs before voiceless consonants. This rule applies only to (ay⁰).

[5] Rules 2, 3, and 4 are given in a slightly different form in Labov, 1974.

1. Labov's rule 1 [= Rule 2]

$$[-\text{tense}] \rightarrow [-\text{back}] \: / \: \underline{\quad} \begin{bmatrix} -\text{cons} \\ +\text{back} \end{bmatrix}$$

2. Labov's rule 2 [= Rule 3]

$$[+\text{low}] \rightarrow [-\text{back}] \: / \: \underline{\quad} \begin{bmatrix} -\text{cons} \\ +\text{back} \end{bmatrix}$$

3. Labov's rule 3 [= Rule 4]

$$[-\text{tense}] \rightarrow [-\text{low}] \: / \: \underline{\quad} [-\text{cons}] \begin{bmatrix} +\text{tense} \\ -\text{son} \end{bmatrix}$$

RULE 4

$$[+\text{low}] \rightarrow [-\text{low}] / \underline{\quad} \begin{bmatrix} -\text{cons} \\ -\text{back} \end{bmatrix} \begin{bmatrix} +\text{tense} \\ -\text{son} \end{bmatrix}$$

These rules represent the simplest alternation that would be necessary to bring a New York City or a non-Philadelphian vowel system into alignment with the Philadelphia system. But, if a child makes these alignments, is reorganization or restructuring taking place? Taking (ay°) as an example, how do we account for the success of the out-of-state children in acquiring (ay°)?

On the one hand, some structural analyses would claim that if /pat/ and /pət/ are a phonemic pair, the /a/ and /ə/ are distinct everywhere else, including their occurrences in complex nuclei. This would not be considered to be ordinary phonetic change. They would claim that the native speaker hears the two sounds as different and, therefore, does not identify [ai] and [əi]. On the other hand, in a generative analysis there is no phonemic difference corresponding to [ai] and [əi]. Instead one finds that what is occurring is an allophonic change and not a phonemic change. The subjective reactions, the speaker's attitudes, and the continuous variation in Philadelphia lead one to accept the latter of these two treatments. Therefore, all (ay) words would be written as /ay/ in the lexicon and a rule would be added on the grammar to apply under the given conditions.

Age of Arrival

A number of scholars have contributed to the literature on age spans, peer group influence on language acquisition, and the "critical period" for language acquisition. The scholars whose contributions have been most significant in terms of this paper are Piaget (1926, 1928, 1971), Erikson (1950), Lenneberg (1967), Ervin (1964), Cazden (1964), Asher and Garcia (1969), Bloom (1970), Kazazi (1970), LeMasters (1970), Wolfram (1974), Oyama (1973), Bee (1975), Labov (1974), Labov et al. (1968).

Further inquiries in King of Prussia involved a search for patterns of socialization and schooling. The emerging data suggested a practical grouping of the ages as follows: 0–4 years, 5–9 years, and 10–14 years. In Table 7.3 the age divisions are used to summarize the effect of age and to give the results for the percentage of children who acquired a given variable for natural speech. The data reveal that the tendency appears to be that the earlier a child moved to King of Prussia the more successful he was in acquiring the Philadelphia phonetic variables. (See Appendix A for the statistical results on the data in Table 7.3 using chi squares).

Although the age at which the child moved to King of Prussia appears to have an effect upon the degree of acquisition of the phonetic variables, it is also important to determine the possible effect on acquisition of the number

TABLE 7.3

Percentage of Acquisition of Phonetic Variables for
Natural Speech for Different Age Spans During which
the Out-of-State Children Moved to King of Prussia

Variable	Number completely acquired	Number of subjects considered	Percentage acquired
Age 0–4			
aw	6	10	60
ay⁰	11	17	64.7
ow	7	10	70
uw	7	10	70
oy	7	10	70
Age 5–9			
aw	2	8	40
ay⁰	7	14	50
ow	7	12	58.3
uw	8	12	66.6
oy	5	8	62.5
Age 10–14			
aw	0	2	0
ay⁰	0	3	0
ow	2	3	66.6
uw	0	3	0
oy	0	2	0

of years a child has lived in King of Prussia. Table 7.4 shows the percentage of acquisition of the phonetic variables according to the age a child was when he moved to King of Prussia and the number of years lived in King of Prussia—4–7 years or 8–16 years. Further subdivisions of years lived in King of Prussia were not made as the number in the cells would have become too small. The groupings for the age at which the children moved to King of Prussia were set so as to correspond to changes in a child's school–and related social–statuses. Thus, 0–4 corresponds to the pre-school years, 5–8 corresponds to kindergarten through third grade, and 9–13 corresponds to the grades up to high school. The percentages were derived by dividing the total number of variables acquired by the children in each cell by the total number of variables which could be considered. The results indicate that children born and raised in King of Prussia, or those who moved to the area by the age of 4 and who have lived in King of Prussia for anywhere between 4 to 16 years, and children who have lived in King of Prussia for 8–16 years and moved between the ages of 5 and 8 have approximately the same degree of success in acquiring the Philadelphia phonetic variables. Children who moved to King of Prussia between the ages of 5 and 8 and who have lived in

TABLE 7.4

The Percentage of Acquisition of the Phonetic Variables by OOS[a] Children According to the Number of Years Lived in King of Prussia and the Age Moved

Number of children	Age moved to area	Years lived in area	Variables		
			Number acquired	Number of variables	Percentage acquired
1	9–13	8–16	—	—	—
6	9–13	4–7	8	24	33
3	5–8	8–16	9	13	69
7	5–8	4–7	13	23	56
12	0–4	8–16	24	36	66
5	0–4	4–7	11	17	64
$N = 33$					

[a] Out-of-state.

the area for only 4–7 years show a slightly less degree of success of acquisition.

The Short-*a* Patterns

Unlike the phonetic variables, the Philadelphia short-*a* pattern cannot be incorporated into the grammar by simple rule addition at the end of the grammar, as there are several serious structural consequences involved in the acquisition of the short-*a* pattern. The success that the out-of-state children have in acquiring the CORE pattern of the Philadelphia short *a* provides an important insight into the ability of children to recognize and/or restructure their dialects as they are exposed to new data; a child needs to learn not only the phonetic conditioning of the short-*a* distribution (represented in what follows by Rule 5), but also the grammatical conditioning and lexical exceptions.

Four general types of short-*a* patterns in Eastern United States dialects and the distribution of the allophones of short *a* (Labov, Yaeger, and Steiner, 1972; Labov, 1974) are displayed in Figures 7.3A–7.3D. Figure 7.3A is the pattern in which the allophones of /æ/ have remained lax in all environments and show no major variants. Figure 7.3B is the pattern of a nasal dialect in which the allophones have a bimodal distribution: That is, /æ/ is raised and tensed before nasals and lax elsewhere (Laferriere, 1974). Figure 7.3C is a complex distribution of the variable (æh) and residual /æ/ which is the pattern found in both the New York City dialect and in the Philadelphia dialect.

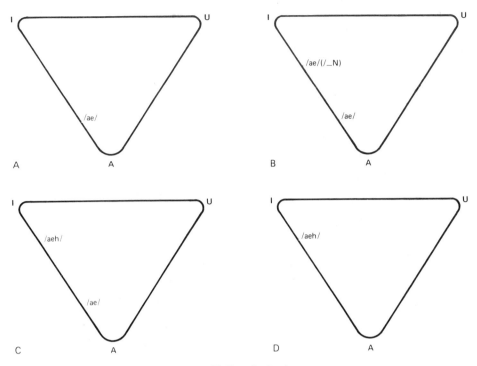

FIGURE 7.3 (A–D) Four basic short a patterns.

In these dialects there is some degree of surface contrast between [e< · ə] and [æ]. The issue as to whether (æh) is a separate phoneme is left open. Figure 7.3D represents the pattern for the Northern City dialects. In this case all the allophones of the short-a class are raised and tensed and /æ/, if it exists at all in the system, is a front allophone of short o.

The foregoing data which have been tabulated suggest that a critical turning point in the ability to acquire the Philadelphia dialect features occurs at about age eight. The findings also reveal that children are strongly influenced by their peers even when parental influence is maximal.

How does one account for the differences in the phonetic patterns in the speech of the children who arrive after the age of eight? Parental influence is one possible source for the deviations since the older children have been exposed to the speech of their parents for longer periods of time than have their younger siblings. But as these data and other studies indicate, the effect of the parents' influence seems to diminish as children grow older. A more probable explanation is that, as a child grows older, he has less ability to reorganize freely the linguistic patterns he acquired early under the influence of both his parents and out-of-state peers. The result is a mixture of the child's first dialect and the Philadelphia dialect.

Although New York City and Philadelphia are represented by the same schematic Figure 7.3C, the distribution of the short *a* is different for each dialect. The central core[6] of the short-*a* pattern in Philadelphia might be formalized as follows:

RULE 5

$$\begin{bmatrix} +\text{low} \\ -\text{back} \end{bmatrix} \rightarrow [+\text{tense}] \,/ \overline{\quad[-\text{weak}]\quad} \left\{ \left\{ \begin{matrix} [+\text{ant}] \\ [+\text{nas}] \\ \begin{bmatrix} +\text{cont} \\ -\text{voice} \end{bmatrix} \end{matrix} \right\} \right\} \left\{ \begin{matrix} \# \\ C \end{matrix} \right\}$$

This rule states that the short *a* becomes tense when it is not in a weak word,[7] and is followed by a front nasal (e.g., *man, ham, hand*), or a front voiceless fricative (e.g., *glass, laugh, path*), and this is followed by either an inflectional boundary or another consonant. There are two major exceptions to this core rule. First, three lexical items that do not meet the standard description of this rule undergo tensing and raising in Philadelphia—that is, the three affective adjectives with final *d*—*mad, bad, glad* (henceforth *mbg*). The other *d* words (e.g., *cad, dad* and *fad*) have lax nuclei. Second, three strong verbs that end in nasals and therefore should meet the structural description of Rule 5—*ran, swam* and *began*—have not undergone tensing and raising.[8]

This represents only the bare outline of the short-*a* distribution. The other details are so complex that it must be problematic that people actually do produce the two sets of vowels by a rule, as there are many categories that require specific grammatical and lexical knowledge.

When one examines the Philadelphia short-*a* pattern in more detail, four general subpatterns emerge:

1. In the core pattern of Philadelphia, /æ/ is INVARIABLY raised and tensed when it occurs in the following environments:

    a. — N^f $\left\{ \begin{matrix} C \\ \# \end{matrix} \right\}$ (i.e., before front nasals followed by another consonant or an inflectional boundary—except for *ran, swam, began, wan*)

    b. — F^o $\left\{ \begin{matrix} C \\ \# \end{matrix} \right\}$ (i.e., before front voiceless fricatives followed by another consonant or an inflectional boundary)

    c. *mbg*   (i.e., in the three affective adjectives in which short *a* precedes *d*)

---

[6] The percentages of correction for the core short *a* pattern for the 36 local children is 5%—(*a*) 2% in the environment __N^F; (*b*) 2% in the environment __F^o; and (3) 1% for the three affective adjectives *mad, bad,* and *glad.*

[7] Weak words are monosyllabic words whose nucleus may be reduced to schwa.

[8] Furthermore, David DePue of the LCV found that in the vernacular speech of white working-class Philadelphians the past tense of *win* is *wan,* which is also pronounced with a lax nucleus.

2. In the following environments, /æ/ is INVARIABLY lax:

a. auxiliary   (e.g., *am, can*), verb
b. __ S°   (i.e., before all voiceless stops)
c. __ Sᵛ   (i.e., before all voiced stops except *mad, bad, glad*)
d. __ Fᵛ   (i.e., before all voiced fricatives)
e. __ /š/
f. __ /r/
g. __ /ŋ/

3. On the other hand, /æ/ is found to be VARIABLE when it occurs:

a. __ N(+)V   (i.e., before a nasal consonant followed by an optional derivational boundary or by a vowel—(for example, *hammer, manage*)
b. __ F°(+)V   (i.e., before front voiceless fricatives followed by an optional derivational boundary or by a vowel—for example, (*halfies, graphic*))
c. __ /l/   (e.g., *pal, personality*)

4. Furthermore, /æ/ is VARIABLE in proper nouns and abbreviations.

The Philadelphia core short-*a* pattern is included within the New York City short-*a* pattern. A core rule for New York City can be roughly formalized as follows:

RULE 6

$$\begin{bmatrix} +\text{low} \\ -\text{back} \end{bmatrix} \rightarrow [+\text{tense}] \Big/ \underset{[-\text{weak}]}{\underline{\quad\quad}} \left\{ \begin{bmatrix} +\text{nasal} \\ -\text{back} \end{bmatrix} \begin{bmatrix} \alpha\text{continuant} \\ -\alpha\text{voice} \end{bmatrix} \right\} \left\{ \begin{matrix} \# \\ C \end{matrix} \right\}$$

In other words, /ǣ/ goes to [æ̃] before front nasals, voiceless fricatives, and voiced stops, when these are followed by an inflectional boundary or another consonant. The environments in which /æ/ is tensed and raised in Philadelphia are thus a subset of those in which it is tensed and raised in New York City.

A closer examination of the New York City short *a* also reveals that the distribution is not without variation. Paul Cohen (1970) carried out a study of the tensing and raising of short *a* in New York City and found "inherent variability" in several classes (see Chapter 3, pp. 63–70, for details).

*Acquisition of the Philadelphia Short-*a* Pattern*

Now the question arises, how can one determine if the Philadelphia core rule is being learned and how much of it is learned at any point in time? For New York City children, the percentage of learning of the Philadelphia pattern (L^P) can be calculated as follows: First it is necessary to consider the degree of laxing in that part of the short-a pattern which is tense in New York City (N^c); that is, short-a words that are lax in Philadelphia but tense in New York City (e.g., *smash, dad, tag*). If one then subtracts from N^c, the percentage of laxing in that part of the Philadelphia pattern which is tense, P^c, one obtains that percentage of laxing (L^P) which is the learning of the Philadelphia pattern for the New York City children.

$$L^P = N^c - P^c$$

This procedure separates the effects of irregular social correction from the systematic learning of the Philadelphia short-a rule. One may argue that the New York City forms are more stigmatized than the Philadelphia forms. That effect, however, is precisely what is meant by "learning the Philadelphia pattern"; that is, the New York City children learn to correct only those short-a words that are tense in New York City and not the tense short a in Philadelphia.

Acquisition of Short a by New York City Children

There are two general questions that apply to all out-of-state speakers trying to learn the Philadelphia short-a pattern:

1. What is/are the actual stages for reorganization?
2. Does the age at which a child moves to King of Prussia affect his ability to acquire the short-a pattern?

New York City children have two basic parts of the Philadelphia core rule to learn:

1. They must learn to retain a tense short a for the class of front voiceless fricatives, /s,f,θ/, and to lax short a before /š/.
2. They must learn to lax short a before d except for the three affective adjectives, *mad, bad, glad*.

If the feature system used in writing phonological descriptions represents the simplest one-to-one correspondence of description of rules and if people actually make use of these features to learn, then one might predict that the New York City children will have more success learning to lax short a before /š/, as this requires a generalization of a rule to exclude BACK voiceless fricatives, whereas the learning of *mbg* requires some special diacritic in the dictionary to mark exceptions to the blocking rule.

The percentages of learning (L^P) of the core Philadelphia short-a pattern by New York City children are given in Table 7.5 for natural speech. Table 7.6 gives the actual numbers upon which the percentages in Table 7.5 were calculated. These children give evidence of a wide but uneven spectrum of

TABLE 7.5
The Percentage of Learning of the Core Philadelphia Short a Pattern of NYC Children for Natural Speech

Name	Age moved/ Age at time of study	NYC Core Pattern			Philadelphia Core Pattern			
		No. tense ÷ token	Total token	= Percentage tense	No. tense − token	Total no. tense	= Percentage total	= Percentage learned
Bob Baker	9/20	0	7	0	0	24	0	0
Ken Baker	7/18	0	15	0	0	82	0	0
Matt Baker	4/15	0	7	0	0	46	0	0
Tom Baker	2/13	0	3	0	0	16	0	0
Don Baker	0/10	2	12	17	0	37	0	17
Mark Miller	11/15	16	23	70	19	115	17	53
Regina Miller	9/13	19	21	91	10	61	16	75
Theresa Miller	4/8	45	49	92	4	47	9	83
Richard Morgan	8/13	5	32	16	3	89	3	13
Liz Morgan	6/11	8	13	62	8	44	18	44
Danny Morgan	5/10	9	45	20	3	72	4	16
Mike Morgan	3/8	6	19	32	5	66	8	24

TABLE 7.6

The Percentage of Tensing of Short a *for Twelve NYC Children in Natural Speech in the Environments* /s,f,θ/, /š/, *mbg,* /d/

Name	Age moved/ age at time of study	No. tense/total tokens = percentage tense			
		/s,f,θ/	/š/	mad,bad,glad	/d/
Bob Baker	9/20	12/12 = 100	3/3 = 100	—	1/1 = 100
Ken Baker	7/18	43/43 = 100	3/3 = 100	11/11 = 100	2/2 = 100
Matt Baker	4/15	13/13 = 100	4/4 = 100	13/13 = 100	1/1 = 100
Tom Baker	2/13	5/5 = 100	1/1 = 100	3/3 = 100	1/1 = 100
Don Baker	0/10	10/10 = 100	2/2 = 100	12/12 = 100	3/5 = 60
Mark Miller	11/15	27/44 = 61	1/4 = 25	21/23 = 91	0/8 = 0
Regina Miller	9/13	17/21 = 81	1/2 = 50	15/21 = 71	1/7 = 14
Theresa Miller	4/8	17/21 = 81	1/3 = 33	8/8 = 100	2/6 = 33
Richard Morgan	8/13	42/44 = 95	2/2 = 100	18/19 = 95	6/8 = 67
Liz Morgan	6/11	12/19 = 63	2/6 = 33	6/7 = 86	1/3 = 33
Danny Morgan	5/10	32/33 = 97	9/9 = 100	8/10 = 80	3/10 = 30
Mike Morgan	3/8	13/17 = 76	3/3 = 100	13/14 = 93	3/8 = 38

learning patterns. One salient in Table 7.5 emerges: the acquisition of short *a* by most of the New York city children is low. The two exceptions are Terry Miller [4 (years when moved)/8 (years at time of study)] who has learned 83% of the short-*a* pattern and Regina Miller (9/13) who has learned 75% of the pattern.

Table 7.5 shows that the Baker family appears to have learned virtually none of the Philadelphia short *a* with the exception of Donald (0/10), who has learned only a little. Laxing has been overgeneralized. This is somewhat surprising considering that the Bakers have lived in King of Prussia for 11 years, which is longer than either of the other two New York City families have lived there, and that all but Bob moved before the age of 8.

The Millers show the highest percentages of learning of the three families. The children follow an expected pattern in which the oldest child, Mark (11/15), shows the lowest percentage of learning; the middle child, the next lowest percentage; and the youngest child has acquired the most.

The Morgan family shows some acquisition of the Philadelphia short-*a* pattern, but the children do not follow a regular increase in percentage of learning from the oldest learning least to the youngest learning most.

In order to obtain a clearer picture of the degree of learning of the short-*a* pattern by the New York City children, the figures have been plotted in scattergrams which show the progress in the acquisition of the two major generalizations—that is, learning to lax short *a* before /š/ and before /d/ in natural speech. One question that arises is, how do the scattergrams display the success of learning of the children? First, we must determine the starting point for the New York City children and where the Philadelphia target is in relation to their starting point.

Figure 7.4 displays the specific results for /s,f,θ/ versus /š/. In this scattergram the percentages of tensing for /s,f,θ/ are located on the horizontal axis and those for /š/ are given on the vertical axis. The children from New York City begin approximately 100% tensing of short *a* before /s,f,θ,š/. They are striving to each the Philadelphia pattern at lower right which is 100% tensing before /s,f,θ/ and 0% before /š/. In Figures 7.4 and 7.6 the point of origin (*O*) of the lines is not 100%—100% for all the speakers, as correction occurs within the core Philadelphia pattern which is shared by the New York City children (see Figure 7.5). In order to display the actual amount of learning of the Philadelphia pattern for each child, the lines begin from a starting point defined by the amount of tensing of the core Philadelphia–New York City short-*a* words. For example, in Table 7.5 we see that the amount of

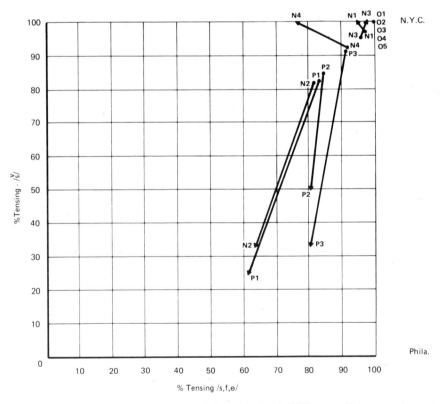

FIGURE 7.4 *The percentage of tensing of short* a *before* /s,f,θ/ *versus* /š/ *in natural speech with the point of origin beginning from the amount of correction in the* core *pattern of Philadelphia and New York City words for New York City children.*

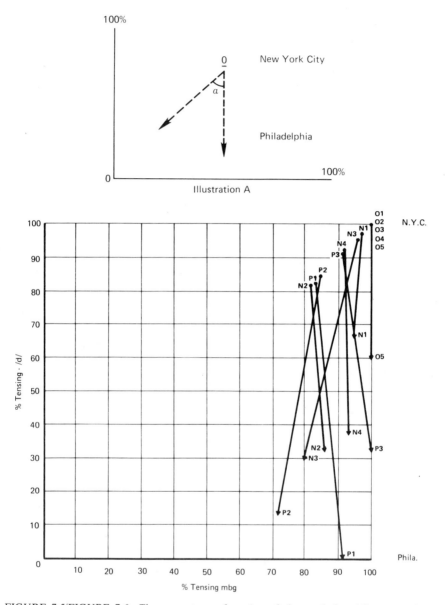

FIGURE 7.5/FIGURE 7.6 *The percentage of tensing of short* a *before* /d/ *versus* mbg *in natural speech with the point of origin beginning from the amount of correction in the* core *pattern of Philadelphia and New York City words by children from New York City.*

correction in the Philadelphia core (P^c) for Mark Miller (P1) is 17%. His point of origin for learning is then $100\% - 83\% = 17\%$ in both environments. From this point a vertical line extending downward or angling to the right would represent learning entirely targeted on the Philadelphia pattern, whereas a line extending diagonally to the left represents no orientation towards the Philadelphia /s,f,θ/ versus /š/ distinction, since it treats them as equal. Thus, an angle of $\alpha \geq 45°$ would represent complete overgeneralization and loss of the target, whereas $\alpha \leq 0°$ is no overgeneralization, but accurate and efficient learning of the Philadelphia pattern.

Figure 7.6 displays the results for the learning by New York City children to lax tense short a for all /d/ words except mbg. The percentage of tensing for mbg is given on the horizontal axis and the percentage of tensing for /d/ is found on the vertical axis. Again the New York City children are seen as shifting toward the Philadelphia pattern in the lower right corner of 100% tensing of mbg and 0% for all other d words.

A comparison of the two scattergrams (i.e., Figures 7.4 and 7.6) reveals the striking difference in the results of the success of the New York City children in learning to lax tense short a before /d/ and before /š/. It can be clearly seen that the New York City children show, contrary to what was expected, a much greater success in learning to lax tense short a before /d/ than before /š/.

The difference becomes more apparent with closer examination of the direction in which the lines and the value of alpha move. For mbg there is a tendency for almost all of the lines to be angled in the direction of the Philadelphia target with $\alpha \leq 0°$. However, for /š/, the lines, although moving downward, are not angled in the direction of the Philadelphia target, but rather they tend to angle slightly toward a general laxing of all four classes—/s, f, θ, š/; that is, $\alpha \geq 0°$. Thus, it appears that for the New York City children, the lexical contrast of mbg with the other d words seems to help in learning and is actually easier to learn than the simple laxing rule laxing [æ] before /š/, which is a simple generalization.

Perhaps one reason the mbg pattern seems to be more easily learned is that the three emotive adjectives occur more frequently in everyday speech than other d words. The frequency of occurrence also seems to affect the percentage of laxing. For example, the word dad is more likely to be in common use among children than, say, words such as cad or fad.[9]

Acquisition of Short a by Children from "Nasal Dialect" Areas

The percentage of learning for New York City children could be determined by a simple formula as the Philadelphia short-a core pattern fits within the New York City short-a core pattern. However, the percentage of learning is not as easily determined for the children from Nasal and Northern City

---

[9] This study will not include a detailed examination of each individual which would allow the effects of frequency to be tested; the data are stored in a form which would make such an examination possible and further studies of lexical learning are indicated. Other types of influence such as sibling, block, family, and age span are discussed in Payne, 1976.

) dialects do not share a core pattern with the Philadelphia

pattern for Nasal speakers can be described as:

$$\begin{bmatrix} +\text{low} \\ -\text{back} \end{bmatrix} \rightarrow [+\text{tense}] \, / \, \_\_ \, [+\text{nas}]$$

That is, in the Nasal dialect, short *a* is tensed and raised before all nasals in all environments including NV. Thus, Nasal speakers must learn three parts of the core Philadelphia short-*a* pattern. First, they must learn to raise and tense short *a* before the front voiceless fricatives, /s,f,θ/, when followed by another consonant or inflectional boundary. Second, they must learn to raise and tense the nucleus of short *a* for the three *d* words, *mad, bad* and *glad*, while maintaining a lax nucleus for all other *d* words (such as *sad, dad, fad*). Third, they must learn to variably lax the short-*a* words that are variably lax in Philadelphia but tense in the Nasal dialect. That is, for Nasal speakers one is interested in the degree of laxing in those words in which short *a* precedes the sequence __NV (as in *planet, manage, damage*). However, in Philadelphia for the class of short-*a* words preceding the sequence __NV, the research project found lexical diffusion occurring. The word *planet* is usually raised and tensed for Philadelphians, although other words of this class are less frequently raised and tensed. The percentage of learning for Nasal speakers, then, for the short-*a* words preceding the sequence__NV, must be determined on the basis of the percentage of laxing occurring in the class of short-*a* words preceding the environment __NV (minus the word *planet*).

That is, if a child shows 100% tensing for NV, then he has not learned the Philadelphia pattern. However, if a child only tenses short *a* in the NV category 25–30% of the time, then he has learned the Philadelphia pattern. If the problem of Nasal speakers is represented as a problem in rule learning these speakers must: (*a*) add a tensing rule for /s,f,θ/; (*b*) mark *mbg* with some special diacritic feature in their dictionary which would include them in the tensing rule, and (*c*) add a lexically variable tensing rule for the category NV. One might anticipate a higher degree of success in learning (*a*) and (*b*), as the former requires the addition of phonetic rules and the latter requires marking only three words in the dictionary. To learn NV would require replacing a phonetic rule with a lexically conditioned variable rule.

The Nasal dialect speakers' percentages of learning patterns for natural speech[10] are given in Table 7.7. The children had 100% tensing in the category__N^F {$^\#_C$} and, therefore, this category is not given in Table 7.7. The three categories in the tables are not averaged together due to the low number of tokens in the NV class for the Castle family.

---

[10] For details on word lists see Payne, 1976.

TABLE 7.7

Percentage of Tense Token of Short a *in Natural Speech for Nasal Speakers in the Environments NV,* /s,f,θ/, *and* mbg

Name	Age moved/ age at time of study	No. tense/total tokens = percentage tense			Average tense/ total of /s,f,θ/ plus mad,bad,glad
		NV	/s,f,θ/	mad,bad,glad	
Max Barnes	9/13	2/5 = 40	13/20 = 43	8/20 = 40	42
Becky Barnes	6/10	4/11 = 36	2/18 = 11	3/12 = 25	18
Tina Castle	0/14	2/2	0/7 = 0	0/5 = 0	0
Rick Castle	0/12	1/2	0/12 = 0	1/6 = 17	8
Sam Castle	0/11	1/1	0/9 = 0	2/13 = 15	6

The data in Table 7.7 reveal that the Barnes children have had some success in learning the Philadelphia short *a* for both /s, f, θ/ and *mbg,* and that the Castles show little or no learning. Both of the Barnes children show considerable learning of the NV patterns. No percentages are given for the Castles as the number of tokens is too small to reveal a distinct pattern, but the fact that Rick (0/12) has one tense and one lax token indicates that he has at least some variation in the NV category.

These results do not agree with any expectations of a correlation be- tween years spent in King of Prussia and success in learning the (æh) pattern. The Castles have learned practically nothing, which is very unusual as they were all born and raised in the Philadelphia area. The Barnes show some learning, but it is about the same for all categories. The most important feature of the acquisition that has taken place is that only the Philadelphia pattern is learned—that is, there is no generalizing of the tensing to /š/ or to /b,d,g/. On the other hand, there is no differentiation of __NV and the other environments, all show about the same degree of tensing.

Acquisition of Short a *by Northern City Children*

The Northern City speaker approaches the learning of the Philadelphia short-*a* pattern with a different set of problems from the New York City or Nasal speaker as his system has tense short *a* in all environments. Thus, he must learn to

1. Retain tense short *a* before /s,f,θ/, while learning to lax tense short *a* before /š/
2. Retain tense short *a* in *mbg,* while learning to lax /æ/ before all other *d* words
3. Learn to variably lax tense short *a* for the NV class 75% of the time
4. Learn to lax tense short *a* when it precedes /b,g,/ and /p,t,k/

Unlike Nasal speakers, who must add a tensing rule, the Northern City speakers must learn to add laxing rules. In this respect they face a situation similar to that of New York City children. If Northern City children attempt to use rules, these rules must block tense short *a* from occurring before /š/ and before /d/. At the same time they must mark the *mbg* lexical items with some special diacritic in the dictionary to exempt them from the laxing rule. Also, the children must learn to add a lexically conditioned variable rule to account for the NV class.

The results of acquisition of short *a* by Northern City speakers are given in Tables 7.8 and 7.9. Table 7.8 gives the percentages of tense/total tokens for the occurrence of short *a* in the following environments: (*a*) /s,f,θ/; (*b*) /š/; (*c*) *mbg*; (*d*) /d/; (*e*) /b,g/ and /p,t,k/; and (*f*) NV. Table 7.9 provides the actual number of tokens. Table 7.8 reveals that 6 of the 17 children have succeeded in learning to retain a tensed and raised short *a* before /s,f,θ/ and to lax tense short *a* before /š/. Judy Kelly (6/17), Karen Cameron (8/15), Paul Jackson (4/16), Joanne (4/11) and John Hunter (8/15), and Bob Burk (0/13) all show 93–100% tensing of short *a* before /s,f,θ/ and 0% tensing of short *a* before /š/.

TABLE 7.8

Percentage Tensing of Short a *in Natural Speech for 17 Northern City Children in the Environments* /s,f,θ/, /š/. mbg, /d/, /b,g/ & /p,t,k/, *and NV*

Name	Age moved/ age at time of study	/s,f,θ/	/š/	mad,bad, glad	/d/	/s,f,θ/ plus mbg	/b,g/ & /p,t,k/	NV
Bill Douglas	6/14	39	14	25	0	32	2	100
Lisa Douglas	4/12	0	0	5	0	3	0	100
David Douglas	0/8	0	0	0	0	0	0	100
David Martin	13/17	64	0	53	20	59	0	—
Linda Martin	11/15	86	25	100	0	93	0	100
Cindy Martin	9/13	11	—	88	75	50	15	100
Judy Kelly	6/17	100	0	100	0	100	0	100
Karen Cameron	8/15	100	0	93	0	97	0	55
Ralph Cameron	7/14	29	0	6	0	18	0	57
Joyce Cameron	4/11	10	0	22	0	16	0	47
Ellen Cameron	2/9	4	0	15	0	10	0	45
Paul Jackson	4/16	100	0	100	0	100	19	100
Dan Jackson	2/13	86	56	50	100	68	0	75
John Hunter	8/15	100	0	100	50	100	0	100
Joanne Hunter	4/11	96	0	100	86	98	0	100
RaeLynn Burk	0/16	50	0	23	0	37	0	100
Bob Burk	0/13	93	0	63	9	78	0	100

TABLE 7.9

The Number of Tense Short a *Tokens over Total in Natural Speech for 17 Northern City Children in the Environments* /s,f,θ/, /š/, mbg, /d/, /b,g/ & /p,t,k/, *and* NV

Name	Age moved/ age at time of study	No. tense/total token					
		/s,f,θ/	/š/	*mad,bad, glad*	/d/	/b,g/ & /p,t,k/	NV
Bill Douglas	6/14	16/41	1/7	7/8	0/6	1/41	12/12
Lisa Douglas	4/12	0/65	0/10	1/20	0/14	0/44	10/10
David Douglas	0/8	0/12	0/1	0/11	0/4	0/26	12/12
David Martin	13/17	3/28	0/9	10/19	1/5	0/50	—
Linda Martin	11/15	6/7	1/4	8/8	0/2	0/13	2/2
Cindy Martin	9/13	7/11	—	7/8	3/4	3/20	4/4
Judy Kelly	6/17	37/37	0/2	10/10	0/4	0/11	4/4
Karen Cameron	8/15	24/24	0/2	14/15	0/4	0/54	5/9
Ralph Cameron	7/14	14/48	0/10	1/17	0/5	0/30	4/7
Joyce Cameron	4/11	5/50	0/1	5/23	0/9	0/37	7/15
Ellen Cameron	2/9	1/28	0/8	2/13	0/11	0/61	5/11
Paul Jackson	4/16	12/12	0/5	12/12	0/6	3/21	6/6
Dan Jackson	2/13	12/14	5/9	3/6	4/4	0/18	3/4
John Hunter	8/15	12/12	0/3	5/5	2/4	0/7	3/3
Joanne Hunter	4/11	23/24	0/1	15/15	6/7	0/25	8/8
RaeLynn Burk	0/16	11/22	0/3	6/26	0/1	0/39	12/12
Bob Burk	0/13	28/30	0/5	10/16	1/11	0/45	4/4

The other children have a strong tendency to lax tense short *a* before /s/, but they also display a strong tendency to lax tense short *a* before /s,f,θ/.

Figure 7.7 and 7.8 are scattergrams, which provide a more abstract view of the pattern of learning that has taken place in the speech of the Northern City children. The two basic categories of the Philadelphia short-*a* rule that must be learned are shown (i.e., /s,f,θ/ and *mbg*).

In Figure 7.7, the percentages for tensing of short *a* before /s,f,θ/ are located on the horizontal axis and those for /š/ are given on the vertical axis. The children from Northern City dialects begin with 100% tensing of short *a* before /s,f,θ,š/. The goal is to achieve 0% tensing for /š/ and 100% tensing for /s,f,θ/. In Figure 7.8 the results for *mbg* versus /d/ are given with the percentages for *mbg* on the horizontal and for /d/ on the vertical. The goal is to achieve 0% tensing for /d/ and 100% tensing for *mbg*. These two scattergrams are interpreted in the same manner as were the scattergrams for the New York City children.

The angle of the lines in the scattergrams for natural speech for *mbg* and for /š/ provide, perhaps, the clearest display of the difference in the success the Northern City children have in learning the two different classes. In this case the expectations that were set forth for the ease of rule formation are

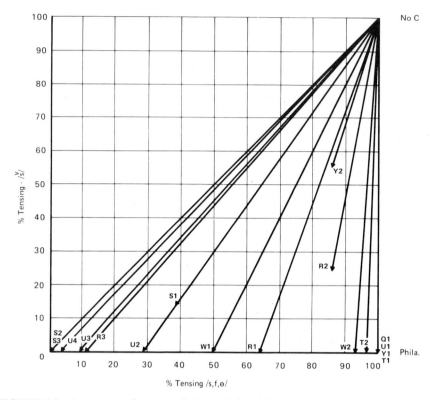

FIGURE 7.7 *Percentage of tensing of short* a *before* /s,f,θ/ *versus* /š/ in natural speech for children from northern city areas.

confirmed. The children seem to have less difficulty learning to retain a tense short *a* for only the front voiceless fricatives. The scattergrams show a less abrupt break or a finer gradation of shift in the learning patterns of the children. That is, even though there is a tendency to apply a general laxing rule, more children come closer to the Philadelphia target more often for /š/ (Figure 7.7) than when trying to learn the exceptions of *mbg* (Figure 7.8).

Tables 7.8 and 7.9 show that the Northern City children on the whole have been completely successful in learning to lax tense short *a* before /b,g/ and before /p,t,k/. Only three children have not completely succeeded. These results indicate that when the Northern City children are confronted with the Philadelphia pattern they tend to apply laxing rules across the board. For those parts of the Northern City dialect that are completely lax in Philadelphia (e.g., /p,t,k/), the Northern City children are very successful in learning to lax tense short *a*. However, when they must learn to block application of a tensing rule for only part of a class they are less successful. And, as was discussed, the Northern City children show a slightly greater degree

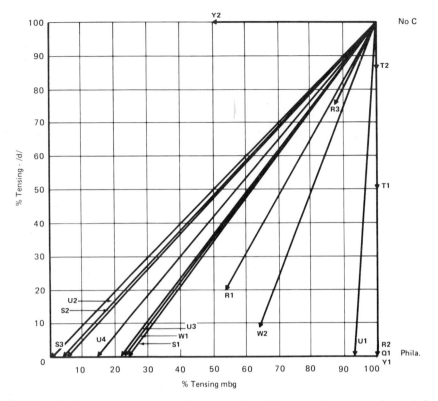

FIGURE 7.8 *Percentage of tensing of short* a *before* /d/ *versus* mbg *in natural speech for children from nothern city areas.*

of success in learning to lax tense short *a* for the whole class /š/, than they do for marking *mbg* with special diacritic features in the dictionary, which was expected.

The data for the learning of the Philadelphia pattern for short *a* in the category NV are also given in Tables 7.8 and 7.9. Except for the Camerons, the Northern City children as a whole have not succeeded in learning the lexically conditioned variable pattern for NV.

One important finding that is very striking is that only one child, Karen Cameron (8/15), appears to have almost completely learned the Philadelphia short *a*. Judy Kelly (6/17) and Paul Jackson (4/16) have also been very successful in the acquisition of the short-*a* pattern; Judy has learned all of the short *a* except for laxing tense short *a* in the environment NV, and Paul, all except for the NV category and a few words in the voiced and voiceless stop categories. Otherwise, the children as a whole have been unsuccessful in learning the Philadelphia short-*a* pattern.

TABLE 7.10
Number of Northern City Children for Whom the Angle of Alpha is Greater or Less Than 22.5° for Variables mbg *and* /s,f,θ/ *versus* /š/

	Number of children	
Variable	>22.5°	<22.5°
mad, bad, glad	10	7
/s,f,θ/ versus /š/	7	9

Comparison of the New York City and the Northern City Children's Learning Patterns

The contrast in learning patterns between New York City and Northern City children despite the similarity in tasks is immediately relevant to the fundamental issue of rule formations. Both groups of children overgeneralize.

A comparison of the difference in degree of success can be obtained from Tables 7.10 and 7.11 in which the angle of alpha is compared for *mbg* and /s,f,θ/ versus /š/. Recall that if $\alpha \geq 45°$ then the child has completely overgeneralized. If $\alpha > 22.5°$ the child is showing a strong tendency to overgeneralize in attempting to learn the Philadelphia pattern. If $\alpha < 22.5°$, then the child is aiming for the Philadelphia pattern. Tables 7.10 and 7.11 show the results for the Northern City and New York City children. Table 7.10 shows the results for the Northern City children. As can be seen the children show more of a tendency to acquire /s,f,θ/ versus /š/ and less acqui-

TABLE 7.11
Number of New York City Children for Whom the Angle of Alpha is Greater or Less Than 22.5° for Variables mbg *and* /s,f,θ/ *versus* /š/

	Number of children	
Variable	>22.5°	<22.5°
mad, bad, glad	0	8
/s,f,θ/ versus /š/	3	4

sition of *mbg*. Table 7.11 shows the results for the New York City children. All of the children who showed learning reveal a high degree of success in aiming for the *mbg* pattern of Philadelphia and considerably less success in acquiring the /s,f,θ/ versus /š/ pattern. The individual angles for alpha are listed in Table 7.12 for natural speech.

TABLE 7.12

The Degree of Alpha for Natural Speech for mbg *and* /s,f,θ/ *versus* /š/ *for Northern City and New York City Children*

Children	Variables	
	mad,bad,glad	/s,f,θ/ versus /š/
Northern City		
Judy Kelly	0°	0°
David Martin	30°	19°
Linda Martin	0°	10°
Cindy Martin	25°30'	—
Bill Douglas	36°30'	34°
Lisa Douglas	43°45'	45°
Mike Douglas	45°	45°
John Hunter	0°	0°
Joanne Hunter	0°	2°30'
Karen Cameron	4°	0°
Ralph Cameron	43°	34°
Joyce Cameron	37°45'	40°45'
Ellen Cameron	40°	43°
RaeLynn Burk	37°	25°45'
Bob Burk	21°30'	4°
Paul Jackson	0°	0°
Dan Jackson	90°	17°
	$N = 17, \bar{X} = 26°60'$	$N = 16, \bar{X} = 19.95'$
New York City		
Bob Cook	—	—
Ken Cook	—	—
Matt Cook	—	—
Tom Cook	—	—
Dan Cook	0°	—
Mark Miller	−5°30'	20°15'
Regina Miller	10°45'	6°
Theresa Miller	−8°30'	9°45'
Richard Morgan	4°	152°
Liz Morgan	−4°30'	21°30'
Danny Morgan	14°	202°
Mike Morgan	−1°	117°
	$N = 8, \bar{X} = 1.°19'$	$N = 7, \bar{X} = 75°41'$

The Northern City children give every evidence of operating with phonetic rules in the following respects:

1. They have greater success in acquiring the simple rule of laxing only before back voiceless fricatives.
2. They have almost 100% success in laxing in environments where New York City is 100% lax.
3. They show further shifting towards generalization in word lists (see Payne, 1976).

New York City speakers reverse the pattern for (1) and have a weaker effect on (3); (2) is not applicable. For these reasons it appears that New York City speakers are more attuned to lexical factors than rule formation.

Conclusion

The Philadelphia short-*a* pattern provides us with an example of one of the most difficult tests for the acquisition of a local dialect. The issue crucial to linguistic theory whether (*a*) the Philadelphia system differentiates tense and lax *a* by rule and (*b*) the out-of-state children are attempting to use a rule to learn the Philadelphia short-*a* pattern.

The examination of the acquisition of the short *a* has revealed several significant findings:

1. The phonetic variables are acquired with greater ease than the short *a*.
2. It is in fact very rare for a child to acquire the Philadelphia short *a*.
3. Unless a child's parents are locally born and raised, the possibility of his acquiring the short-*a* pattern is extremely slight even if he were to be born and raised in King of Prussia.

It was found that the children from the Northern City, Nasal, and New York City dialects have demonstrated differing degrees of success in acquisition of the Philadelphia short-*a* pattern and apparently different approaches. The data on the Northern City and New York City children provide the clearest example. The Northern City child whose short-*a* pattern falls in a continuum of detailed phonetic conditioning applies phonetic generalizations in his attempt to learn the Philadelphia short-*a* pattern. The fact that his short-*a* pattern is a rule governed continuum may make him more attuned to treating the word class as a unit rather than as individual lexical items. The only way we can explain learning patterns of the New York City children is through the complex conditioning of their short-*a* pattern. That is, because of not only phonetic conditioning but also the lexical and grammatical exceptions to the tensing of short *a*, the New York City children are more oriented toward learning words.

A comparison of the two types of variables—that is, the phonetic variables versus the short-*a* pattern—reveals that there are two different learning patterns.

Almost all of the out-of-state children show some learning of the Philadelphia pattern. The phonetic variables were acquired or partially acquired by almost all of the children. The age of arrival had the strongest effect on the success of acquisition, age 8 being the cut-off point. Acquisition of the short *a* was usually irregular, sporadic, and incomplete. The incomplete acquisition indicates that children do not freely restructure and/or reorganize their grammars up to the age of 14 but that they do have the ability to add lower level rules. Although parental influence is dominant in the learning patterns for the phonological variables, the acquisition patterns of the out-of-state children revealed not only that they were strongly influenced by their peers but also that they employ other modes of learning besides rule formation.

Appendix

TABLE 7.A.1
The Acquisition of (ay°) *According to the Age at Which a Child Moved to King of Prussia*[a]

Age	No. of subjects who acquired (ay°)	No. of subjects who did not acquire (ay°)	Total
0–4	11	6	17
5–9	7	7	14
10–14	0	3	3
N	18	16	34

[a] $X^2 = 4.66$, $p = .10$.

TABLE 7.A.2
The Acquisition of (aw) *According to the Age at Which a Child Moved to King of Prussia*[a]

Age	No. of subjects who acquired (aw)	No. of subjects who did not acquire (aw)	Total
0–4	6	4	10
5–9	2	6	8
10–14	0	2	2
N	8	12	20

[a] $X^2 = 3.74$, $p = .20$.

TABLE 7.A.3

The Acquisition of (uw) *According to the Age at Which a Child Moved to King of Prussia*[a]

Age	No. of subjects who acquired (uw)	No. of subjects who did not acquire (uw)	Total
0–4	7	3	10
5–9	8	4	12
10–14	0	3	3
N	15	10	25

[a] $X^2 = 2.95$, $p = .30$.

TABLE 7.A.4

The Acquisition of (oy) *According to the Age at Which a Child Moved to King of Prussia*[a]

Age	No. of subjects who acquired (oy)	No. of subjects who did not acquire (oy)	Total
0–4	7	3	10
5–9	5	3	8
10–14	0	2	2
N	12	8	20

[a] $X^2 = 1.68$, $p = .50$.

TABLE 7.A.5

The Acquisition of (ow) *According to the Age at Which a Child Moved to King of Prussia*[a]

Age	No. of subjects who acquired (ow)	No. of subjects who did not acquire (ow)	Total
0–4	7	3	10
5–9	7	5	12
10–14	2	1	3
N	16	9	25

[a] $X^2 = .59$, $p = .80$.

Social scientists generally use a probability level of .05 or less when reporting "statistically significant" findings. The results of the chi square tests on the preceding data indicated no statistically significant difference based on age. However, the differences that do appear indicate that age is least important in the acquisition of (ow) and most important in the acquisition of (ay^o). The conclusiveness of the data is limited by the small size of the sample.

References

Asher, J. J., and Garcia, R. 1969. The optimal age to learn a foreign language. *The Modern Language Journal, 53,* 334–342.

Bee, H. 1975. *The developing child.* New York: Harper and Row.

Bloom, L. 1970. *Language development: Form and function in emerging grammars.* Cambridge, Mass.: MIT Press.

Brown, R. and Bellugi, U. 1964. Three processes in the child's acquisition of syntax. In E. Lenneberg (Ed.), *New directions in the study of language.* Cambridge, Mass.: MIT Press.

Cazden, C. 1964. *Environmental assistance to the child's acquisition of grammar.* Unpublished doctoral Ph.d. dissertation, Harvard University.

Cohen, P. S. 1970. *The tensing and raising of 'short a' in the Metropolitan area of New York City.* Masters Thesis, Columbia University.

Erikson, E. H. 1950. *Childhood and society.* New York: Norton.

Ervin, S. M. 1964. Imitations and structural change in children's language. In E. Lenneberg (Ed.), *New Directions in the study of language.* Cambridge, Mass.: MIT Press.

Ferguson, C. 1968. Short *a* in Philadelphia English. Mimeographed.

Halle, M. 1962. Phonology in a generative grammar. *Word, 18,* 54–72.

Johnson, B. L. 1971. The Western Pennsylvania dialect of American English. *Journal of the International Phonetic Association, 1* (2), 69–73.

Kazazi, K. 1970. The relative importance of parents and peers in first language learning. *General Linguistics, 10,* 111–120.

Kurath, H. and McDavid, R. I., Jr. 1961. *The pronunciation of English in the Atlantic states.* Ann Arbor: University of Michigan Press.

Labov, W. 1966. *Social stratification of English in New York City.* Washington, D.C.: Center for Applied Linguistics.

Labov, W. 1972a. *Socioloinguistic patterns.* Philadelphia: University of Pennsylvania Press.

Labov, W. 1972b. *Language in the inner city.* Philadelphia: University of Pennsylvania Press.

Labov, W. 1974. The relative influence of family and peers on the learning of language. In A. Mioni (Ed.), *Proceedings of the 1974 Meetings of the Societadi Linguistica Italiana.* A cura di, Rafaele Simene i qiulianella Ruggiero Estratto, Bulzoni, Roma, 1977. (Quotes taken from unpublished English draft.)

Labov, W. Cohen, G., Robins, C., and Lewis, J. 1968. *A Study of the non-standard English of Negro and Puerto Rican speakers in New York City.* Philadelphia, U.S. Regional Survey, 2 Vols. USOE Final Report, Research Project No. 3288.

Labov, W., Yaeger, M., and Steiner, R. 1972. *A quantitative study of sound change in progress.* Philadelphia: U.S. Regional Survey.

Laferriere, M. 1974. Boston short *a:* Social variation as historical residue. Paper presented at NWAVE 3 Conference, Georgetown University.

LeMasters, E. E. 1970. *Parents in modern America: A sociological analysis.* Homewood, Ill.: Dorsey Press.

Lenneberg, E. 1967. *Biological foundations of language.* New York: John Wiley and Sons.

Oyama, S. 1973. *A sensitive period for the acquisition of a second language.* Unpublished doctoral dissertation, Harvard University.

Payne, A. C. 1976. *The acquisition of the phonological system of a second dialect.* Unpublished doctoral dissertation, University of Pennsylvania.

Piaget, J. 1926. *Language and thought in the child.* New York: Harcourt, Brace.

Piaget, J. 1928. *Judgement and reasoning in the child.* New York: Harcourt, Brace.

Piaget, J. 1971. *Biology and knowledge: An essay on the relations between organic regulations and cognitive processes.* Chicago: University of Chicago Press.

Trager, G. L., and Smith, H. L., Jr. 1951. An outline of English structure. *Studies in Linguistics, Occasional Papers 3.* Norman, Okla.

Wolfram, W. 1974. *Sociolinguistic aspects of assimilation: Puerto Rican English in New York City.* Arlington, Va.: Center for Applied Linguistics.

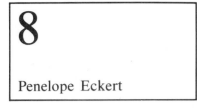

Penelope Eckert

THE STRUCTURE OF A LONG-TERM PHONOLOGICAL PROCESS: THE BACK VOWEL CHAIN SHIFT IN SOULATAN GASCON[1]

Introduction

The greatest recent breakthrough in the study of linguistic change has been the recognition that some variation found in the everyday use of language is itself historical change in progress. This provides us with the means to study historical change *in vivo* and thus to observe the inner workings of historical process. The development of variable rules has already shown that any change can be governed by a variety of variably weighted constraints, and that categoricalness is not part of the definition of a linguistic rule. Variability cannot be set aside from the rest of linguistic phenomena—not only because it is systematic, but because it stands in a feedback relation with the rest of the system: It is the potential for variability in linguistic rules that allows the linguistic system to change systematically. Systematicity, in turn, can only be defined in terms of the patterns shown in variable rules. C.-J. Bailey (1972) has pointed out that "everyone always speaks what traditional dialectologists labeled a *transitional dialect* [p. 26]." In his insistence on a dynamic view of linguistic systems, he has built into his model of a grammar the obvious fact that change is built into language design. Thus any treatment of linguistic competence that ignores change, and any treatment of change that ignores the role of speakers' transitional competence, cannot answer many of the essential questions of linguistic theory.

[1] The research was supported in part by National Science Foundation dissertation research Grant NSF-GS-3211.

Weinrich, Labov, and Herzog (1968), in the context of a proposal for more broadly based studies of linguistic change, argued that a great deal of progress in the understanding of phonological change can come from investigation of the minute progress of individual sound changes. Investigating only changes that have occurred in the past provides a limited understanding of the processes involved, for a sound change viewed in its completed form tells us relatively little about how it came about. A bird's-eye view of phonological change allows linguistic theory to maintain the fiction that a phonological rule actually progresses through classes of sounds under the conditions stated in the finished rule. Only the combination of insights gained in the observation of linguistic change over long periods of time and of the minute progress of one change through a community will yield a complete understanding of the ·constraints in historical process.

One area that needs to be examined with as wide a variety of data as possible is that of long-term phonological process. It is frequently found that sequences of individual phonological changes are clearly linked by their similar phonetic characteristics (lenition, vowel raising or lowering, etc.) and by their related movements in phonological space (Martinet, 1955). What has not been closely investigated is the manner in which the individual changes in such a sequence are related in the competence of the speakers who effect the transition. The actual degree and kind of relatedness between rules in such a sequence is still an open question.

This paper will examine just such a long-term process—a back vowel chain shift in a dialect of Gascon, spoken in southwestern France. Map 8.1 shows the location of the dialect in question, which is spoken in the commune of Soulan in the department of Ariège. The large number of closely bundled isoglosses running southeast from the Gironde along the Garonne River to the eastern range of the Pyrenees represents a major dialect division of southern France, separating the two important southwest regions of Gascony and Languedoc. Soulan, represented by a star on Map 8.1 (and all subsequent maps), lies within the southernmost part of the Gascon–Languedocien isogloss bundle.

Haudricourt and Juilland's treatment of certain Romance languages (1949) interprets major vowel changes in these systems as responses to pressures set up in the proto vowel system with the replacement of Latin vowel length by a new distinction between high and low mid vowels. The simple vowel system of what Hall reconstructs as Proto-Italo-Western Romance (1976, p. 188) contained seven vowels: *i, *eˆ, *e, *o, *oˆ, *u (the symbols are those used by Hall). According to Haudricourt and Juilland, this system was overcrowded, particularly among the back vowels, which function in a smaller articulatory space. In the subsequent evolution of Romance, the two forms of reaction to the overcrowded proto vowel system were (a) diphthongization of the mid vowels and (b) an upward chain shift of the back vowels. All Romance dialects in France show the effects of both processes. The predominance of one of these two processes over the other varies considerably from area to area in such a way as to leave little question that they interact as alternative "releases" of structural pressure.

This chapter will examine the progress of the entire chain shift, using historical, geographic, and current variable data to arrive at a closer understanding of the relations between the individual vowel raisings that make up the chain. Historical data are all from the *Atlas linguistique de la France* (Gilliéron and Edmont, 1902–1910), hereafter abbreviated as *ALF*. Data on the current state of Soulatan (the name used for the Gascon dialect of Soulan) were gathered during 18 months of participant-observation in that community. All modern data used in this chapter are from taped interviews consisting of free-flowing conversation and narrative. The informants are all bilingual natives of Soulan. Soulatan is their first language; French, which they learned in school, has progressed in their lifetime from the position of a language reserved for contact outside the community to the first and only language of all people born in Soulan within the past 30 years.

The Vowels of France

The first stage of the back vowel chain shift, the fronting of *u to [y], is the only Romance vowel change common to all dialects of France. Although this change must have occurred relatively early in order to have affected such a large area uniformly, its relation to certain other changes (i.e., palatalization)[2] shows that it was not complete in Late Latin (Bourciez, 1956, p. 152). As shown in Map 8.2, this change spread throughout France and into northern Italy, but it stopped in the southwest of France at the border of the Catalan dialects (shown in the southernmost section of Map 8.2). Modern forms in some areas show a subsequent diphthongization or lowering to [œ]—these are modern developments rather than a failure to undergo the original fronting (Ronjat, 1930, p. 131). The following stages of the back vowel shift form a pull chain which differed in extent from place to place. Diphthongization of the mid vowels and the back vowel chain shift interacted throughout France to disperse the back vowels; the balance between these two kinds of change varied considerably from one region to another.

The North

Diphthongization was at its most extensive in northern France: All stressed mid vowels in open syllables diphthongized, the back diphthongs

[2] The argument is that if *u had been fronted in the protolanguage, the early palatalization of *k and *g before front vowels would have occurred before *u as well as before *i, *eˆ, and *e.

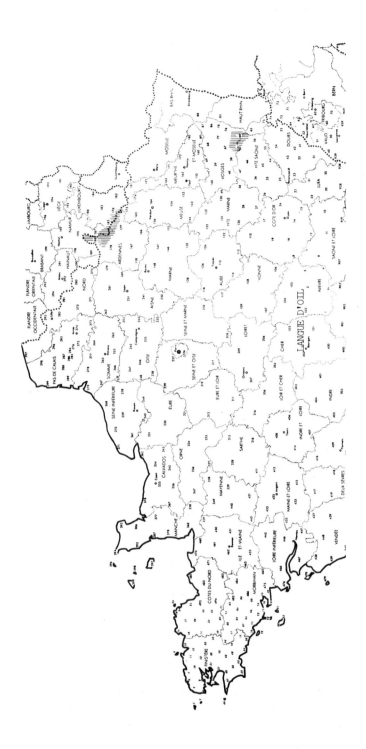

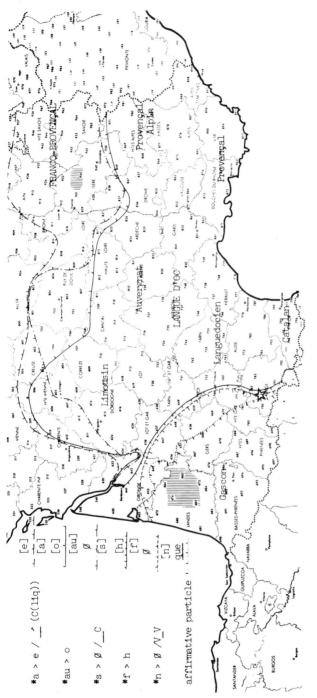

MAP 8.1 *Major language d'Oc—langue d'Oil and Gascon—Languedocien isoglosses.*

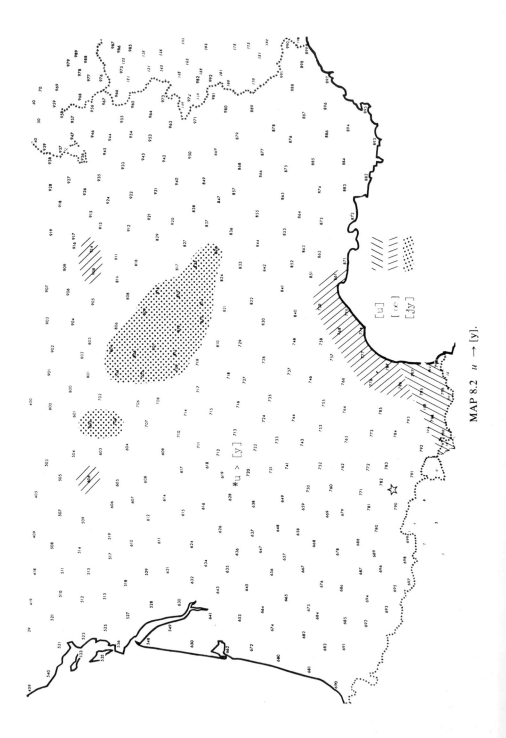

MAP 8.2 $u \to [y]$.

later becoming mid front rounded monophthongs:[3]

*coˆlóre	(> oṷ)	>	F kulǽr	'color'
*nóvo	(> ṷo)	>	F nǽf	'new'
*péde		>	F pi̯e	'foot'
*péˆra	(> ei̯)	>	F pṷar	'pear'

Beyond the initial stage (*u > y), the back chain shift in northern France only affected remaining occurrences of *oˆ (i.e., those that had not diphthongized: unstressed occurrences and stressed occurrences in closed syllables). It should be noted that movements of unstressed *oˆ included unstressed *o, as the unstressed mid vowels had merged. These all raised to [u]:

*colóre	>	F kulǽr	'color'
*póˆlla	>	F pul	'hen'

The South

There are two small sets of occurrences of vowels that diphthongized throughout southern France in the eleventh and twelfth centuries (Bourciez, 1956, p. 294): All low mid vowels (front and back) diphthongized (a) before palatals and (b) before [ṷ]. Other diphthongizations varied considerably according to location.

The back chain shift was more complete in the south than in the north, spreading from the stressed to the unstressed vowels. The first two stages of the chain shift, in both north and south, affected both stressed and unstressed occurrences:

stressed *u	*lúna	>	S lýo	'moon'
unstr. *u	*mutáre	>	S mydá	'shed' (inf)
stressed *oˆ	*póˆllo	>	S puč	'rooster'
unstr. *oˆ	*stoˆffáre	>	S estuhá	'smother'

Since Late Latin had only high mid vowels in unstressed position, all occurrences of the back mid vowel (i.e., unstressed *oˆ and *o) moved up to [u] along with stressed *oˆ (Ronjat, 1930, p. 143, 295). This left only one mid back vowel, which will be represented as [o]. Bourciez (1956, p. 290) attributes this raising to the thirteenth century, although Ronjat (1930, p. 295) claims that it was later, being reflected only sporadically in the southwestern texts of the fourteenth and fifteenth centuries:

*jocáre	>	S žugá	'play' (inf)

[3] F = French, S = Soulatan, O = unidentified Occitan (Southern French) dialect.

As a result of the merger of the unstressed mid vowels, then, there remained a stressed mid back vowel after these shifts (as *o moved up to [oˆ] in stressed position), but a 'case vide' at this position among the unstressed vowels. The result was that the chain shift continued in the unstressed vowels alone, with the raising of some occurrences of *a to [o] beginning in the fifteenth century (Bourciez, 1956, p. 301).

This latter stage of the chain shift began in the north-central part of Occitania and spread out, especially to the south and southeast. The waves of spread of *a > [o] are shown in Map 8.3. Although these waves primarily represent grammatical morphemes (see Eckert, 1969 for a detailed study of this spread), occurrences of unstressed *a within lexical roots also raised in the core area of this change, shown on Map 8.4. Furthermore, in a small highly variable area, shown on Map 8.5, occurrences of stressed *a have raised to [o] before nasals.

It is important to note that diphthongization interacts geographically with the area where *a raised to [o]. The geographic configurations of the changes undergone by stressed *o and by unstressed *a in the north-central region of Occitania provide confirmation of the systemic interrelation between these two changes.

Occurrences of *o following nasals and *o preceding blocked *r diphthongized to [u̯o] and [u̯a] in areas shown in Map 8.6. Ronjat speculates (1930, p. 162) that diphthongization may have been more widespread at one time, and is receding, with the diphthongs simplifying in some places to [o]. This is borne out by the geographic data under consideration. Map 8.7 shows a pattern typical of a number of lexical items, where an area of [o] (Area X) separates two areas of [u̯o] (Areas Y and Z). These three areas are, furthermore, opposed to a large area of [u] (Area Q). This indicates that in Area X, probably after *o had raised to [u] preceding a nasal, occurrences of [u̯o] simplified to [o].

Area Y in Map 8.7, where *o diphthongized, corresponds to the easternmost part of the core area of *a > [o] (hatched area of Map 8.3). As can be seen in Maps 8.3, 8.4, and 8.5, somewhat to the east of this core area, around points 824 and 833, there is an area where the intensity of *a > [o] is somewhat comparable to that in the core area itself; whereas in between there is an area of greater conservation. This middle conservative area corresponds to Area X in Map 8.7—the cut in the area of diphthongization; whereas the core area and the eastern area of intensive *a > [o] correspond to Areas Y and Z, where there is regular diphthongization. It is undoubtedly the case that the simplification of the diphthongs to [o] is in covariation with the raising of *a to [o] or to a reversal of that change to [a]. (Exactly what is the status of this latter change in that area beyond the scope of the present study.)

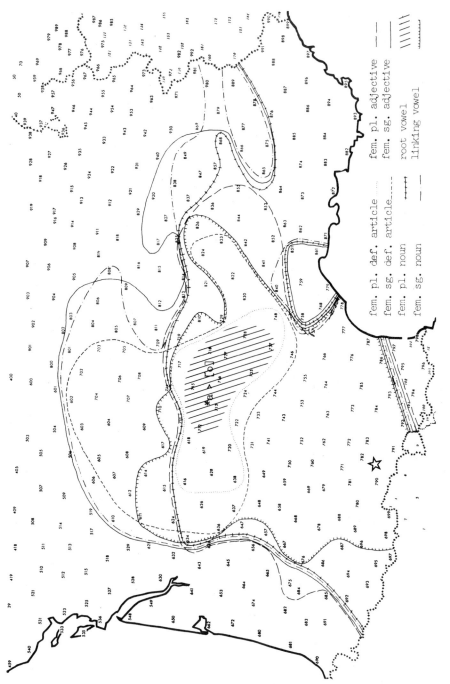

MAP 8.3 $a \rightarrow$ [o].

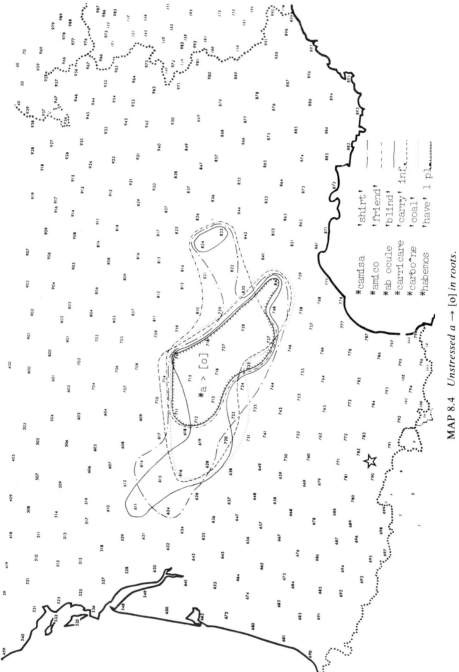

*a > [o]

*camisa	'shirt'
*amico	'friend'
*ab oculē	'blind'
*carri care	'carry' inf.
*carbō^ne	'coal'
*habemos	'have' 1 pl.

MAP 8.4 *Unstressed a → [o] in roots.*

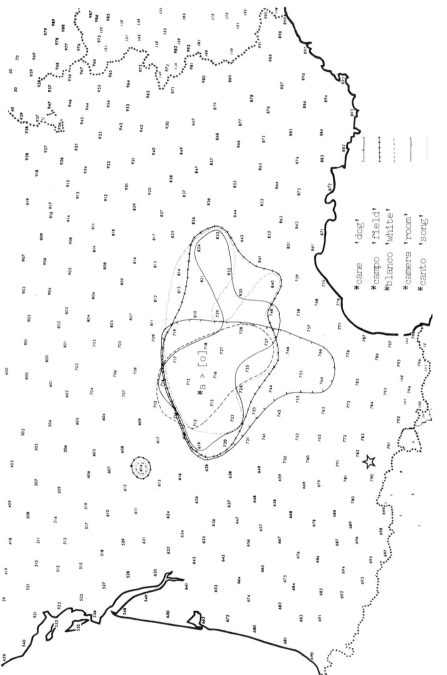

*a > [o]

*cane   'dog'
*campo   'field'
*blanco   'white'
*camera   'room'
*canto   'song'

MAP 8.5 $a \rightarrow [o] / \_ N$.

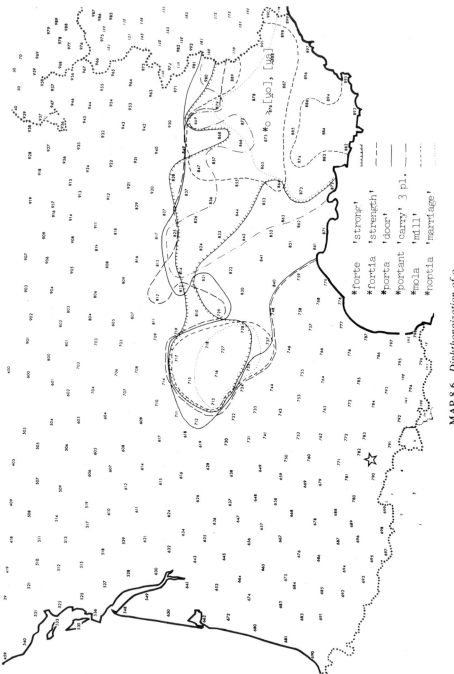

MAP 8.6 *Diphthongization of o.*

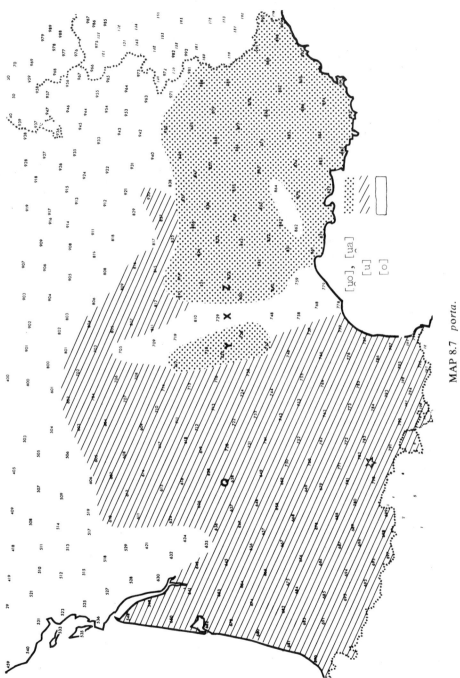

[u̯o], [u̯a]

[u]

[o]

MAP 8.7 *porta*.

Soulatan Vowels

There was as little diphthongization in Soulan as in any dialect of France. On the other hand, the back chain shift has advanced further in some respects in the area around Soulan than anywhere else in France.

Diphthongization

The only diphthongization that occurred in Soulatan is in those sets of occurrences common to all of the South:

1. The stressed low mid vowels diphthongized before all palatals, according to Bourciez (1965, p. 295) in the eleventh to twelfth centuries:

*lécto	>	S ļiet	'bed'
*cócto	>	S ku̯et	'cooked'
*média	>	S mi̯ézo	'half'
*lónge	>	S lu̯eñ	'far'

2. The stressed low mid vowels diphthongized before [u̯]:

| *méu | > | S mi̯eu̯ | 'mine' (pn) |
| *bóvo | > | S bu̯eu̯ | 'steer' (n) |

The only exceptions to this are occurrences of *o that had previously lowered to [a] (Bourciez, 1956, p. 294) before *-ve:

*plove	>	S plau̯	'rain' (3 sg)
*nove	>	S nau̯	'nine'
*die jóves	>	S dizáu̯s	'Thursday'

This development affected all such occurrences, in a wide geographical area.

The Chain Shift

Aside from the diphthongizations, there were no changes among the Soulatan front vowels. The back vowels, however, are still completing the chain shift.

THE HIGH AND MID BACK VOWELS

1. As elsewhere, *u fronted to [y] in all of its occurrences:

| *mutáre | > | S mydá | 'shed' (inf) |
| *lúna | > | S lýo | 'moon' |

2. All occurrences of *oˆ raised to [u]:

| *flô^re | > | S *hlu* | 'flower' |
| *bo^llicáre | > | S *burí* | 'boil' (inf) |

3. Some occurrences of *oˆ went beyond [u], fronting to [y] (thus merging with occurrences of *u) when followed by a palatal nasal:

*po^gnáre	>	S *pyñá*	'hit' (inf)
*pó^gno	>	S *pyñ*	'fist'
*có^neo	>	S *kyñ*	'corner'
*pó^ncto	>	S *pynt*	'tack'
*ó^ngola	>	S *ýŋglo*	'fingernail'

4. Stressed *o raised to [u] when preceding a nasal:

| *pónte | > | S *punt* | 'bridge' |
| *bóno | > | S *bu* | 'good' |

According to Bourciez (1956, p. 296) this *o raised to [oˆ] when preceding a nasal, prior to the fifth century. This then raised to [u] with occurrences of *oˆ around the fifteenth century (Bourciez, 1956, p. 297). This change was generalized geographically.

5. Stressed *o following a nasal has also raised to [u]:

| *mórto | > | S *murt* | 'dead' |

This has occurred in only a small part of Gascony: an area in the southwest (Map 8.8) and an even smaller area around Soulan. This change is not shown at all for the area around Soulan in the *ALF* since apparently the change has not reached any of the local *ALF* points, but it shows up in Bec's more detailed and recent maps (1968, phonetic map no. 6). This is associated with an ongoing change, which will be discussed further in what follows.

*a > [o]

Posttonic *a has raised categorically to [o]:

| *bélla | > | S *béro* | 'pretty'(f) |

and a class of pretonic occurrences are currently in the process of raising—the "linking" vowels that precede the adverbial and deverbal suffix -*ment:*

| S *sul* | 'alone' | S *sulamént* | ~ | *sulomént* | 'only' |
| S *enseñá* | 'teach' (inf) | S *enseñamént* | ~ | *enseñomént* | 'teaching' |

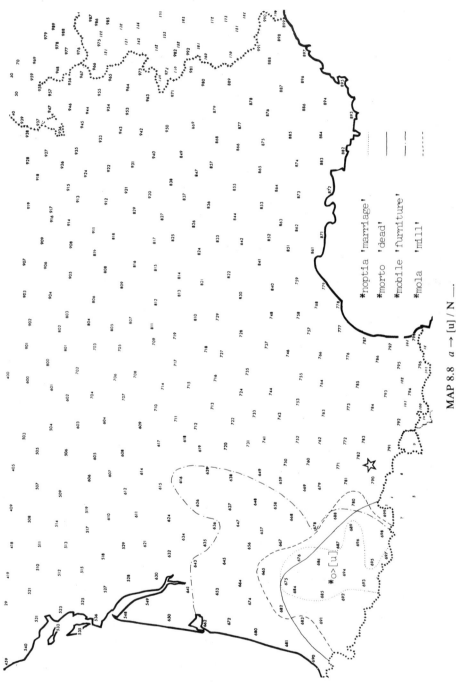

MAP 8.8 $a \rightarrow [u] / N$ __.

*noptia 'marriage'
*morto 'dead'
*mobile 'furniture'
*mola 'mill'

*o>[u]

Soulan is at the absolute southernmost edge of the waves of this change *a >
[o] emanating from northern Occitania. As shown in Map 8.3, the disposition
of the geographic waves for this change show clearly defined word classes.
These word classes divide differently as the change spreads to the north as
opposed to the south. Moving south toward Soulan in order of increasing
size of waves, these classes are

1. Posttonic occurrences (feminine morpheme in nouns and adjectives,
   thematic vowel in first conjugation indicative and second and third
   conjugation subjunctive verbs)
2. Intertonic linking vowels
3. The feminine definite article, which is posttonic in the article itself
   (*ella > S era) but pretonic in the context of this change by virtue of its
   enclitic position
4. Pretonic stem vowels
5. Stressed *a preceding nasals

Of these five, only the first two waves have reached Soulan.

Wave 1. It is unequivocally documented in Limousin (605) in the fifteenth
century (Ronjat, 1930, p. 212). It has now spread all the way to the Pyrenees,
reaching parts of this region recently enough that it is still in progress in a few
locations. Ronjat notes that posttonic *a is variably raised to [o] after labial
occlusives in Arrens, and after labials and syllables containing [u] in Ossau.
Castet (1895, p. 7) notes that [a] and [o] are in variation in the valley of Biros.
In Soulan, the change has been complete in this word class long enough for
the following stage in the chain (raising of [o] to [u] after nasals) to have
occurred. There are no signs of [a] in this position, and speakers are unaware
that [o] is an innovation.

Wave 2. Wave 2 is in its final stage of raising in Soulan. There is little geographic material on this class of occurrences, and no discussion of it in the
literature.

The change in Soulan is complete in this class among the younger
speakers, and the class is undergoing the next stage of the change, [o] > [u]. A
couple of instances of [a], however, have emerged among the older speakers;
but in a limited set of items. Specifically, the item *sulamént* 'only' shows
variability between [a] and [o] in the speech of two older inhabitants, and [a]
appeared in two out of two utterances of *emplasamént* 'setting' and one out
of two utterances of *akučamént* 'birth' in the speech of one of these two older
speakers. These occurrences are all shown in Table 8.1. This behavior is
reflected also in the small amount of available geographic material. The three
maps that are available for this vowel show a solid area of [o] for two words
sulamént and *dusamént* (Map 8.9) and this same area shows considerable
variability for a third, *talamént* (Map 8.10).

TABLE 8.1
Number of Realizations of [a], [o], [u] in Each Class of Occurrences of Posttonic and Linking a

Informant		Linking a			Imperfect verb endings[a]								
		N_	~N_	—N	—~N	b_	~b_	b_N	~b_~N	—m	—n	—ŋ
1 Female 92 years	[a]	0	0	0	0	0	0	0	0	0	0	0
	[o]	0	97	26	45	19	45	6	32	5	14	7
	[u]	6	3	14	1	7	9	6	0	6	2	6
2 Male 86 years	[a]	1	0	0	0	0	0	0	0	0	0	0
	[o]	10	129	54	48	18	86	14	44	19	25	10
	[u]	0	10	31	3	21	31	21	3	22	7	2
3 Female 80 years	[a]	7	0	0	0	0	0	0	0	0	0	0
	[o]	11	133	78	134	48	176	23	109	20	38	20
	[u]	16	9	49	6	49	66	32	3	27	13	9
4 Female 72 years	[a]	0	0	0	0	0	0	0	0	0	0	0
	[o]	1	132	105	0	39	66	39	0	25	71	9
	[u]	1	2	80	0	45	32	45	0	42	24	14
5 Male 65 years	[a]	0	0	0	0	0	0	0	0	0	0	0
	[o]	1	86	17	31	7	41	4	28	6	7	4
	[u]	0	10	13	4	10	7	9	3	11	1	1

		1	2	3	4	5	6	7	8	9	10	11	12
6 Female 60 years	[a]	0	0	0	0	0	0	0	0	0	0	0	0
	[o]	9	1	211	70	110	26	154	15	99	13	40	17
	[u]	0	9	2	75	12	60	27	54	6	40	17	18
7 Male 50 years	[a]	0	0	0	0	0	0	0	0	0	0	0	0
	[o]	34	1	81	78	94	51	121	35	78	9	59	10
	[u]	3	9	0	53	1	27	26	27	1	12	28	13
8 Female 48 years	[a]	0	0	0	0	0	0	0	0	0	0	0	0
	[o]	0	1	10	35	53	19	69	9	43	6	18	11
	[u]	0	0	0	39	0	13	39	13	0	6	29	4
9 Female 38 years	[a]	0	0	0	0	0	0	0	0	0	0	0	0
	[o]	9	1	151	73	61	44	90	33	50	20	48	5
	[u]	4	20	3	36	8	19	25	18	7	14	11	11
Column		1	2	3	4	5	6	7	8	9	10	11	12

[a] Columns 4–12 represent phonetic environments in imperfect verb endings:

	Conjugation 1 (b__)	Conjugation 2 (~b__)	*be* (~b__)
3 sg. (__~N)	-abo	-io	ero
1 pl. (__N)	-abom	-iom	erom
3 pl. (__N)	-abon	-ion	eron

(Forms shown are base forms. Point of articulation of final nasal in Columns 10–12 is assimilated to following consonant.)

197

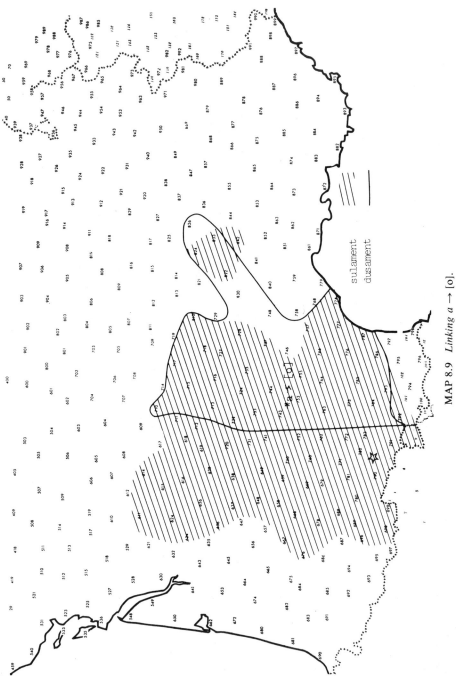

sulament
dusament

MAP 8.9 *Linking a → [o]*.

198

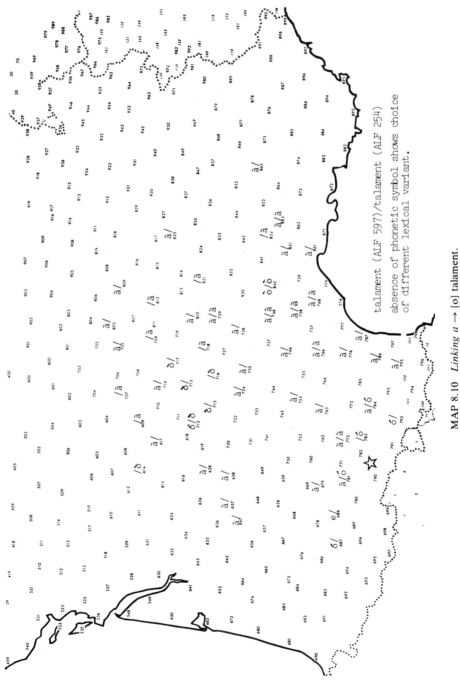

talament (ALF 597)/talament (ALF 254)

absence of phonetic symbol shows choice
of different lexical variant.

MAP 8.10 *Linking a → [o] talament.*

199

The behavior of this set of occurrences can perhaps be explained by its association with the feminine and verbal morphemes:

S *súlo*	'alone' (f)	S *sulomént*	'only' (adv)
S *akúčo*	'give birth' (3 sg)	S *akučomént*	'birth'

This set of occurrences has probably been split off from other intertonic occurrences (note that no other pretonic or intertonic occurrences raise in or near Soulan) by analogy with related posttonic occurrences. The wave of the change of "linking *a" is not defined by any phonetic criteria: Other occurrences of pretonic *a, even when followed by [m], do not change in a similar area (e.g., *kamisa* 'shirt', *amiko* 'friend'; Map 8.4). The wave of raising of linking *a follows closely behind that of posttonic *a: It is a small class of occurrences defined by its pretonicity on the one hand and its grammatical relation to posttonic *a on the other.

Items lagging behind in the change remain in the speech of older Soulatans as stylistic variants. The circumstances under which the occurrences of [a] were uttered were where maximal attention was being paid to speech—either where the word was being stressed, or where the speaker had had to search for the word or phrase. The occurrences of *sulamént* were embedded in speech as follows[4]:

Informant 2: a. *Que serbishion a bebe sulament*
  '*They served drinks **only***'

Informant 3: a. *Suloment que costabo dets sows*
  '*But it cost ten sous*'
  b. *Suloment no bengio cap ets boushes com awe*
  '*But the butchers didn't come by like nowadays*'
  c. *Mes Sulament . . . Hesto . . . que las calio mete . . .*
  '*But . . . feast . . . you had to put them . . .*'
  d. *Que bengio et diminge sulament porta biando*
  '*He came on Sundays **only** to bring meat*'
  e. *Que tiro: sulament que cal . . . se bie trop gros que . . .*
  '*You pulll but you have to . . . if it gets too thick . . .*'

In all these cases, [a] occurs in emphatic position or in hesitant speech, where the speaker is groping for words. Where the word occurs before the main verb in rapid speech, it is pronounced with an [o].

A similar situation is implied in the *Atlas* cases of *talament*. Map 8.10 represents two instances of *talamént* in two separate *ALF* maps. These maps

---

[4] These sentences are written in my own orthography (there are several extant Gascon orthographies). Only the occurrences of *a in question, which appear in bold face, are rendered phonetically.

show great variation not only between [a] and [o], but also between the lexical items *talamént, ta* 'so', and *trop* 'very'. There is considerable variation between locations within each map and at any location between the two utterances represented by the two maps. But this variability is more frequently between different lexical items than between [a] and [o]. These forms were elicited by a request to translate from French *si chaud* 'so hot' (*ALF* map 254) and *si fort* 'so strong' (*ALF* map 597). There is no cognate of French *si* 'so' in Soulatan: This would be rendered normally with *ta* (F *tant*). *Talamént* would be used more in tonic position, especially in response to such a statement: S *que he caut* 'it's hot'—*talamént!* 'it sure is/really!' It is possible that the large number of occurrences of *talamént* in this map are due to the translation task, and that its very presence is idiomatically incorrect. And it is further possible that this translation task is also responsible for the high degree of variability in the forms between [a] and [o].

The kind of phonological variation reflected in these two maps, also, indicates that this is not part of the regular spread of change. At the edge of the spread of *a > [o], there is normally variation between gradual stages of raising, represented in the *ALF* by the symbols *à, ò* and *ó*. Comparison of *ALF* maps 254 and 597 (Map 8.10) shows variation between *à* and *ó* near the edge of the change (point 784) and *à* and *ò* at the center of the change (point 717). This is a picture not of gradual vowel raising, but rather of variation between two separate phonemes.

I have observed over and over in linguistic maps that there is often great lexical variability in the area of the frontier of a phonological change. It is often difficult to trace isoglosses, precisely because a number of informants have used an alternative lexical item in just that locality. This is common enough to suggest a causal relation between the lexical variability and the phonological change: Rather than deal with a phonological variable, the informants choose an alternative lexical item. The *ALF* data for *talamént* appear to reflect a related situation: The informant is requested to give a form that requires a complicated translation task, and he/she responds with a hypercorrect version.

If all this is so, then what is particularly interesting about it is that, while the change *a > [o] in this class of words has spread all the way to the Pyrenees, it is still alive throughout the territory that it has affected. This would seem to indicate that a historical rule does not necessarily "die" after it passes through an area, but can remain active in some way.

*a > [o] > [u]

At the present time, [o] resulting from *a is in the process of raising to [u] when following, and to a lesser extent when preceding, a nasal consonant.

1. The raising of this [o] after nasals is now almost categorical in Soulan, while in nearby Bonac and Sentein (Bec, 1968, p. 66) it is still quite

variable. As shown in Column 2 of Table 8.1, most informants showed some occurrences of [o] in this environment.

Bec associates this with the raising of postnasal stressed *o (*morto > murt), finding that in the Soulatan area, the two changes cover similar geographic areas. This area is too small to be reflected in the *ALF*. The only raising shown near Soulan in the *ALF* is a raising of *all* posttonic [o] < *a at point 791 (Auzat). Bec (1968, p. 65) refers to the area in Map 8.8 as an area of "predilection" for the raising of [o].

The stressed change appears to be older and more widespread than the posttonic change: It is categorical in Soulatan although it was still variable in Bethmale in 1933 (Schönthaler, 1937, p. 19). The stressed change (but not the posttonic) also occurs to the west, originating in south-central Gascony (Map 8.8). Since the western area in the *ALF* does not touch Soulan, one might wonder if the change has spread since the compilation of the *Atlas* data. This is unlikely, since the change has gone too far in Soulatan for this to have been an extension of the western area. Fifty years is not long enough for the rule to have gone nearly to completion in the area between that shown in the *ALF* and the area around Soulan. According to Bec's more recent data, furthermore, the eastern and the western areas are separated by a considerable area of [o] retention. It appears, then, that this new stage of the chain shift began independently in both areas. This is important to the theory of phonological change, and will be discussed further.

2. The raising of [o] after nasals applies to the pretonic linking *a in the speech of younger people—although less categorically than to posttonic [o]. The speakers who show variation between [a] and [o] show no occurrences of [u] for this variable, whereas the younger speakers who show no [a] show a switch into the [o] > [u] pattern. It appears that the identification of [o] with [a] via the patterns of variation was preventing this vowel from being identified with the variable (o). This appears to indicate that the raising of [a] to [o] and the raising of [o] to [u] are discrete stages in the chain shift, and that only once the first shift becomes categorical does the following shift begin. This is an illustration of Bailey's claim that variation will not begin in an area until the change is complete in the preceding area.

3. The third class of occurrences of [o] < *a that is raising to [u] consists of posttonic occurrences before nasals. These appear most frequently in imperfect endings and in first conjugation present indicative endings:

1st conjug. pres. indic. 3 pl.	*-ant	>	on ~ un
1st. conjug. imperf. indic. 1 & 3 pl.	*-abamo	>	abom ~ abum
	*-abant	>	abon ~ abun

2nd & 3rd conjug.

imperf. indic.	*-ebamo	>	iom ~ ium
1 & 3 pl.	*-ebant	>	ion ~ iun

'to be'

imperf. indic.	*eramu	>	erom ~ erum
1 & 3 pl.	*erant	>	eron ~ erun

This change is part of still another geographic wave, shown in Map 8.11. While these endings are direct outcomes of the Late Latin forms in Soulatan, there are large areas in southern France where the third person plural endings in both the present and the imperfect were remodelled by analogy with *−oˆnt (Classical Latin −ŭnt) (Ronjat, 1937, p. 159–160). This accounts for the large areas of [o] and [u] shown in this map for these forms. The area to the northeast, where [o] is shown for these forms, was affected neither by the raising of *oˆ to [u] nor by the raising of *a to [o]. The [o] shown in this area is the regular phonetic outcome in that area of the *o in the analogical formation. In the central area, by the same token, the [u] that is represented for this ending is a raising of *oˆ to [u]; not a raising of *a. However, the location of the isogloss between [o] and [u] to the south raises an interesting problem: Soulan is near the border of [o] and [u], and although its own third person plural ending descends from *-ant, and is raising to [u] via [o], it is near an area where the [u] is raising from *oˆ. Here, grammatical analogy has undoubtedly facilitated the merger of *a and *o.

4. As shown in Column 3 of Table 8.1, there is a small amount of raising of posttonic [o] < *a to [u] when not adjacent to a nasal. The small numbers involved do not indicate any conditioning.

5. Among the current occurrences of *a in modern Soulatan, there is a tendency for unstressed (i.e., pretonic) occurrences to be more back than stressed occurrences. Furthermore, backness in both stressed and unstressed *a is favored by labials.

Table 8.1 is a composite of the realizations of occurrences of unstressed *a in modern Soulatan. The degree of raising of *a to [o] can be measured in terms of a height index as developed by Labov (1966, pp. 52 ff). A value of 1 is given to [a], 2 to [o], and 3 to [u]. The index for a class of occurrences is the average index of all occurrences, multiplied by 100. For ease of comparison, a separate table (Table 8.2) is provided with the index for each speaker in each class of occurrences.

While the position of *a in the posttonic occurrences is relatively stable among the age groups, the progression of the raising of the linking vowel is clearly shown: Younger speakers consistently produce a value of over 200, whereas older speakers stay below 200.

A general set of constraints for the raising of [o] to [u] is clearly apparent from these data. In all cases, raising is favored by nasals—both preceding

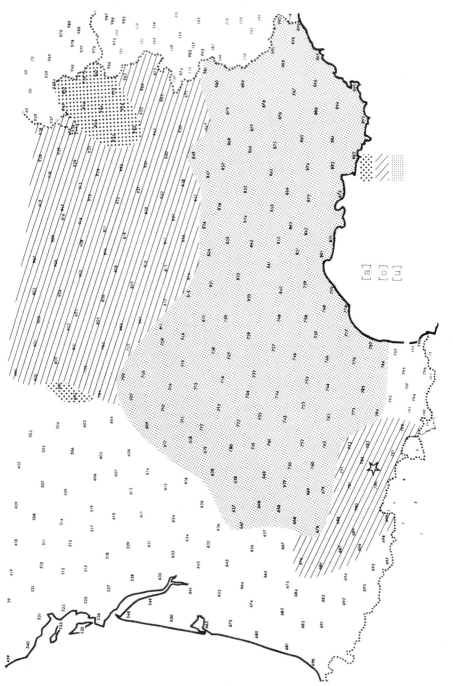

MAP 8.11. *Imperfect Ending -ont.*

TABLE 8.2
Average Height Index for Each Class of Occurrences of Posttonic and Linking a[a]

Informant	Linking a	N_	~N_	_N	_~N	b_	~b_	b_N	~b_~N	Imperfect Verb Endings		
										_m	_n	_ŋ
1	—	300	203	235	202	227	217	250	200	255	213	246
2	191	279	207	237	206	254	227	260	206	254	222	217
3	161	276	206	239	204	251	227	258	203	258	226	231
4	250	300	202	243	—	254	233	254	—	263	225	261
5	200	300	210	243	211	259	215	269	210	265	213	220
6	200	—	—	252	210	270	215	278	206	276	230	251
7	208	290	201	240	201	235	218	244	201	257	232	257
8	—	291	200	253	200	241	236	259	200	250	262	227
9	231	295	202	233	212	230	222	235	212	241	219	269
Column	1	2	3	4	5	6	7	8	9	10	11	12

[a] [a] = 100; [o] = 200; [u] = 300.

and following, although primarily by preceding. And in all cases, raising is favored by labials—both preceding [b] and (with the exceptions of informants 8 and 9), following [m].

The Form of the Chain Shift

Labov, Yaeger, and Steiner (1972, p. 159) have suggested that phonological space may be curved in such a way that the high front rounded vowel [y] is actually higher than the high back rounded vowel. Such a finding would simplify the representation of the shift of the Soulatan (and French) back vowels, which could be represented as a simple shift upward rather than as two kinds of shifts—fronting of *u and raising of the rest of the back vowels. But this is not the only Soulatan phenomenon that such a conception of phonological space would clarify.

In a historical vowel deletion rule, high vowels were found to be weaker than low vowels; but futhermore, front vowels were found to be weaker than back vowels[5]. If a vowel height assignment rule were to be devised for the purposes of the upward chain shift of the back vowels, frontness would be given more strength than backness. The feature [+front] would add a degree of height, so that [y] would be one degree higher than [u]. Such a height assignment rule could also account for the vowel deletion rule, since front vowels would be consistently assigned a greater height (and thus weakness) value than back vowels.

The upward chain shift and the weak vowel deletion rule—along with certain others—can best be described following the format of Labov, Yaeger, and Steiner (1972) whereby a value corresponding to relative height is assigned to segments according to certain of their features. These values can then represent points on a continuum in phonological space or discrete steps in a phonological system. This has the advantage of allowing for the dialectic between the discrete and gradual nature of synchronic phonological systems and diachronic shift. The height assignment rule will assign a maximum height of 4 to all segments that are [+vocalic] [−consonantal], and the height adjustment rule will lower that value by one level for each feature a segment possesses that participates in lowness:

(1)
$$\begin{bmatrix} +\text{voc} \\ -\text{cons} \end{bmatrix} \rightarrow [4 \text{ high}]$$

(2)
$$[x \text{ high}] \rightarrow [x - 1 \text{ high}] \, / \, \underline{\hspace{2cm}}$$
$$\begin{array}{l} [-\text{front}] \\ [-\text{high}] \\ [+\text{low}] \\ [+\text{central}] \end{array}$$

[5] Ronjat mentions (1930, p. 231, footnote) having attempted to assign weakness coefficients to vowels on the basis of height and frontness, but he does not explain how they worked or what kinds of predictions he was intending to make with them.

These two rules assign the following values to the Late Latin vowels:

i, y	4
eˆ, u	3
e, oˆ	2
o	1
a	0

The upward chain shift of the back vowels could, then, just add a given degree of height to all back vowels:

(3)
$$\begin{bmatrix} +\text{voc} \\ -\text{cons} \\ +\text{back} \\ x\text{ high} \end{bmatrix} \rightarrow [x + y\text{ high}]$$

The actual value of y is the pivotal question in establishing the constraints in this rule, and will be the focus of the following discussion.

Linguistic Rules and Linguistic Process

In this chain shift, all back vowels raised one level, and some raised two levels. In a grammar restricted to categorical rules, each stage of this shift would be described separately. If an alternative approach is to be taken to the writing of these rules, it must tell something about the chain shift that could not be told in separate categorical rules.

It is apparent from the data presented in the preceding sections that the raising of the various back vowels in Soulatan and the surrounding dialects were related, and that in some way the raisings of all the vowels were linked. It is also clear that chain shifts of this sort occur often, and that the participation of phonological change in larger processes is more the rule than the exception. A theory of phonological change should tell us how isolated a change can be: whether all changes are part of larger processes; and within any process, what the relation is between the individual changes, that is, how the process exerts its pressure. The selection of a noncategorical mode of description of phonological change assumes the responsibility of dealing with these questions. The examination of the changes that constitute the Soulatan back vowel shift should dictate the form of the rule or rules that will be written to describe them.

The model of phonological change that underlies this study shows a passage of any given change through classes of occurrences, taking time periods of variable length. At the time of the change, this passage will be characterized by variability among continuous stages as it passes through a community. The speakers of the community possess, as part of their linguistic competence, "knowledge" of this change—sometimes even conscious knowledge. The knowledge may be in the form of "higher" or "lower" (socially), "more" or "less," rather than "earlier" or "later" (as discussed, for example, in Fasold, 1973), but the working of the historical change is part of the individual's competence.

A speaker acquires a knowledge of linguistic structure and social structure together. It has been shown that dialect patterns take form in early adolescence: This is also the time when young people are developing competence in adult social structures. The development of dialect goes hand in hand with the positioning of the speaker within the social system. This involves, then, positioning with respect to the progress of any linguistic innovation that may be in progress in that community. A young individual's eagerness to identify with that social choice may in fact be an important source of social energy in the progress of change. What the individual acquires, then, is a range of performance within a much larger set of possibilities. This acquisition is in some sense a choice from at least part of the larger set that makes up the totality of speech patterns within the community, and as the range is chosen from a larger set, so it functions within the larger set. In the case of a phonological change, although the range of one speaker's pattern may reflect a small area along the chronological continuum of the change, this pattern occurs within the context of other patterns that reflect adjacent areas along the continuum. Thus, in his or her awareness of the totality of speech patterns within the community, the speaker is also aware in some sense of the relation between the stage of a phonological change reflected in his or her speech, and preceding and following stages.

What is variable at the time of the actual occurrence of the rule will become categorical if and when the rule goes to completion. However, this variability is as much a part of the change as the subsequent categoricalness, and whether the variability is reflected in later stages of the language depends on what else is happening at the time. The writing of a variable rule in a historical reconstruction, then, has the same relation to historical fact as the writing of a categorical rule: A categorical rule represents the application, in the past, of one change as if it had applied all at once. A variable rule is simply an expansion of a categorical rule: It reflects the chronological relation between and within the application of change to different word classes. Of course, in any historical treatment, some facts will be lost. The purpose of substituting a variable rule for a categorical one is to "pick up" facts related to the progress of the change that are of particular importance to the description and theory of change.

The purpose of a categorical treatment is to "generate" the correct modern forms from a protocorpus. Here, as in Chomsky's synchronic model, simplicity is the primary basis for judging rules, so that categorical historical rules cut the phonetic inventory into the largest chunks that can yield the correct results. If phonemes change one class of occurrences at a time, this will not be reflected in a categorical rule unless an interruption—either within the rule itself or from another rule—makes it unavoidable. In this case, the phoneme will be broken into as few classes as possible to restate the events in a series of categorical rules. By the same token, the chunks of phonetic material treated in categorical rules may be subclasses of an inventory of phonemes affected by one change. The failure of this rule to affect uniformly all phonemes in a class may require the categorical treatment to split up the process. Thus the unit of description in a categorical treatment is that unit that allows the generation of the modern corpus with the fewest and simplest rules.

The present description assumes responsibility for the relation between the form of the individual rules, speakers' linguistic competence at any time during the change, and the actual historical processes. This means that, expressed in a given rule should be the major forces in that change, with some explanation of how that change passed through the generations.

Weinreich, Labov, and Herzog (1968) have discussed the relation, in the synchronic linguistic system, of different vowels that are participating in a single chain shift. Labov (e.g., 1972) has shown that in one synchronic system, variable rules may account not only for two stages of a chain that are occurring at once, but also for the relation between these two changes. Thus, there is a connection between what might look later on, in retrospect, like a series of separate shifts. It is in this sense that these changes can be said to constitute a process—not in any abstract sense independent of the linguistic competence of the successive speakers.

All of these phenomena could be treated with individual categorical rules, supplemented by metarules to bind them together into processes.[6] The disadvantage of such a treatment is that it sets up a complicated cognitive structure that has no justification elsewhere. Variable rules are known to function as part of a speaker's competence. There is plenty of evidence of such rules in everyone's everyday speech, and of the relation of such rules to diachronic change. There is, on the other hand, no such clear evidence of metarules. The inclusion of metarules in historical description, then, implies that there are processes occurring in change that do not exist in synchronic linguistic competence. This leaves historical process to a heretofore unidentified external force. The forces of linguistic change must be in the linguistic system itself, and given a model of this system in which rules are variable, and in which this variation is a manifestation of historical change, variable rules must express the forces of change. At any given point in time in the course of a long process, at least some constraints participating in that process must be present in the synchronic rules. Any shift of constraints in the course of the process must, furthermore, be explainable in terms of the

---

[6] This is a device suggested by Foley (1972).

previous set of constraints. A historical process, then, is not describable by a series of categorical rules, nor by a series of variable rules; but rather by a variable rule that may itself evolve in time.

The problem in establishing a rule or rules for the Soulatan back vowel chain shift is to understand the interactions between the successive stages of the shift. Since this shift does not occur in a vacuum, certain aspects of the evolution of the rules themselves may be interlocked with other processes. Thus the practical choices in the actual writing of rules range from a separate statement of the rule for every occurrence of raising to one statement for the entire shift. In between, it must be decided whether all stages are related to the same degree and in the same way, and what the relation is between those occurrences that raised two steps and those that raised only one. In this latter case, it would be possible to establish (a) one rule for the first raising, and an additional rule or rules for the second raising; or (b) one rule for all raising, the additional raising being accounted for by variable constraints. Option 2 would imply that the boundaries between all the phonemes were relatively fluid—that the degree of raising of one vowel phoneme in relation to another was due entirely to the constraints built into the rule, and that phonemic membership is of negligible effect. A separate rule for the second raising, on the other hand, would imply that there were in fact two distinct stages in the change. Which of these options is correct is, of course, an empirical matter, and the data on which such a decision will be based are somewhat scattered. The following discussion will draw on these data to approximate the various states of affairs existing across time.

To the degree to which these changes were related, one would expect to find a similar form of rule affecting them all; if they were separate, one would expect to find separate sets of constraints and varied relations between these constraints. It is important to reconstruct the variable nature of the early stages of the raising rule, in order to see whether there are correspondences with current stages of the change. All indications show that the phonological constraints operating in the modern variable rule for the raising of *a to [u] also operated in the raising of *u, *oˆ and *o, although they all ultimately became categorical—that is, went to completion. If, then, it is true that the same constraints applied at all stages of this change, the variable constraints have only to be added to Rule (3). If the rule specifies that it applies to vowels in order of their height, then the current variability will be a function of its height, thus a function of time. The rule, therefore, could be modified as follows, awaiting the additional variable constraints:

(3a)
$$\begin{bmatrix} +\text{voc} \\ -\text{cons} \\ +\text{back} \\ x\ \text{high} \end{bmatrix} \rightarrow \langle x + y\ \text{high} \rangle\ /\ \underline{\qquad\qquad}_{\langle z\ \text{high} \rangle}$$

The Individual Constraints

STRESS

Meillet (1900) discusses the raising effect of weak position on vowels, and Ronjat (1930, pp. 289–290) continues this discussion in the context of Occitan vowels. Stress placement is clearly a factor throughout the chain shift, and at all stages that are known about, the unstressed vowels raised earlier than the stressed vowels. In other Romance dialects, only unstressed *oˆ raised to [u]; stressed occurrences remained [o] or diphthongized.

In this chain shift, *a is the only vowel that is affected in only some occurrences, that is, in a subset of unstressed occurrences. In Soulan, *a > [o] has not yet affected all the unstressed vowels—only posttonic and a small class of pretonic vowels. As *a is also the only vowel that occurred in posttonic position at the time of these shifts, there is no point of comparison of the relation between these two positions in other vowels. The literature on the higher vowels shows that in the cases of *oˆ and *o, also, unstressed occurrences raised before their stressed counterparts and at least in the center of the area of *a > [o], this rule is now affecting the stressed vowels after having worked through all the unstressed occurrences, suggesting that the pattern unstressed–stressed is common to much of the shift. A constraint whereby, among the occurrences of a given vowel, posttonic, then pretonic, then stressed occurrences are raised, will account for all stress phenomena among the back vowels. Two things make this analysis difficult to accept: (a) there is no evidence that occurrences of *u fronted in the same order; and (b) it is not clear whether or not stress is responsible for the distinction between posttonic and pretonic occurrences of *a in modern Soulatan (or in earlier raisings of *a).

Spectrographic work on the neighboring dialect of Ercé (Eckert, 1969b) shows that in isolated words in that dialect, word accent is correlated only with sudden drop in pitch, and that intensity is the greatest at the beginning of the word and decreases progressively toward the end. Length, on the other hand, progresses in the opposite direction, and the vowels become increasingly longer toward the end. This corresponds to statements in the Romance literature attributing greater strength to word-initial syllables, separating vowels in these syllables from other pretonic vowels. This pattern is reflected in spectrograms of Soulatan speech. However, in the flow of speech, the length of the final syllable is decreased, to become about equal or inferior to that of the stressed syllable. This provides no clear correlation with the order of syllables affected by *a > [o]: posttonic–pretonic–stressed.

It appears, then, that the raising of *a to [o] and [u], anyway, is not constrained by vowel strength beyond perhaps the distinction between stressed and unstressed; and that within the category of unstressed vowels, the distinction between occurrences is made according to other parameters.

GRAMMATICAL CONSTRAINTS

The geographical data show clear grammatical constraints in the raising of *a to [o], both in posttonic and pretonic occurrences. Although the pretonic linking vowel has raised in Soulatan, there are no signs of the raising of other occurrences of *a in phonologically similar environments [e.g., *medasí* 'doctor', *lapasú* 'tick', *estamá* 'tin' (inf.), *estamáįre* 'tinker']. In the geographic data, furthermore, the wave represented by the change of the linking vowel is considerably larger than that represented by the change of other pretonic vowels. The constraint for the raising of these occurrences, therefore, must be morphological.

NASALS

The raising effect of nasals on vowels has been copiously discussed elsewhere (see in particular Labov, Yaeger, and Steiner, 1972). For all raising beyond the first stage, nasals were a necessary environment, and in many occurrences, raising to the first stage was earlier in a nasal environment:

1. *o raised early to [oˆ] before nasals (*pónte* > punt), allowing this to merge with *oˆ and raise to [u].
2. *oˆ went beyond [u] to [y] when followed by a palatal nasal (*cúneu* > kyṇ).
3. *a raises beyond [o] to [u] only when preceded or followed by a nasal.
4. In the center for the change of *a > [o], stressed *a raises to [o] only before nasals.

Perhaps the most important is the fact that the raising of *o after nasals began independently in two areas. This is perhaps the strongest confirmation of commonality of constraints in the various stages of the chain. Short of sheer coincidence, the only plausible explanation of two independent beginnings of the same change is a common predisposition to certain kinds of change. This predisposition to raising after nasals is the result of previous sensitivity to this constraint in the context of current stages of the vowel shift. The raising of *o, then, was a "logical" next step in the chain.

POINT OF ARTICULATION

Point of articulation served as a secondary constraint in a number of these changes, and is also the primary constraint in some related changes elsewhere:

1. As was mentioned, *oˆ went to [u] and then [y] only when followed by a palatal nasal. Thus the front point of articulation combined with the nasal appears to have been adequate to bring the vowel forward and thereby higher. There is one occurrence of this vowel fronting to [y] before a non-nasal palatal, but the preponderance of cases were be-

fore nasal palatals. It appears that in this case, the point of articulation was slightly more important than the nasality, but that a combination of the two was normally required to effect the change, and in this combination comprised a categorical change.

2. In Soulan, where posttonic [o] < *a raises to [u], although nasals form the primary constraint, labiality and velarity serve as a secondary constraint.

3. In Ossau, where the raising of *a to [o] is currently taking place in posttonic position, this occurs only after labials (Ronjat, 1930, p. 207).

4. Currently in Soulatan, both stressed and unstressed *a are backed when preceding and following labials.

The Form of the Chain Shift

The evidence so far indicates that one variable rule could be written to describe the entire chain shift: The constraints of nasality, point of articulation, and stress *could* all be incorporated into one statement. However, if such a rule is to be more than a notational innovation, it has to correspond to the actual events. The constraints have to have been the same throughout, or else any change in the constraints has to be explainable internally to the rule.

A particular difficulty in this rule is the raising of posttonic *a. If these occurrences were truly "weaker" than pretonic occurrences, a rule wherein increasing weakness constrained raising would adequately account for the raising of posttonic *a and pretonic *ô and *o as two instances of the same phenomenon. However, neither the modern data nor the historical data indicate without a doubt that final *a is weaker than pretonic *a. On the contrary, there are indications that *a tends to move back to [ɑ] as a function of length in a number of Romance dialects. In the north, this occurred around the sixteenth century before *s, giving the now-disappearing distinction in French between *pâte* (< *pasta) [pɑt] and *patte* (< *patta) [pat] (Bourciez, 1956, p. 639). Length has also been shown to be a property of final Soulatan vowels. In this case, the statement that simplifies the description of the chain shift may be falsifying the facts about the latest shift, and certainly in that case says nothing of importance about how the entire shift occurred. Although the raising of *a is linked to the other raisings, it involves factors (including a positional class) that were not present in other raisings.

One rule for the entire shift would entail not only the inclusion of height, stress, nasality, and point of articulation as variable constraints—the rule would also have to account for the apparent shift of the primary constraint from the following segment to the preceding. The influence of the preceding and following segment changed as the shift moved from higher to lower vowels: Thus, *ô fronted to [y] only before nasals; *o raised to [u] first before nasals but eventually after nasals too; *a raises to [u] first after nasals, and only in the later stage before nasals. A single rule for this chain shift, then, will have to account for a sliding difference in weight between a preceding and following nasal environment.

An added complication is the fact that the influence of following over preceding labials and palatals also shifts, like that of nasals. In this case, only following palatals have an influence on ([u] < *oˆ) > [y], and, although following labials have a greater effect on ([o] < *a) > [u], the preceding labials also have some effect. Finally, preceding labials have more effect on modern unstressed *a than following ones do.

These shifting constraints could be handled in one rule by something similar to a minus alpha rule, replacing alpha with a continuous value, co-varying with the height of the vowel. The coefficient of the following constraint would vary directly with the height of the vowel, and that of the preceding would vary inversely with height. The rule would look something like Rule (3b):

(3b) $\begin{bmatrix} +\text{voc} \\ -\text{cons} \\ +\text{back} \\ x \text{ high} \end{bmatrix} \rightarrow \langle x + y \text{ high} \rangle / 4 - z \langle w \text{ feature} \rangle \dfrac{}{\langle z \text{ high} \rangle} z \langle y \text{ feature} \rangle$

The choice between this rule and a more pluralistic alternative depends on the relative capacity of each to explain the phenomena that they are describing. In this case, the phenomena that complicate the rule and thus need explaining are the shift in importance between the various constraints. The convention within the variable rule implies that there is a connection between the height of the vowel itself and the shifting of the constraint. The constraints shown in this rule are all phonetic. Unless there is some phonetic explanation of why preceding segments should affect lower vowels more than higher, this complicated variable rule is roughly equivalent to a metarule, that is, it describes the long-term contours of the constraint, but it does not relate them to the rest of the material in the rule—thus to linguistic competence at any one time. The addition of the grammatical constraint for the raising of posttonic and pretonic *a, furthermore, will complicate the rule with a constraint that only applies to one of the four protovowels involved in this change.

The raising of *a had to begin with the backing of the vowel. According to Bourciez (1956, p. 297), the raising of *a before nasals in the north began with velarization of the vowel. Although current backing of *a is constrained by weakness and by a labial environment, it is not constrained by nasals. The raising rule so far does not provide for the backing of *a, but only for its raising to [o]. There is every reason to expect that backing, although related to raising, may have been a quite separate process. Establishing a separate rule for the backing of *a would leave the raising rule free to operate with constraints having to do only with raising (e.g., nasals). Since the grammatical constraints are special to *a, a fact that in itself could justify a separate treatment of this protovowel, this notion is strengthened. This creates a situation strikingly similar to the distinction between the tensing and raising rules of Labov, Yaeger, and Steiner (1972, pp. 70–72).

Rounding represents a major difference between low central vowels and back vowels. For although rounding increases with height among the back vowels, the jump in rounding from [a] to [o] is considerably greater than any of the increases in rounding moving up from [o] to [u]. Insofar as rounding is a redundant feature of Gascon back vowels, it could be said that the development of rounding is a major step in moving a vowel into the back series. Therefore, while the shift from [a] to [o] is a step upwards and backwards in a continuum from [a] to [u], there is a major step between [a] and [o] in the development of rounding, by which the vowel acquires a redundant feature of backness. This interpretation is supported by the fact that a labial environment predominates in the shift backwards of [a] to [o], whereas in the shift upwards to [u], although labial environment remains important, it is surpassed in importance by preceding nasal environment. The change in primary constraints represents a change in the predominant perceptual change between central and back, and low back and high back. Thus while there is no low back position that is separate from central and in line with the higher back vowels, there is undoubtedly a transitional area, characterized by the fast onset of rounding, perhaps, wherein a central vowel enters perceptually a back series. This initial backing rule, then, represents this transition, but not a sudden qualitative shift.

The backing rule can be quite simple, with nonstress, membership in a grammatical morpheme, and preceding and then following labials all serving as variable constraints:

$$(4) \qquad [+\text{central}] \rightarrow \langle +\text{back}\rangle \; / \; \langle +\text{lab}\rangle \underline{\hspace{3cm}} \langle +\text{lab}\rangle$$
$$\langle +\text{grammatical}\rangle$$
$$\langle -\text{stress}\rangle$$

It remains to explain the shift between preceding and following constraints.

The back vowel chain shift began with the shifting forward of *u to [y]. This has been frequently attributed to the Celtic substratum, but it is noteworthy that this change coincided with later stages of a long process of palatalization. It is possible that there were palatal constraints in this change, but there is no clear evidence, the change having occurred earlier than the appearance of Romance texts. Such is, however, the hypothesis argued by Jacoby (1916, p. 59 ff), whereby [u] fronted to [y] earliest in second conjugation nouns by umlaut conditioned by the plural ending in -*i. This then spread by analogy to other occurrences of *u until all occurrences shifted. The first constraints that are clearly reflected in the chain shift are involved in the second part of the shift to [y], of occurrences coming from *o. This shift is conditioned by a combination of following nasal and palatal.

Like [a] and [i], [u] is on the borderline between two vowel subsystems: front and back. Whereas the nasal constraint operates fully elsewhere, it does not in the fronting of *u or the backing of *a. These are, rather, primarily constrained by point of articulation. This works occasionally in the other direction in Soulatan, with labials attracting the high front vowel to front rounded: *priméru > [prymé] 'first.'

The secondary constraint provided by the nasal in the fronting of [u] < *o to [y] could be regarded as a combination of the constraints raising back vowels and the articulatory (palatal) constraint fronting back vowels. This conforms to the reality of this shift as both fronting and raising.

The raising rule illustrates an important difference between synchronic and diachronic variable rules. At any particular time, a constraint may predominate in a change. Normally, we assume that this is explainable in phonetic terms. When the change has occurred in the environment of that primary constraint, however, the change continues in the environment of the remaining constraints. Although the remaining constraints may be less powerfully phonetically, they gain systemic power by the pure fact of being in operation. If, then, a new class of occurrences of the segment being affected by that rule arises, the secondary constraint for the initial change may become the primary constraint for a new set of changes.

This is undoubtedly what has happened in the later stages of the Soulatan chain shift. In the shift, *oˆ raised two steps to [y] before nasals (some nasals, to be exact), and *o raised two steps to [u] before nasals and then later after nasals. Nasals commonly have more of a nasalizing and raising effect on preceding than on following vowels, thus it is phonetically logical that *o should have raised before nasals prior to raising after nasals. However, the rule for the raising of [o] < *a to [u] has as its primary constraint a preceding nasal, and as a secondary constraint, a following nasal. This is undoubtedly because of the chronologically preceding raising. The last stages of the raising of *o to [u] coincided with the last stages of the raising of posttonic *a to [o]. It is highly probable that the new occurrences of [o] fell into the old rule, although without merging with *o. Thus the secondary constraint of the rule *o > [u] became the primary constraint of ([o] < *a) > [u]. This conclusion corresponds to observations made in the context of the raising of the *a of third person plural morphemes.

It is clear that the chain shift is in some sense a single occurrence, that is, a similar force is producing all the separate raisings that make up the back chain shift. On the other hand, these changes are linearly arranged in relation to each other both insofar as each stage provides the case vide that occasions the following, and insofar as they feed constraints to each other. As shown in the case of the raising of the linking vowel, two stages of the shift in a given class of occurrences do not overlap in the speech of any one person: The previous stage must end before the following one begins. Since it has been established above that the backing rule is separate from the raising rule, the general picture is a chain shift rule overlapping with a backing rule. Here the backing rule (*a > [o]) occurs late enough in the progress of the chain shift to feed the later stage of the chain shift rule (*oˆ > [u]). Since this later stage of the chain shift is at the stage of the later constraints (preceding nasal), these constraints become the primary constraints of the later occurrences of [o] > [u].

The chain shift itself is introduced by an umlaut rule, possibly, and the palatal constraint of this umlaut rule itself carries over to front some occurrences of *oˆ. Therefore, the entire chain shift is a series of three overlapping rules: (*a*) a fronting rule, whose palatal constraint remains to front certain occurrences of [u] raising from *oˆ; (*b*) a raising rule for back vowels that applies in sequence from highest to lowest back vowel; and (*c*) a backing rule for *a that overlaps with the raising rule in such a way that the preceding nasal constraint picks up those occurrences of [o] as they are backed according to the several constraints of the backing rule. These rules would look as follows:

(5)
$$\begin{bmatrix} +\text{vocalic} \\ -\text{consonantal} \\ 4\ \text{high} \end{bmatrix} \rightarrow \langle +\text{front}\rangle\ /\!-\text{C}_0 \left\langle \begin{matrix} +\text{high} \\ -\text{back} \end{matrix}\right\rangle$$

(3c)
$$\begin{bmatrix} +\text{vocalic} \\ -\text{consonantal} \\ +\text{back} \\ x\ \text{high} \end{bmatrix} \rightarrow \langle x+y\ \text{high}\rangle\ /\ \gamma\ \langle +\text{nasal}\rangle\ \underset{\alpha\ \langle z\ \text{high}\rangle}{\rule{2cm}{0.4pt}}\ \beta\ \langle +\text{nasal}\rangle$$

(4)
$$\begin{bmatrix} +\text{vocalic} \\ -\text{consonantal} \\ +\text{central} \end{bmatrix} \rightarrow \langle +\text{back}\rangle\ /\ \langle +\text{labial}\rangle\ \underset{\substack{\langle +\text{grammatical}\rangle \\ \langle -\text{stress}\rangle}}{\rule{2.5cm}{0.4pt}}\ \langle +\text{labial}\rangle$$

Rule (5) is a rough approximation of what a palatalization rule might look like for *u and later occurrences of [u]. It simply fronts [u] when followed by a palatal (whether a consonant or a vowel) in the following syllable. Rule (3c) is the main chain shift rule which can be said to grow out of Rule (5) and which raises *oˆ to [u] earliest before a nasal. In the case of palatal nasals, these occurrences of *oˆ then continue forward by Rule (5). Rule (4), by overlapping with Rule (3c), provides additional occurrences of [o] to be picked up by the later stage of Rule (3c), at the point where that rule is affecting *o by the gamma constraint, preceding nasal. The exact sequence of application of each rule to each segment or class of segments could only be directly represented by a spelling out of the chronology of the application of the constraints. The precise time of overlapping of constraints of two rules could then be reflected, allowing a rough prediction of most lexical items.

These rules represent a compromise, or combination of pressures that undoubtedly make up a series of related phonological changes. A chain shift can provide its own impetus by the consecutive opening of cases vides, but it must originally have been set in motion by some other force—possibly palatalization in this case. As the chain shift procedes through classes of occurrences, it procedes through sets of constraints, and the very passage of time adds a sequential aspect to what might otherwise be repetitions of identical constraints. It is thus that overlapping rules may reflect reversals or reweightings of constraints. This solution to the problem of the back vowel chain shift has the advantage of capturing the relations between the successive stages of the shift, but showing no constraint out of context. One or the other of these advantages would have to be sacrificed in a description based on more particulate or more general rules.

References

Bailey, C.-J. 1972. The integration of linguistic theory. In R. P. Stockwell and R. K. S. Macaulay (Eds.), *Linguistic change and generative theory*. Bloomington and London: Indiana University Press.

Bailey, C.-J. 1973. *Variation and linguistic theory*. Washington, D.C.: Center for Applied Linguistics.

Bec, P. 1968. *Les interférences linguistiques entre Gascon et Languedocien*. Paris: Presses Universitaires de France.

Bourciez, E. 1956. *Eléments de linguistique romane* (4th ed.). Paris: C. Klincksieck.

C., J. 1895. *Etude grammaticale sur le dialecte de Couserans*. Foix.

Eckert, P. 1969a. *Grammatical constraints in phonological change: The vowels of southern France*. Unpublished Master's thesis, Columbia University.

Eckert, P. 1969b. The acoustic correlates of stress in the dialect of Ercé. Unpublished paper.

Fasold, R. 1973. The concept of 'earlier–later.' In C.-J. Bailey, R. Shuy (Eds.) *New ways of analyzing variation in English*. Washington D.C.: Georgetown University Press.

Foley, J. 1972. Rule precursors and phonological change by meta-rule. In R. P. Stockwell and R. K. S. Macaulay (Eds.), *Linguistic change and generative theory*. Bloomington and London: Indiana University Press.

Gilliéron, J., and Edmont, E. 1902–1910. *Atlas linguistique de la France*. Paris: H. Champion.

Hall, R. A., Jr. 1976. *Proto-Romance phonology*. New York: Elsevier.

Haudricourt, A. G., and Juilland, A. G. 1949. *Essai pour une histoire structurale du phonétisme français*. Paris. C. Klincksieck.

Jacoby, E. 1916. *Zur Geschichte des Wandels von lateinische u zu y in Galloromanischen*. Braunschweig: Westermann.

Labov, W. 1972. On the mechanism of linguistic change. In W. Labov, *Sociolinguistic patterns*. Philadelphia: University of Pennsylvania Press.

Labov, W. 1966. *The social stratification of English in New York City*. Washington, D.C.: Center for Applied Linguistics.

Labov, W., Yaeger, M., and Steiner, R. 1972. *A quantitative study of sound change in progress*. Philadelphia: U.S. Regional Survey.

Martinet, A. 1955. *Economie des changements phonétiques*. Berne: Francke.

Meillet, A. 1900. D'un effet de l'accent d'intensité. *Mémoires de la Société Linguistique, 11,* 165–172.

Ronjat, J. 1930. *Grammaire istorique des parlers provençaux modernes.* (Vol. I.) Montpellier: Société des Langues Romanes.

Ronjat, J. 1937. *Grammaire istorique des parlers provençaux modernes* (Vol. 3). Montpellier: Société des Langues Romanes.

Schönthaler, W. 1937. *Die Mundart des Bethmale-Tales.* Tubingen: Eugen Gobel.

Weinreich, U., Labov, W., and Herzog, M. 1968. Empirical foundations for a theory of language change. In W. P. Lehmann and Yakov Malkiel (Eds.), *Directions for historical linguistics.* Austin: University of Texas Press.

9

Geoffrey Nunberg

A FALSELY REPORTED MERGER IN EIGHTEENTH-CENTURY ENGLISH:[1] A STUDY IN DIACHRONIC VARIATION

Introduction

A good number of the first principles of historical reconstruction are based on the premise that true merger of contrasting word classes is irreversible. That is, given a sound change whereby two word classes A and B are merged as C, it is assumed that no subsequent change can operate in such a way as to affect only those members of C that are etymologically derived from A; after all, how could speakers, ignorant of etymology, ever come to diffuse a word class along etymological lines? In the words of Bréal (1900): "The public has a feeling for utility, but does not trouble at all about history."

Occasionally, however, historical linguists encounter evidence that suggests that just such a reversal of merger may have taken place. Examples are rare, but it must be remembered that a perfectly reversed merger would leave no trace in the subsequent stages of a language, and could hence be observed only when careful records of pronunciation were being made during the period of actual confusion of the word classes; a reversed merger could not be reconstructed. Given that such records are available only for the recent histories of a handful of Western languages, the scarcity of instances of apparent reversal of merger should not be surprising.

And yet, even if we restrict the field entirely to English, a surprisingly large number of potential examples can be cited. Some of these have occasioned discussion in the literature, such as the case of seventeenth-century

[1] I am grateful to Paul Cohen, William Labov, Scott Parker, Robert Newsom for their comments, and particularly Patricia Wolfe, who provided a number of helpful criticisms.

LOCATING LANGUAGE IN TIME AND SPACE

221

reflexes of Middle English /a:/ and /ẹ:/, as in *hate* and *heat*. Others are more obscure, but there is at least some evidence for reversal of merger of sixteenth-century short /o/ and short /a/, as in *pot* and *pat;* of sixteenth- and seventeenth-century dental stops and interdental fricatives in the environment __[ɚ] #, as in *ladder* and *lather*; and of late eighteenth- and early nineteenth-century London /w/ and /v/, as in *west* and *vest*.[2]

The best-documented instance of reversal of a reported merger, however, involves late seventeenth- and early eighteenth-century pronunciations of such pairs as *line* and *loin, pint* and *point,* representing the ME /i:/ and /oy/ classes. Middle English /i:/ fell to [ey] in the first stage of the Great Vowel Shift, and was subsequently backed to [əy]. The Modern English /oy/ class is largely the reflex of ME [oy] and [uy]; the [uy] allophones fell to [əy] in the seventeenth century, probably as a part of the general lowering of [u] to [ə]. We can sketch these developments as follows:[3]

	loin	line
1400	[luyn]	[li : n]
1600	[luyn]	[leyn]
1700	[ləyn]	[ləyn]

For a century after 1650, *line* and *loin* were apparently perceived by speakers as having identical nuclei. In the second half of the eighteenth century, however, the pronunciation of such words as *loin* and *point* with a central nucleus came to be stigmatized, and speakers began to restore a back nucleus to the *loin* class; by the end of the century the two word classes were again wholly distinct:

1800	[layn]	[lɔyn]

Thus, by the nineteenth century, confusion of *line* and *loin* had wholly vanished from polite speech, though it remained a feature of many rural and lower-class dialects, and survives to this day in Ireland and the county of Essex.

---

[2] Evidence bearing on the confusion of /θ, ð/ and /t, d/ can be found in Jespersen (1909, I, 7.2). A number of late-eighteenth-century sources mention confusion of /w/ and /v/ in the London dialect, such as Walker (1791); Dickens uses this to comic effect in *Pickwick* and elsewhere.

Wyld (1937) cites a number of inverse spellings involving /a/ and /o/ in the late-sixteenth-century, including Queen Elizabeth's "I pray you stap the mouthes." This confusion left in its wake such doublets as *god–gad* and *strop–strap*.

[3] This analysis is by no means universally agreed upon, and will be justified at length below.

Some Explanations of Apparent Mergers

Before going deeper into the somewhat complicated details of this reported merger, we might look briefly at some of the ways in which apparent reversals of merger could be analyzed and explained. With respect to some of the instances that have been mentioned, such as nineteenth-century *heat* and *hate*, it has been suggested (as by Dobson, 1968) that the evidence for merger having taken place is equivocal, and that the seventeenth-century reflexes of the ME [a:] and [ę:] classes remained distinctive to speakers, in which case the late seventeenth century raising of *heat* from [ę:] to [i:] would present no problem for the analyst. In the case of *heat* and *hate,* Dobson's position may be tenable, for the testimony of the grammarians is by no means univocal, and is often contradictory; the assumption that the phones were merged is based primarily on the evidence of rhymes and misspellings, which are not always reliable indices of pronunciation. Certainly, it is easier to believe that this evidence may have been misinterpreted than to assume that a merger could have been inexplicably reversed.[4]

In the case of *line* and *loin,* however, the evidence is unexceptionable that speakers felt that the phones were identical. We not only have inverse spellings, and the rhymes of such as Pope:

> And praise the easy vigour of a line
> Where Denham's strength and Waller's sweetness join.
>
> *Essay on Criticism,* 161–162

but we also have spellers, often with appended lists of homonyms; grammars of English written for foreigners; and, most important, the testimony of several generations of careful phoneticians, including Cooper, Bailey, Nares, and Kenrick. These sources often differed as to which words of the two classes were confused, and as to the social markedness of the merger; and these differences are significant, as will be seen in what follows. But the grammarians are unanimous in their insistence that merger of some of the words in the *line* and *loin* classes had taken place. The combined weight of the evidence for merger is so overwhelming that none of the philologists and linguists who have addressed themselves to the *line–loin* problem have ever thought to deny that the merger took place.

[4] Among the grammarians and orthoepists, I have found only one who actually indicates that reflexes of ME /ę:/ and /a:/ were pronounced identically; and he—Mauget (1679)—was a native Frenchman. Price (1665) distinguishes *e* from "*e* drawl'd out long" and Cooper (1687) distinguishes *e* from "*a* slender." Identification of the two vowels is commoner in the lists of homonyms that were often appended to spellers and dictionaries, but these tend to be unreliable; Price, for example, also identifies as "sounded alike" the words *ken* and *keen, fair* and *far* (see Note 12).

For a more extensive discussion of this problem, see Labov and Nunberg, 1972.

But if speakers did in fact perceive the phones as identical, then it must be explained how they could have come to reseparate the original word classes; that is, how they might have contrived access to the etymologies. Several possibilities suggest themselves. Etymology could have left its mark internally, in a regular series of morphophonemic alternations, in which case it might be argued that the two word classes retained distinctive underlying representations. It is not certain, however, that this sort of argument could have any psychological validity even under the most favorable circumstances, as when all members of a word class undergo the same regular alternation. And in the case of *loin–line*, there is no basis whatsoever for the postulation of distinctive underlying segments; what alternation does exist is irregular and often recondite. Some reflexes of ME /i:/, it is true, do alternate with /i/, as in *line* and *linear,* but many more do not, such as *pint* and *tile.* Similarly, some reflexes of /oy/ alternate with /ə/ and /u/ (e.g., *point* with *punctual, joint* with *junction*), but others alternate with /o:/ (e.g., *oil* and *oleic, foil* and *foliate*), and still others do not show even such obscure alternation, (e.g., *poison,* and *broil*). The merger of a pair like *toil* and *tile,* consequently, could not possibly have been undone by analogical reformation of one of its members.[5]

Etymology is also accessible in external sources, such as spelling, or in neighboring dialects in which a contrast is maintained. Spelling pronunciation is, in fact, the solution most often proposed for the *loin–line* problem (Jespersen, 1909; Luick, 1914; Wyld, 1936; and Kökeritz, 1953). By the eighteenth century, spelling was largely standardized, and although inverse spellings do occur, words of the *loin* class continued for the most part to be written with *oy* and *oi*; these spellings, it is argued, provided the model for restoration of the back nucleus. But this analysis presents some problems of its own. It is true that orthography—and dialect borrowing—can operate to change pronunciation, but both tend to work in an idiosyncratic and anecdotal fashion, especially when unsupported by regular morphophonemic alternation, and to respond to such factors as word meaning and frequency, unlike regular sound change. Examples are plentiful: We sometimes hear the American pronunciations [ælmond], [sælv] for *almond, salve,* but we do not encounter [sælmn] for *salmon,* or [hælv] for *halve.* Jespersen (1909, I, 2.622) mentions the substitution of [θ] for [t] in some names with orthographic *th*, such as *Anthony, Theodore,* and *Catherine;* these are contrasted with *Tony, Ted, Kate,* and *Thomas,* where the retention of [t] may be due to greater familiarity or frequency. Similarly with dialect borrowing; Bloomfield (1933) cites the well-known example (after Kloeke) of Dutch words for *house* and *mouse:*

---

[5] In Labov and Nunberg, 1972, the stronger argument is made that morphophonemic alternation is never relevant to the reconstitution of a word class unless all members participate in the alternation. For the present purposes, however, it suffices to show that, if reflexes of ME /oy/ and /i:/ were actually merged, there would be no grounds for the postulation of distinctive underlying phones.

In some rural dialects, speakers have borrowed from a prestige dialect a front vowel in *house* but not in *mouse* which is less likely to occur in official or commercial conversation. Closer to home, Paul Cohen (1971) notes some exceptions to the New York City tensing of /æ/ to /æh/—speakers may say /mæhd/ "angry," but /mæd/ "crazy," or /bæhd/ but /kæd/. The excepted forms are those whose use is associated with "educated" speech, and thus the more prestigious untensed vowel is used.

What is more, the argument that spelling pronunciation or dialect borrowing was responsible for restoration of [oy] runs afoul of the well-established dialectological principle that mergers expand at the expense of distinctions, as convincingly demonstrated by Herzog (1965) and Garde (1961). In fact, all evidence seems to suggest that spelling and dialect borrowing alone are insufficient to restore a distinction once it has been lost, even where there is pressure from teachers and peers who regularly make the distinction. For example, speakers of American dialects in which *marry*, *merry*, and *Mary* are pronounced identically are unable to identify these forms when pronounced in isolation by a speaker who does distinguish them, even when they have been exposed to dialects in which the forms are un-merged, and, more surprisingly, even when the analogy of spellings before *l* has been pointed out to them—in such words as *salient, selling,* and *Sally,* these speakers do, after all, distinguish the spellings *aCV, eCCV,* and *aCCV* as [e(y)], [ɛ], and [æ], respectively. (I have confirmed this inability to identify *marry, merry,* and *Mary* in an informal experiment.)[6] In still another instance, Western Pennsylvania speakers cannot utilize a consistent spelling difference to distinguish such pairs as *hock* and *hawk.*[7]

The argument that spelling pronunciation was responsible for the restoration of the *loin–line* distinction must thus be viewed with a certain amount of scepticism. Certainly, it is a mistake to generalize from a handful of anecdotal instances to the categorical re-formation of an entire word class, in the absence of empirical support, and to proclaim, as Jespersen did that "the disappearance of [ai] for *oi* in polite speech is no doubt due to the influence of the spelling (1909, I, 11.53)." Nevertheless, given the basic assumptions of historical linguistics, it is hard to see what other explanation there could be for the restoration. There is recent evidence, however, that disputes some of these assumptions and that suggests another solution to the *loin–line* prob-

[6] Randomized lists of *marry, Mary,* and *merry* were read by the author to five subjects, all of whom were college-educated (two were teachers of college English), and all of whom had lived in the East, where the distinction is maintained, for at least two years. The subjects identified tokens correctly only 39% of the time, which is just slightly better than random. Even when the analogy of spellings before /l/ was pointed out, and after they had had some practice, they could identify only 49% of the tokens. Yet native New Yorkers who were present successfully identified all tokens, and were astonished that the Midwesterners could not hear the difference.

[7] For a fuller discussion of this and other examples, see Labov, Yaeger, and Steiner (1972) and Labov and Nunberg (1972).

lem. This evidence grows out of the investigations of sound change in progress conducted by William Labov and his associates, some of the findings of
which have been discussed in Labov and Wald, 1969, Labov and Nunberg,
1972, and, in greater depth, in Labov, Yaeger, and Steiner, 1972.

Another Explanation for Reported Mergers

Labov, Yaeger, and Steins (henceforth LYS) examined a number of
English dialects for which merger of two word classes had been reported;
these included Albuquerque *pool–pull,* New York City *source–sauce,* Norwich (England) *too–toe,* and Essex (England) *loin–line.* In each instance, it
was determined that, although speakers reported the pairs as "sounding the
same" and were unable to identify tokens with any consistency in minimal
pair and commutation tests, they nonetheless distinguished the pairs in production. One Essex speaker, for example, was wholly unable to identify his
own productions of *loin* and *line;* in fact, when his own reading of a list of
pairs was played back to him, he misidentified more than 50% of the tokens.
Yet he consistently showed a higher first formant in *line* than in *loin,* and
when he was asked to make an effort to maximally differentiate the pairs, the
difference in formant heights was increased. This pattern of misidentification
combined with distinct production appears repeatedly in LYS.

It has long been known that speaker reports cannot be taken as infallible
indices of differences in pronunciation; a speaker might, for example, be
misled by spelling to report that his tokens of *prince* and *prints* were "not the
same" when in fact the tokens were identical acoustically. The work of
Labov and his associates suggests that the opposite is also true—speaker
reports of sameness cannot be taken as assurances of merger. Speakers can
produce differences that, in Labov's words, "they cannot hear, or, at least,
are not aware of hearing."

It might be argued that these observations merely reflect a stage in a
gradual sound change just prior to merger of two word classes, and that
succeeding generations of speakers would necessarily show merger in both
perception and production; but, in at least one case, this could not be the
explanation. Merger of Essex *line–loin* has been reliably reported on a number of occasions, starting with Ellis's (1874) English dialect survey of 1868,
and almost certainly dates back to the original late-seventeenth-century
merger. Many generations must have learned to produce a nonfunctional
distinction without allowing collapse of the two word-classes.

We must, then, admit the possibility that the original merger of the
line–loin classes was not a true one; that a production difference was retained, notwithstanding the reports of the contemporary grammarians. In the
case of reported merger of Albuquerque *pool–pull,* even linguists with phonetic training have considerable difficulty in identifying tokens; there can be no

insult to the memory of Cooper in suggesting that if the difference between the vocalic nuclei of his *loin* and *line* was equally slight, he would have been unable to tell them apart. But in so suggesting, we appear to be painting ourselves into a corner; how can we ever distinguish between real and reported merger in the history of a language, if none of the available evidence shall be sensitive to the difference?

A Model for Reversal of Merger

It is true that nothing short of spectrographic evidence could resolve the problem beyond doubt, but we can still go beyond mere speculation. By examining the first-hand reports of the grammarians, we can show that the chronological pattern of merger and reseparation is incompatible with the assumption that spelling pronunciation was responsible for the change, while consistent with a model of merger and reversal based on the data gathered by Labov and associates.

Figures 9.1A–9.1E schematize such a model. In Figure 9.1A, the inner (solid) ellipse represents the constant probability/error contour for tokens of vocalic nuclei of a given word class. In other words, if we ask a speaker to repeat the same word several times, and map the first two formants of the vowel, this ellipse will best describe the distribution of tokens; Points A, B,

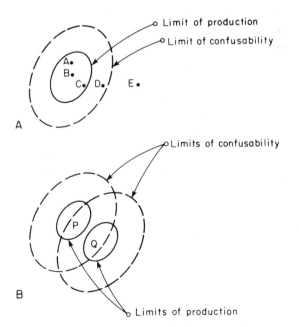

FIGURE 9.1 *A model for reversal of a perceptual merger.*

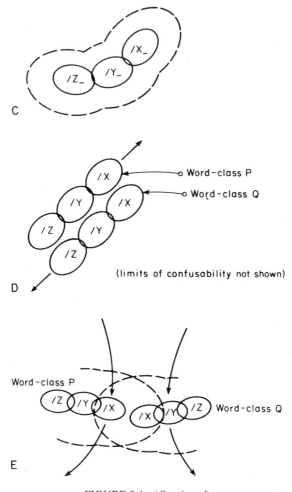

FIGURE 9.1 (*Continued*)

and C may be taken as representative of such tokens. Let us call this inner ellipse the LIMIT OF PRODUCTION. The fact that a speaker produces no tokens whose nuclei fall outside this limit does not necessarily entail, however, that he is capable of distinguishing any token whose nucleus falls outside the ellipse from one whose nucleus falls within it. If, for example, we play for him two tokens, one of which falls within the solid ellipse, at C, the other of which falls just outside it, at D, he may find it difficult or impossible to tell them apart; whereas a third token, at E, much farther from the limit of production, he will always be able to distinguish from C. We can thus establish a scale of points from C to E such that the average rate of misidentification of C and P_n, a point on the scale, declines from 50% to 0%. As with other perceptual phenomena, we can then establish as the just noticeable difference (JND) the distance between C and that point at which the error rate drops below 50%. The broken ellipse describes the locus off all points P_i such that P_i is just noticeably different from some point within the word class.[8] Let us call this the LIMIT OF CONFUSABILITY, recognizing its rough equivalence to Martinet's "margin of safety."[9]

It is important to note that the JND should not be regarded as reflecting only the perceptual capabilities of the subject, though such capabilities clearly fix its inner limit; such variables as the subject's reward for correct identification, and the task he is ultimately asked to perform to effect identification, can be manipulated to increase or decrease the JND.[10] Nor would any linguist wish to call "functional" a distinction that speakers were capable of identifying only 51% of the time.[11] It is difficult or impossible to say how different two targets must be so that speakers can learn to discriminate them in production, or, worse yet, to be able to identify them under given circumstances. The critical point is that these two JNDs need not be identical; two points might be discriminable for a child learning to produce the phones of his language, and at the same time not discriminable to an adult who is casually asked to identify two tokens.

The reported mergers observed by LYS can now be schematized as in Figure 9.1B. Word classes P and Q are distinct in production, but the limit of production for each class falls within the limit of confusability of the other; the speaker reports that the two classes are "the same," and is unable to identify tokens consistently.

---

[8] It might be argued that the limit of confusability should be defined in terms of points that cannot be distinguished from all, rather than some, points that fall within the limit of production, but this seems to me too stringent a definition. If, for example, some point p_i, which falls outside the limit of production, can be distinguished from some point p_j, which falls within the limit of production, we would then have to say that p_i was distinct from points within the word class, even though it is clear that a good many tokens falling within the word class could not be distinguished from it. Note that this proposal might also force us to draw the ellipse of confusability so that it intersected the limit of production, so that two tokens whose nuclei were in free variation would have to be labeled as distinct, which is a contradiction in terms.

[9] If two classes of vocalic nuclei are distinguished by some feature other than their first and second formants, then these can overlap as much as possible without confusion. We are, of course, interested here in cases where production differences are not reported by speakers, and not in cases where speakers are capable of distinguishing two vowels whose first and second formants are the same, but which are distinguished by a difference in length, *etc*. If, for example, a speaker cannot identify tokens of word classes A and B, and their first and second formants are different, then any difference in length will be redundantly nonfunctional.

[10] For a cogent review of the psychological literature dealing with this issue, see Galanter, 1962.

[11] Nor would we want to claim that a distinction must be identifiable in isolation 100% of the time in order for it to be labeled "functional." Obviously, if the term is to have any meaning, then it must be defined with respect to context. Most linguists admit the artificiality of testing in isolation for minimal differences, but continue to use the procedure.

Figure 9.1C represents precisely the same situation as in Figure 9.1A, except that here a single word class is shown as a series of ellipses, which represent its characteristic allophones. This is a more realistic representation for most word classes, whose vocalic nuclei will be realized differently according to their phonetic environment. In Figure 9.1C, /__X, /__Y, and /__Z represent environments in complementary distribution.

Let us suppose, now, that two word classes P and Q pass close by each other on parallel tracks, moving in opposite directions, as schematized in Figure 9.1D. This is the configuration that has been proposed as an alternative to flip-flop rules, and which correlates closely with the mechanism proposed for the Great Vowel Shift development of [i:] > [ay] and [ay] > [e:] (LYS, p. 201). If the allophones of P and Q are distributed symmetrically—if, for example, nuclei in both classes are highest in /__X—then each allophone in P will pass for the same length of time through the limit of confusability of its corresponding allophone in Q, and vice versa. Thus, we would predict that speakers would confuse allophones in /__X, /__Y, and /__Z for the same length of time. We can compare this configuration to the passage along parallel tracks of two trains; each car in train A will be lined up for the same length of time with its opposite number in train B.

If the two word classes are not moving along parallel tracks, however, or if the allophones of one word class are not distributed symmetrically with respect to the allophones of the other, then the extent and duration of confusion may vary for different subclasses. In Figure 9.1E, for example, one word class passes close to another on oblique tracks, and their allophones are arranged asymmetrically. Accordingly, the allophones in /__X of word class P must pass through a greater portion of the ellipse of confusability of its corresponding allophone in word class Q than allophones in /__Y, and allophones in /__Z do not pass through each others' ellipses of confusability at all. Thus, allophones in /__X of P and Q will be confused for a relatively longer period than allophones in /__Y, and allophones in /__Z will not be confused at all. In this type of reported merger, then, the extent and duration of reports of merger should vary according to the phonetic shape of the pairs involved.[12]

Application of the Model to the *Line–Loin* Merger

It must now be demonstrated that the *line–loin* merger fits the hypothetical schema of Figure 9.1E. In order to do this, we must be able to determine,

---

[12] This argument is couched in terms of a picture of sound change as taking place gradually in continuous phonological space, though perhaps less in a series of infinitesimal movements than in a series of small jumps. Most of the observations made by LYS support this view. Note, however, that these jumps could be rather large without compromising the model, and that, as long as we have testimony that two word classes were confused at a certain stage, we must assume that they remained in close proximity for some period.

first, the premerger distributions of allophones, and second, the chronology of reports of confusion. Let us turn, accordingly, to the details of the merger.

What I have been calling the "*loin* class" consists of a group of words of various origins, all of which are reported with Early Modern English [oy] or [uy]. The vast majority of these words are French borrowings, and were introduced in the Middle English period; their ultimate origins were (after Jespersen, 1909) (*a*) from Lat. *au* + *i*, as *joy, cloister*; (*b*) from Lat. *ǒ* + *i*, as *oil, oyster;* (*c*) from Lat. *ǒ* or *ǔ* + *i*, as *moist, point;* (*d*) from late Fr. *oi*, earlier *ei*, as *royal, loyal;* and (*e*) from anomalous or obscure sources, as *joist* (from OF *giste*), and *toy* (origin uncertain; perhaps from M. Du. *toi*). Owing to the Romance origin of the word class, E. Mod. Eng. [oy] and [uy] appear only word finally and before apical consonants.

Words of the *loin* class appear in Middle English spelled with both *u* and *o*, and the earliest orthoepists (Hart, 1569; Mulcaster, 1582; Bullokar, 1588) all distinguish two diphthongs, apparently [oy] and [uy]. Luick (1914–1940) claimed to find an etymological basis at least for Bullokar's classification, but the distribution of [oy] and [uy] does not appear to have been made along etymological lines, except insofar as these influenced the phonetic shape in French. For example, *toil* and *voice* share etyma of Class (*c*), yet *toil* is assigned [uy] by both Mulcaster and Bullokar, whereas *voice* is assigned [oy] by Hart and Bullokar. (It is rare, of course, to find a single word cited by all sources.) Similarly, Mulcaster assigns [oy] to *avoid* and [uy] to *foil*, yet both belong to Class (*b*).

If the assignment of [uy] or [oy] had been based on etymology, then we might expect to find minimal pairs for the two diphthongs, and to be able to distinguish two surface phonemes. However, as will be demonstrated in what follows, the height of the nucleus was in fact conditioned by the phonetic environment; the (orthographic) *oy* class formed a functional and psychological unit for Early Modern English speakers (although they may have been more sensitive to the difference between [oy] and [uy] than to most other allophonic variants, since [o] and [u] were elsewhere distinctive).

Around the middle of the seventeenth century, the [uy] allophones began to fall to a mid-central position, probably as a part of a general shift of short [u] to [ə]. At this point, it ran into the [əy] < [ey] < [i:], so that *line* and *loin* were realized with approximately the same nucleus; hence the confusion of the two. The shift of [uy] > [əy] did not, however, affect the [oy] allophones of the *oy* class; the nucleus of these words remained in a non-high back position, and, accordingly, these words were not reported as merged with reflexes of ME /i:/. These shifts are schematized in Figures 9.2A and 9.2B. Finally, around the middle of the eighteenth century, the [əy] from [uy] was again backed to [oy], while the [əy] from [ey] began to descend to [ay], so that the two phones were again discriminable; this situation is represented in Figure 9.2C.

We can now note the similarity between this situation and the hypothetical schema of Figure 9.1E. The *loin* and *line* classes passed on tangential

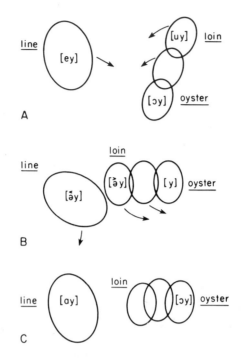

FIGURE 9.2 *Projection of hypothetical model onto* line–loin *merger: (A) c. 1600, (B) c. 1700, (C) c. 1800.*

tracks, and we will accordingly predict that, if they remained distinct in production, then the chronology of their reported merger and reseparation will have varied according to the distribution of their allophones. If, on the other hand, the merger was a true one, and the word classes were produced, as well as perceived, identically, then we must predict that the chronology and extent of merger and reseparation will reflect such factors as word frequency, and will show no close correlation with the phonetic shape of the word involved.

Testimony on the *Loin–Line* Merger

Let us now turn to the problem of determining the premerger distribution of allophones in the *loin* and *line* classes. As [u] and [o] were distinctive in Early Modern English, most phoneticians and orthoepists had little difficulty in distinguishing the diphthongs [uy] and [oy], and there is a good deal of testimony with respect to these diphthongs. In looking at this testimony, we will be concerned with establishing two points. First, what phonetic factors, if any, governed the height of the precentralization nucleus of the *loin* class? Second, how many allophones were there? If every word in the class was realized with either [oy] or [uy], and it was only those words in [uy] that were centralized, then the chronology of merger and reseparation could tell us nothing, for all those words that were centralized would have been centralized at the same time and we would observe no differential effect. And if the reseparation also took place simultaneously, as we would assume, then we could mount against an explanation via spelling pronunciation only the weaker argument that factors of word use and meaning had NOT been observed to affect the chronology of merger, but we could not show that the chronology had been affected by phonetic shape.

When we turn to the testimony of the contemporary grammarians and orthoepists, however, we find apparent chaos: One source shows an original [uy] in *boil,* another [oy]; some writers report merger of *kine* and *coin,* and others do not; the bulk of the evidence seems to be hopelessly and haphazardly contradictory. This disorder is the traditional lot of the student of Early Modern English, and there has been a traditional solution: to select two or three of the "best" grammarians as representative of their speech communities, using the others for the ancillary purposes of settling differences, filling in lacunae, etc. This is the procedure followed by Jespersen, Dobson, and Chomsky and Halle—researchers whose approaches to theoretical problems are otherwise quite disparate. Even when an attempt has been made to treat a broader range of data, as by Wyld, or Wolfe (1969), it has not been possible to generalize systematically over the testimony.

The problem of reconciling these data is in fact very like the problem of establishing a coherent grammar for a group of individual speakers, and may admit of the same solution. The techniques devised by Labov and other researchers for the systematization of synchronic variation can also be applied to the diachronic data that concern us here. It is true that we do not have the large numbers of speakers and elicitations that such studies have used, but we do have some 40 or 50 grammars, spellers, and dictionaries written during the relevant period, certainly a respectable sampling. For purposes of this study, I have selected 19 of these sources—written between 1569 and 1799—and tabulated all citations of pronunciations of words in the *oy* class.[13] The grammars were selected on the basis of clarity, completeness, and, in some cases, availability. Together, they yielded almost 200 separate

---

[13] This procedure has, of course, the weakness of allowing inferior, derivative sources the same standing as the great orthoepists like Hart and Cooper. In particular, we have no way of determining to what extent a source is citing his own pronunciation, and to what extent he is citing the pronunciation established by some previous source. For instance, Aicken (1693) is clearly influenced by Cooper (1687), and uses much of the same terminology. There is some discrepancy, however, in the choice of citation forms, albeit not as much as we might wish. This is the most egregious example; most writers of spellers and school grammars, even when mightily influenced by an earlier source, did vary the forms cited. There is no sure way to do away with this uncertainty; we can only assume that a derivative source would not have cited the same pronunciation as the model unless such a pronunciation was reasonably general. In any

citations, which were then characterized in terms of variable-input rules.[14] A complete summary of the data can be found in Table 9.1.

The sources vary enormously, of course, in both manner and clarity of presentation, and each source required some analysis and interpretation. For the most part, however, it was relatively easy to determine whether a writer had a high or mid nucleus in a given form, though often impossible to determine its precise phonetic value. Mulcaster (1582) may be regarded as more or less typical:

> [y should be used in place of i]. . . . Thirdlie, oi, the diphthong sounding upon the o, for difference sake, from the other, which soundeth upon the u, wold be written with a y, as ioy, anoy, toy, boy, whereas anoint, appoint, foil and such seme to have an u. And yet when i goeth before the diphthong, tho it sound upon the u, it were better oy, then oi, as ioynt, ioyn . . . likewise if oi with i, soundeth upon the o, it may be noted for difference from the other sound, with the streight accent, as, boíe, enoíe.

Mulcaster's orthography is impossibly obscure, but it is clear from this passage that he had a high nucleus in some words, those which "soundeth upon

---

event, there is sufficient agreement among sources that were clearly original to ensure that most of the statistical generalizations are justified.

Another related problem is that we have no way of controlling for dialectal differences among the sources; here again, we can only hope that such differences will be absorbed in the statistical wash, while excluding obvious cases of Irish or Scottish dialect from the sample.

A number of sources, including some of the best orthoepists, had to be excluded from the sample because they cited only a handful of forms, or because their notation was insufficiently clear to me. For all sources used, only forms actually cited were included in the sample; if a writer said that oy was pronounced like "i long" in words X, Y, and Z, but with o elsewhere, only forms X, Y, and Z were included.

The lists of homonyms often included in spellers and grammars were felt to be too unreliable to be used in the sample. For instance, Price (1665) gives us the following couplet, which might lead us to assume homonymy of beat and bait:

> Then the make-bait began to beat,
> When he could do nought with his bait.

But a few lines down, we encounter the following:

> Fair mayds do use to feast, and fare,
> Without all fear, in the far fair.

where it is clear that far and fair could not have been pronounced with identical vowels. Another problem with such lists is that they would have skewed the lists in favor of citations of lexical items for which minimal pairs existed, such as loin–line and oil–isle, to the expense of forms like join and broil. There is an inherent skewing in all texts in favor of a few of the most common lexical items, of course, but about that we can do nothing.

[14] Given the nature of the data, it is not surprising that they could be characterized as easily by implicational scales as by variable rules. We will want to claim, however, that the variable rules involved determined, not the probability of application of a single raising rule, but rather the relative height of the nucleus along a continuum; for these purposes the Bickerton–Bailey model would be awkward.

the u," and a low nucleus in others, those "sounding upon the o." Later, when we come to the period of actual confusion of the *loin* and *line* classes, it becomes even easier to determine which words of the *loin* class were centralized, for these are almost always identified as "sounding with i long," or the like.

Table 9.2 summarizes the testimony of the grammarians with respect to the height of the nucleus of words in the *oy* class for the precentralization period. The word class has been broken down into phonetic subclasses, and the index of [uy] (/[oy]) computed for each subclass. Where variation between two pronunciations is indicated, with no stigmatization assigned to either variant, the citation has been split and counted as half [uy] and half [oy]. Clearly, the presence of a high nucleus was favored in certain environments and not in others; we have only 25 citations of [uy] for words in which the diphthong is not either preceded by a labial stop or followed by a liquid or a nasal. We can make the effects of the phonetic environments even more explicit if we broaden the data base, and allow the citations of precentralization nuclei to be combined with the citations for the postcentralization period. In order to do this, we must be able to establish that the same factors that governed the height of the pre-1650 nuclei of the class also governed its subsequent centralization. Table 9.3 gives the correlations between citations of [uy] and later [əy], according to the relevant phonetic environments. These indices are not significantly different; we can therefore make the assumption that the same factors that raised the nucleus before 1650 favored its subsequent centralization, or, in other words, that those nuclei that were high were most likely to have been centralized. Accordingly, we may feel justified in lumping together the citations of [uy] and [əy], in order to increase the data base upon which more precise assessments of the effect of the phonetic environments can be made; this will, in turn, allow us to tease out the factors that have created the slight discrepancies in Table 9.2.

Table 9.4 shows the effect of the phonetic environments on combined citations of [uy] and [əy]. With the larger sample, we can demonstrate two further conditioning factors: the environments [j]__ and __#, the latter of which operates to disfavor [uy] and [əy]. We might also wish to add to this list that [uy] and [əy] were favored in closed syllables ending in voiceless stops, as in *point* and *joist*; the index of [uy]/[əy] here is .86 ($N = 30$). However, all but two of the citations are for words in which a nasal precedes the voiceless stop, so that it is difficult to establish whether or not this phenomenon is restricted exclusively to nasals.

If we now reanalyze the data in Table 9.3, allowing for the added conditioning environments revealed in Table 9.4, we discover that the discrepancies between citations of [uy] and citations of [əy] virtually disappear. The index of [uy] in the environment [p,b]__, for example, is .53, and that of [əy] is .67. If, however, we omit from each column citations of *boy*, in which the disfavoring environment __# is present, we find that the indices for [uy] and

TABLE 9.1

Reports of Grammarians on oy *Class Nuclei*

Number of favoring environ- ments	Word	Precentralization period						Centralization			
		Ety- mol- ogy	Hart, 1569*	Mul- caster, 1582*	Bull- okar, 1586*	Gil, 1621*	Hodges, 1653	Cooper, 1687*	Aicken, 1693	Jones, 1701	Green- wood, 1711
*2	appoint	3		u			u				i
*2	point	3		u		u	u	i	i		i
*2	anoint	3		u				i	i		i
*2	joint	3		u	o	u		i			
2	join	3	u	u	o	ʊ			i	i	i
2	boil	3	ʊ			ʊ	o	i	i	i	ə
2	broil	3				ʊ		i	i	i	ə
2	spoil	2			o	u	o			i	
1	coin	3	o	u				o		i	
1	loin	3								i	
1	foil	3		u	u	ʊ	o			i	
1	oil	2				o		i	i		ə
1	toil	3		u	u			i	i		ə
*1	joist	5		u			u				
1	poison	2						i	i	i	
1	boy	5	u	o	o	o					
1	joy	1		o	o	o		o		o	o
0	toy	5		o					o		
0	oyster	2		o						o	
0	noise	1			o		o				o
0	voice	3	o	ʊ	o	o	o				
0	void	2			o	o					
(1)	loyal	4			o	o		o		*i	
0	voyage	4			o	o		o		*i	

Number of favoring environments
  2—Both preceding and following environments favor original [uy] or subsequent [əy]
  1—Either preceding or following environment favors original [uy] or subsequent [əy]
  0—Neither preceding nor following environment favors original [uy] or subsequent [əy]
  *—Syllable shape in / __ [+cons] [+cons/+tens] #
  (1)—Environment favorable to original [uy] or subsequent [əy] in some dialects
Etymology (after Jespersen, 1909)
  1—From Latin *au* + *i*
  2—From Latin *ŏ* + *i*
  3—From Latin *ō* or *ū* + *i*
  4—From Late OF *oi*, earlier *ei*
  5—From other sources
Sources
  An asterisk after a source (as "Kenrick, 1773*") indicates that this is generally considered to be one of the "better" or "more reliable" grammarians or orthoepists.

[əy], respectively, become .63 and .64. A similar pattern emerges when we break down the citations for __[n]: The index of [uy] for words in the environment __[nt] is .88; for [əy], .82. The index of [uy] for words in the environment __[n]# is .58, that of [əy] is .58. Finally, we note that the

Centralization			Retreat of centralization							Number of u/ə/i	Total number of citations
Lediard, 1725*	Tuite, 1726	Douglas, 1740*	Rudd, 1755	Bailey, 1755*	Fenning, 1751	Kenrick, 1773*	Nares, 1784*	Walker, 1791*	Adams, 1799*		
i										3.5	4
i							*i	*i		8.5	10
i		i		i						6.5	7
i			*i				*i			5	7
i		i	*i	i		i	*i		i	9.5	14
i	i	i	o			i	*i	*i	i	9	15
i	i	i	o		i		*i			8	11
i					i			*i		4	7
i		o					o	o	o	2	9
i		i								2.5	3
i			o		o				o	3.5	8
	o	i	o	o		*i	o			4	10
	o	i	o	o	o	*i	o			6	11
										2	2
i							*i			4	5
o	o			o						1	7
o										—	7
o										—	3
o		o								—	4
	o	o		o			o			—	7
	o	o					o			0.5	8
										—	2
										0.5	4
										0.5	2

Citations

i—Indicates that the word is identified as being "sounded with i long" or in some other way assigned the pronunciation of the ME /i:/ class

ə—Indicates that the word is assigned a central nucleus, but is not identified with the pronunciation of reflexes of ME /i:/

ə,i,u—Indicate that the pronunciation given is cited with nucleus [ə], [i] or [u] alternating with [o]; neither form is stigmatized

*i—Indicates that a pronunciation with the vowel of the ME /i:/ class occurs and is cited as "vulgar," etc.

Numbers of citations

The first figure is the total number of citations of the word for which u or i are given. Where u or i are cited as being in alternation with o, that citation has been counted as 0.5. The second figure gives the total number of citations for the word among the sources used.

References

References for all sources can be found in the bibliography.

category "elsewhere" in Table 9.3 includes words in the environment [ǰ]__; when these are excluded, the index of [uy] becomes .04, and that of [əy], .06.

Lest it be thought that the correlation of these phonetic factors with an original high nucleus is merely an accident of the etymology of the forms involved, we can further demonstrate that the effect of favoring environ-

TABLE 9.2

Effects of Phonetic Environment on Height of Precentralization Nucleus of oy *Class*

Phonetic shape	Number of citations	Index of [uy]
/__[n(t)]	15	.76
/__[l]	14	.50
/[p,b]__	16	.53
Elsewhere	18	.14

TABLE 9.3

Correlation of Environments Favoring [u] (Pre-1650) with Environments Favoring [ə] (Post-1650)

Phonetic shape	Index of [uy] (*N*)	Index of [əy] (*N*)
/__[n]	.76 (15)	.69 (39)
/__[l]	.50 (14)	.57 (48)
/[p,b]__	.53 (16)	.67 (38)
Elsewhere	.14 (18)	.04 (21)

TABLE 9.4

Indices of [uy]/[əy], According to Environment

Phonetic shape	Index of [uy]/[əy]	Number of citations
/__[n(t)]	.70	53
/__[l]	.56	62
/__[s,z,d]	.43	28
/__#	.06	17
/[p,b]__	.63	54
/[j]__	.55	30
/[t,k,f,v]__	.36	71

ments was additive, exactly as we would predict if we were dealing with weighted variables. Table 9.5 shows that the index of [uy]/[əy] was highest where both preceding and following environments were favorable to it. To a good first-order approximation, the relationship between the number of environments favorable and the index is linear; the Pierson correlation coefficient is .98. The discrepancy between the indices for preceding and following environments is not significant (by chi square, $p > .25$).

There is nothing surprising in this distribution; we would expect to find [uy] exactly where we do find it; that is, in the environments [p, b, ǰ]__ and __[l,n]. Vowels tend to be most back before [l]; we could cite the Early Modern English development of [al] > [ɔl], as in *tall*, or the development of French [al] > [ɔw] > [o], as in *paume*, or the alternation in Philadelphia English of [ɛow] ~ [o] in *go-goal*, among numerous examples. Similarly, we would expect to see a rounded variant after a labial stop, especially if we remember that there was a sixteenth- and seventeenth-century tendency to insert a labiovelar glide in these environments; Wallis (1653) gives us *pwot* for *pot*, and the pronunciation [bwoy] has survived for some 400 years as a variant of *boy*, though the history of this word is somewhat uncertain, and this may represent a special case. Raising after a preceding palatal is by no means uncommon, as witness palatal diphthongization in Old West Saxon, or the Standard American pronunciation of *just* (adv.) as [ǰist]; we would assume that this would have held for [č], as well as for [ǰ], but we have surprisingly few citations for *choice*, though these all show it as centralized. The raising of vowels before nasals, especially [m, n], is more problematic; as LYS put it, "vowels before nasal consonants generally rise. The explanation for this principle is not yet clear, though one can advance various speculative arguments for particular cases." As examples, LYS cite tensing

TABLE 9.5
Effects on Nucleus of Multiple Environments

Environments favoring [uy]/[əy]	Index of [uy]/[əy]	Number of citations
None (as in *oyster*, *toy*)	.05	30
Only preceding (as in *boy, poison*)	.33	21
Only following (as in *toil, coin*)	.44	41
Both preceding and following (as in *boil, join*)	.71	75

of NYC /æ/ before [m] and [n], and raising of [en] to [in] in Southern American English. To these examples we could add the Early Middle English development of /an/ > /ɔn/, as *stan* > *stone,* and the frequent raising of Pr. Gmc. /o/, /e/ to /u/, /i/ before /n/ and raising of Gascon a, o before nasals (Eckert, Chapter 8, this volume).

Formulation of the Centralization Rules

We are now in a position to write a rule to describe the pre-centralization distribution of [oy] allophones:

$$(1) \quad \begin{bmatrix} +\text{voc} \\ -\text{cons} \\ +\text{back} \end{bmatrix} \rightarrow \langle x \text{ high}\rangle \, / \, \begin{array}{c}\left\langle\begin{array}{c}+\text{ant} \\ -\text{cor} \\ -\text{cont}\end{array}\right\rangle \\ \langle +\text{del rel}\rangle\end{array} \underline{\quad} \begin{bmatrix} -\text{voc} \\ -\text{cons} \\ -\text{back} \end{bmatrix}\left\langle\begin{array}{c}+\text{seg} \\ +\text{son} \\ +\text{nas}\end{array}\right\rangle\langle +\text{cons}\rangle$$

Rule (1) states that /oy/ was variably realized as [uy]; the value of x will be highest for [p, b]__ and __[n], and somewhat lower for [č, ǰ]__ and __[l]. This formulation is neutral, however, with respect to the second question we asked earlier, the question of how many height distinctions there were. The variables in Rule (1) could be construed as giving us the probability that one of two discrete targets, [oy] or [uy], would be realized in a given form; or they could be construed as establishing for each form a position on a continuum stretching from [o] to [u].[15] Here, unfortunately, the grammarians can be of no direct help to us, because the phonetic distinctions are simply too subtle; we can only argue from analogous synchronic data. Labov, Yaeger, and Steiner examine in detail the spectrographic records of a number of word classes having similarly complex distributions of allophones; they find that these allophones tend to be spread out along a continuum. For New York City /æ/, for example, they state: "front tense vowels are raised in height to a variable degree, and this increase in height is favored by varying degrees of peripherality [3.2.2.5]." There is no reason to suspect that the seventeenth-century /oy/ class was in any important regard different from the instances observed by LYS; accordingly, we will assume that Rule (1) operated to array the nuclei along a continuum from [ɔ] or [o] to [u].

We can turn now to the centralization of [uy]. We have already noted that this development has been linked by Jespersen and others to the EModE centralization of short [u] to [ə] in such words as *but* and *hunt.* But there are too few early attestations to enable us to fix the chronology of these changes

---

[15] Whether the low variant was in fact [oy] or [ɔy] is difficult to determine. I have transcribed it throughout as [oy], since the pre-1650 sources tend to identify it with short [o]. Later sources tend to give [ɔy]; this lowering would in fact be one of the consequences of the rule formulation that will be given to the change; but the argument is in any event irrelevant to the main points being made here.

beyond doubt, and an extensive discussion of the evidence would take us rather far afield. So I will treat the centralization of [uy] as an autonomous development.

The centralization rule will be formulated in terms of the apparatus made available by LYS, as was Rule (1) which stated the distribution of precentralization allophones of /oy/. It will not be necessary here to defend this approach against other presentations, such as Chomsky and Halle's; it is sufficient to note that the treatment of systematic variation is intractible in the Chomsky–Halle framework, and that Chomsky and Halle have either ignored reports of variant pronunciations of EModE /oy/, or dismissed them.[16]

On the basis of widespread synchronic observations, LYS have established three general principles of vowel shifting:

1. In chain shifts, tense vowels rise.
2. In chain shifts, lax vowels usually fall, particularly the lax nuclei of upgliding diphthongs.
3. In chain shifts, back vowels move to the front.

It is, of course, the second principle that interests us here. Although this principle is formulated with respect to chain shifts, it is not limited to them; LYS write: "Principles I and II . . . operate generally in sound change, but without the compelling force that we see in chain shifts [4.3]." They suggest that these principles can best be formulated with respect to Stockwell's feature [peripheral], which they correlate with extreme formant differences: Front vowels are described as [+peripheral] when their nucleus shows high F2 values relative to neighboring front vowels, and back vowels as [+peripheral] if they show low F2 relative to neighboring back vowels. Although vowels that are [+tense] will generally be realized as [+peripheral], the features retain some independence, as it is recognized that there can be central vowels that are long and monophthongal, and consequently [+tense], but with respect to which the peripherality feature cannot be applied. Peripherality corresponds to the outside of phonological space, and vowels that are [−peripheral] are hence more central than those that are [+peripheral], but an independent feature [central] must still be used.

Labov, Yaeger, and Steiner devote considerable space to a discussion of the Great Vowel Shift; there is not space here to present either their arguments or their full conclusions. Within the context of their formulations, however, we can account for the centralization of [uy]; the relevant rules require only minor adjustments. The peripherality of [uy] will be established by LYS's rule (P6):

(P6) Laxing of diphthongal nuclei
$$[2 + z \text{ high}] \rightarrow [-\text{peri}] / \_\_ [+\text{peri}]$$

---

[16] Chomsky and Halle in fact ignore Hart's citation of [u] in *boy* and (as a variant) in *boil*.

Since upglides are automatically [+peripheral], and since a vowel cannot be followed by another vowel, this rule affects only the nuclei of upgliding diphthongs. The notation "2 + z high" indicates vowels of height 2—the height of [e] and [o]—or greater; this rule will thus operate to render [−peripheral] the nuclei of [iy] and [uw], but not of [ɔy], which LYS find to be [+peripheral] in most dialects. Since /iy/, /uw/, and /oy/ were the only upgliding diphthongs at this historical stage of English, this rule will provide the right input for the vowel shift rule (P7) that follows it:

(P7) Vowel Shift

$$[z \text{ high}] \rightarrow [z + \alpha \text{ high}] / \begin{bmatrix} \overline{\alpha \text{peri}} \\ -\text{cen} \\ +\text{str} \end{bmatrix} \left\{ \begin{matrix} [\alpha \text{cons}] \\ [+\text{cen}] \\ \emptyset \end{matrix} \right\}$$

Rule (P7) will raise by one degree of height all peripheral vowels, while lowering [−peripheral] vowels that are followed by segments that are [−cons]—the nuclei of upgliding diphthongs. The effect of (P7) can be schematized as follows:

Tense vowels	Lax vowels
ē → ī	iy → ey
ǣ → ē	uw → uẃ
ɔ̄ → ō	
ō → u	
ɔ̄y → ōy	

This formulation, however, does not take into account the presence of [uy] allophones for the /oy/ class. These would be made [−peri] by (P6), and then changed to [oy] by (P7). After the application of (P6) and (P7), [oy] allophones would wind up as [ɔy], and [ɔy] allophones as [oy]. Although these outputs are not greatly different from what actually obtained, and could certainly be corrected by a few adjustment rules, it is important to note that the lowering of [uy] took place some 100 years after the lowering of [iy] to [ey]. At the same time, we may wish to specify the tensing of [ɔy] in a later rule than (P6), so that we will be able to account with the same rule for the backing of [əy] to [ɔy].[17] Accordingly, let us emend (P6) as follows:

(P6′) Laxing of diphthongal nuclei

$$[+\text{voc}] \rightarrow \langle -z \text{ peri} \rangle / \begin{bmatrix} \underline{\hspace{1cm}} \\ x \text{ high} \end{bmatrix} [+\text{peri}]$$

[17] In fact, most sources indicate that the nucleus of [ɔy] was short; tensing must have been a late-eighteenth-century development.

Rule (P6′) now states that the nuclei of upgliding diphthongs will be increasingly nonperipheral as in accordance with their height. This change will affect only [ɔy], which will now be realized at some intermediate level of peripherality; the nuclei of [iy] and [uw], which are high, will still be minimally peripheral. Note that, in eliminating the specification of height from the input to (P6), we have simplified the rule. This correlation of peripherality to height for the nuclei of upgliding diphthongs is by no means ad hoc; LYS have observed that the nuclei of [ay], [aw], and [oy] are almost always more peripheral than those of [iy], [ey], [uw], and [ow].

If we now allow the vowel shift rule to operate on the output of (P6), we will see the allophones [uy], [oy], and [ɔy] all lowered by equal degrees. But, here again, since the only other nuclei to be affected are those of [iy] and [uw], both high, there will be no loss of descriptive adequacy if we make this also a variable rule, sensitive to degrees of peripherality. The vowel shift rule may now be represented as:

(P7′) Vowel Shift

$$[z \text{ high}] \rightarrow \langle z + \alpha x \text{ high} \rangle \, / \, \left[\underline{\quad \alpha \, y \text{ peri} \quad} \right] \begin{Bmatrix} \emptyset \\ [\text{ cons}] \\ [+\text{cen}] \end{Bmatrix}$$

with a stipulation that when the degree of peripherality is maximal, as with tense vowels, $x = 1$. Since [uy] and [oy] will have been differentiated with respect to peripherality by (P6′), (P7′) will operate to lower [uy] more than [oy], and to lower [ɔy] least of all. The three allophones will now be distinguished less in height than by their degree of peripherality, as assigned by (P6′); in other words, the reflexes of [uy] will be more central than those of [oy]. A rounding adjustment rule such as (2) will now apply:

(2) Rounding adjustment

$$\begin{bmatrix} +\text{voc} \\ +\text{back} \end{bmatrix} \rightarrow \langle -y \text{ round} \rangle \, / \, \left[\underline{\quad -x \text{ peri} \quad} \right] [-\text{round}]$$

Rule (2) would have the effect of unrounding nonperipheral (back) vowels to the degree that they were nonperipheral. Note that it would affect not only [uy] and [oy] reflexes, but [u] and, to a lesser extent, [o] as well. This unrounding is attested; we will return to it in what follows.

Note that, throughout this process, we have not changed the feature assignment [+back]; the "centralization" of [uy] has been handled entirely in terms of degrees of nonperipherality. For the final stage of the sound change, we need merely reapply (P6). As reflexes of [uy], [oy], and [ɔy] are now all the same height, they will be assigned the same intermediate level of

FIGURE 9.3 *Stages in the lowering of* [uy] *and* [oy]. *1 = Position after laxing of diphthongal nuclei. 2 = Position after vowel shift.*

peripherality that [ɔy] has maintained throughout the process; the rounding adjustment can now reapply so that all /oy/ allophones are realized as [ɔy].

It must be re-emphasized here that the phonological rules presented by LYS are based on empirical observations, and that these observations show that sound change occurs as movements in continuous phonological space, which may occur in a series of stages. There is thus no compelling force in the argument that the lowering of [uy] could not have been a part of the Vowel Shift since it happened a hundred years later; according to LYS, the Vowel Shift operated first on vowels that were [+peripheral], and then on [−peripheral] vowels, and this same ordering is observed with respect to the ongoing shifts observed by LYS for a variety of English dialects. The lowering and rebacking of [uy] can thus be represented as a series of stages, schematized in Figure 9.3. This formulation produces results that correlate phonologically with the models sketched in Figures 9.1 and 9.2.

Let us turn now to the *line* class. Here we have far less evidence to go on; at least, there is little discussion by the grammarians and orthoepists of any allophonic variation like that of [uy] and [oy], or [əy] and [oy].[18] This should not be taken to mean, of course, that such variation was absent; it is more probable that the orthoepists found it difficult to distinguish among diphthongal nuclei when the nucleus and glide were both [αfront]. It is clear that there was never for the /i:/ class the extreme variation we have seen for /oy/; but this is as expected. The diphthong [iy] would have been created from [i:] by a diphthongization rule, and the laxing rule (P6′) would have applied to all nuclei to an equal degree, since, unlike /oy/, the /i:/ class allophones were not distributed along a continuum of heights. Then the Vowel Shift (P7″) would have applied to lower all nuclei to an equal degree, and the rounding adjustment rule would not have applied to this group. These rules operated to differentiate the /oy/ class allophones along three parameters—height, peripherality, and roundness—but the allophones of /i:/ would have remained together to a much greater degree.

Labov, Yaeger, and Steiner find ample synchronic evidence to support the "traditional" view of the Vowel Shift—as advanced by Jespersen, Luick, and Chomsky and Halle—that [iy] was lowered to [ey] and [æy] before it was

---

[18] Gil (1621), among others, does indicate a difference between the nuclei of *aye* and *mine*, but it is not clear from his presentation just how these were realized.

centralized. Wolfe (1969), in her extremely thorough review of the primary sources, finds that there is no testimony of a central nucleus in the /i:/ class before 1650. The Vowel Shift formulations of both Chomsky and Halle and LYS are lowering rules, though they differ in detail. Chomsky and Halle (1968) suggest that [ey] became [əy] by application of a rule of diphthong laxing and rounding adjustment. But LYS hold that the /i:/ diphthong was throughout probably a front vowel, but was perceived as central in its final stages because of its extreme nonperipherality. They write: "When the vowel descends far enough, there is very little distance between front and center [4.8.2.3.]." We will assume that LYS are correct in their assumption that the seventeenth-century reflex of ME /i:/ had a nonperipheral front nucleus, like that of /ey/ in many English dialects ([e$^{>i}$], [ɛ$^{>i}$]). For the present purposes, we will also assume that there was relatively little allophonic variation among reflexes of ME /i:/, mostly for want of evidence. Note that, in order to falsify the model of reported merger that was sketched, we would need a situation in which allophones of /i:/ were all equidistant from their corresponding /oy/ allophones—the reverse of Figure 1E. But for this to have been the case, we would have to assume that [ey] nuclei were fronted in precisely those environments in which /oy/ allophones were raised and backed—that is, in the environments [p, b, ĵ, č]__ and __[l, n]. In the absence of evidence, there is no reason at all to make such an assumption; the fronting of [ey] would scarcely be "natural" in any of these environments, and in some of them, such as __[l], we must assume that it was backed, as the backing of vowels before [l] is close to a universal phenomenon.

Reports of Merger: Chronology and Social Evaluation

Let us turn now to the chronology of reports of merger, in an effort to show that confusion of the *line* and *loin* classes was most extended, and lasted longest, for words likely to have had an original [uy]. The data presented in Table 9.1 support this contention. The table shows the citations for all 19 grammarians of 24 of the most frequently cited lexical items in the /oy/ class, which are arranged from top to bottom according to the number of environments present that tended to favor [uy]/[əy]. We would predict that merger would have been longest lasting for those words listed at the top of the column, in addition to being most frequently cited for these forms. Although there are not sufficient citations to generalize about the onset of merger, we can note the effect of the phonetic shape; no source shows merger of a word with one favoring environment who does not show it for all words with two. This hierarchy is especially evident in the case of Greenwood (1711), who alone among these sources distinguishes three degrees of centralization: In Greenwood, whereas words with two favoring environments are identified with "*i* long," words with one favoring environment pertain to an intermediate class that is assigned the pronunciation of "*u* obscure" (Greenwood identifies "*u* obscure" with the vowel of *but*).[19]

When we move to the post-1750 period, during which the merger was in retreat in polite speech, we observe that the restoration of a back vowel occurred first in those words with only one environment favoring original [uy]. Only one source (Kenrick, 1773) allows merger in words having only one favoring environment, whereas all seven show some merger for words in which two favoring environments were present. We must assume that, by 1750, words with an original [oy] had moved outside the limit of confusability of their corresponding allophones in the ME /i:/ class, whereas words within original [uy], which were more nonperipheral, still remained within this ellipse.

We can adduce still more evidence for the phonetic conditioning of the confusion of the word classes if we look at the assignments of social markedness to various pronunciations. Many of the sources used here commented on the "correctness" of a pronunciation of /oy/ class words with a central vowel, though these assessments do not always agree. The only pre-1750 grammarian to discuss this issue is Jones (1701), who allows unstigmatized pronunciation with "*i* long" except for *loyal, royal,* and *voyage,* which are "sometimes abusively sounded with an *i.*" This pronunciation is probably the consequence of the presence in nonprestige dialects of a rule that deleted schwa after diphthongs, so that these words had /oyC/; the nucleus would then have been more amenable to raising, and then to laxing, so that in these dialects the vowel would have been perceived as more central.

But this is a special case; stigmatization of centralization does not really begin until the second half of the eighteenth century. Rudd (1755) allows no merger at all:

> [An exception to the pronunciation of *oy* with a back vowel is] that *oi* sounds *i* in join, and its derivatives . . . tho' this I take to be intirely a *corrupt pronunciation,* borrowed from *vulgar use;* and therefore, cannot but think, it would be much better to give the *oi* in these words the full sound of a PROPER DIPHTHONG.

Rudd mentions the centralized vowel only in *join*. In view of the fact that a number of more reliable later sources—such as Nares, Kenrick, and Bailey— all allow some merger in other forms, such as *point* and *boil,* we must assume that Rudd was either sensitive only to the more extreme examples of centralization, or that he was exposed to a dialect somewhat different from theirs, one in which the laxing of diphthongal nuclei had not proceeded to such a degree.

[19] Greenwood's work is largely a translation of Wallis (1653), and may be suspect. Wallis, however, does not distinguish three degrees of centralization.

Note also that Greenwood appears to have had a more centralized nucleus before nasals than before [l]; this would agree with the difference in the variable coefficients for these two environments as shown in Table 9.4.

As earlier sources make no mention of any stigma attached to a pronunciation of *join* with a high or centralized vowel, we may assume that the original raising, laxing, and lowering were upper-class innovations. Gil (1621), for example, who was an Oxford scholar, rails against the pronunciation of a word like *capon* with a raised vowel, which he takes to be a rusticism characteristic of the *Mopsae* (after Sydney's shepherdess). But he nowhere criticizes the pronunciation [uy], as we might expect him to do if this had been an instance of change from below. The remark of Jones that has been quoted is the first indication we have of stigmatization, and this, as we have seen, reflects, not a stigmatization of centralization, but rather of an independent rule of schwa deletion. Nonetheless, Jones's remarks do suggest that, by the beginning of the eighteenth century, the centralization had spread to lower-class dialects, perhaps in a more generalized form, and that its presence, especially in forms for which the upper class had a back nucleus, was coming to be associated with nonprestige dialects. We would then have a pattern of change from above with subsequent correction from above; as centralization became more frequent among the lower classes, it would come to be stigmatized. Hence the remarks of Rudd and of other grammarians, such as Nares (1784):

> OI . . . has a full, rich, and masculine sound, peculiar to itself and its substitute OY. It is distinctly heard in *noise, voice, rejoice,* etc. Those who are zealous for the harmony of our language have lamented that this sound is in danger of being lost, by a corrupt and vicious mode of pronunciation. It has been, indeed, the custom to give this diphthong in several words, the improper sound of *I* long, as in *boil, broil, choir, join, joint, point, poison, spoil.* The banished diphthong seems at last to be upon its return, and there are many now who are hardy enough to pronounce *boil* exactly as they do *toil,* and *join* like *coin,* etc.

Note that Nares attributes a central vowel only to those words in which two environments favoring original [uy] are present, with the exception of *poison* and *choir* (which has been spelt with *oi* only since the late seventeenth century; the BCP has everywhere *quire*). In such words as *coin* and *toil*, which are shown by earlier writers with a centralized vowel, he finds only a back nucleus.

The most interesting discussion of social markedness is that of Kenrick (1773), who regards centralization as variously vulgar or standard:

> This sound approaches the nearest to a practical diphthong in our language. . . . A vicious custom now prevails, especially in common conversation, of sinking the first broad sound entirely, or rather of converting both into the sound of *i* or *y*; thus *oil, toil* are frequently pronounced exactly like *isle, tile.* This is a fault which the poets are inexcusable for promoting, by making such words rhime to each other. And yet there are some words so written, which by long use, have almost lost their true sound. Such are *boil, join,* and many others, which it would now appear affectation to pronounce other than *bile, jine.*

Kenrick thus stigmatizes centralization where only one environment favored original [uy], but accepts it where there are two such environments. The fact

248 : GEOFFREY NUNBERG

that he regards the presence of a back vowel in this latter group as affected indicates that it was among the upper classes that rebacking was first completed; within 25 years, [ɔy] would be the standard for all forms in polite speech.[20] But this rebacking cannot have been merely the result of correction on the model of spelling, else the phonetic shape of the word would have been irrelevant.[21]

Conclusion

As has been noted, in many popular and rural dialects, a centralized vowel was retained in many forms well into the nineteenth century; in some dialects, it survives to this day. But centralization was by this time a stigmatized feature; Dickens, for example, puts such forms as *spile, jine,* and *rejine* into the mouths of lower-class characters like Cap'n Cuttle and Joe Gargary.[22]

---

[20] In this connection, we might note also the remarks of Walker (1791), whose treatment of pronunciation was based to a degree on that of Kenrick. Walker stigmatizes the practice, "very prevalent . . . among the vulgar," of pronouncing *boil, spoil, joint* and *point* as if written *bile, spile, etc.* He goes on to say: "I remember, very early in life, to have heard *coin* pronounced as if written *quine* by some respectable speakers, but this is now justly banished as the grossest vulgarism." Evidently, by Walker's time, the rebacking of *coin* and other words with only one environment favoring original [uy] had proceeded to such a degree that it was no longer heard as centralized among upper-class speakers, whereas the class of words with two such environments was still pronounced with a centralized vowel frequently enough to occasion censure. Note that this also supports the assumption that rebacking began among higher-ranked speakers.

[21] The role of social markedness in motivating the rebacking of words with original [uy] is not at issue here, but a distinction must be drawn, after Weinreich, Labov, and Herzog (1968), between the presence of social forces that might motivate a sound change (the "actuation problem") and the presence of a linguistic system that allows change to be effected (the problem of "constraints").

Another external pressure for reseparation is suggested by Vachek (1962), who notes that most words in the *oy* class were of Romance origin, and hypothesizes that orthographic *oy* came to be "a signal of synchronically foreign origin," which resisted the "domestication" of a merger with the ME /iː/ class. This is not entirely unreasonable—we note that /ž/ is similarly marked in Modern English, and tends to be retained only in words whose meaning suggests a foreign origin, such as *beige* and *rouge,* while words that have been more completely assimilated, such as *garage,* often show up with /ǰ/. But the application of this principle to the *loin* class raises several problems. First, a number of words in the class, such as *point, boil,* and *oil,* were so common that it is hard to see how they could have retained a foreign flavor for over 400 years. Second, not all words in this class have Romance origins; we also have *boy, toy,* and *hoy.* We would expect, then, that if Vachek were right, we would see in the *oy* class the same sort of lexical diffusion we see now with /ž/, but this is conspicuously absent.

[22] However, Dickens allows centralization of *oy* only when the word is likely to have had an original high nucleus. For example, I am assured by R. Newsom, of the New York City Dickens Fellowship, that *oyster* is never used as a dialect form, which word is extremely common in his work; similarly *voice* and *noise.*

The analysis presented here is doubtless incorrect in many details; in particular, it is probable that a larger sample of grammars would have allowed the clarification of some points, and that the formulation of the rules for laxing and lowering of [uy] must remain a moot subject. Nonetheless, these points are not critical to the bones of the argument. There can be no doubt that the reversal of the reported merger of *loin* and *line* behaved in the orderly fashion that we have come to expect of regular *Lautlehre*, and showed none of the capriciousness that we would have anticipated had spelling pronunciation or dialect borrowing been responsible.[23] It is worth noting that the techniques used here, and the principles applied, have been derived in the main from recent empirical investigations of sound change in progress; it is hoped that similar investigations may provide the means by which other vexing problems in historical linguistics can be resolved.

References

Bloomfield, L. 1933. *Language*. New York: Holt.
Chomsky, N., and Halle, M. 1968. *The sound pattern of English*. New York: Harper and Row.
Cohen, P. S. 1971. The tensing and raising of 'short *a*' in the metropolitan area of New York City. Unpublished manuscript.
Dobson, E. J. 1968. *English pronunciation 1500–1700*. Oxford: Oxford University Press.
Ellis, S. J. 1874. *Early English pronunciation* (Vol. 4.). London.
Galanter, E. 1962. Contemporary psychophysics. In R. Brown, E. Hess, G. Mandler, and E. Galanter (Eds.), *New directions in psychology*. New York: Holt, Rinehart and Winston.
Garde, P. 1961. Réflexions sur les différences phonétiques entre les langues slaves. *Word, 17*, 34–62.
Herzog, M. I. 1965. *The Yiddish language in Northern Poland*. Bloomington, Ind.: Research Center in Anthropology, Folklore, and Linguistics.
Jespersen, O. 1909. *A modern English grammar* (Vol. 1). Heidelberg: C. Winter.
Kökeritz, H. 1953. *Shakespeare's pronunciation*. New Haven: Yale University Press.
Labov, W. 1966. *The social stratification of English in New York City*. Washington, D.C.: Center for Applied Linguistics.

[23] Although the restoration of the word classes was surprisingly neat, there was some small diffusion of words from one word class to the other. All of the cases, however, are for one reason or another equivocal. Only one word shifted from the *loin* class to the *line* class: *eyelet* (< OF *oilet*), but this is an obvious example of folk etymology. From the *line* to the *loin* class went *boil* "tumor" (< OE *byl*), *groin* (< OE *grynde*), and *joist* (< OF *giste*). In each case, however, the first citation with *oy* considerably antedates the centralization of [uy] (*joist* in 1494, *boil* in 1529, and *groin* in Shakespeare). It is worth noting, however, that each of the forms involved has a phonetic shape favorable to confusion; if the new forms in *oy* were introduced through dialect borrowing, for example, then the period of confusion might have helped to entrench them.

The fact that the *line–loin* break was so clean does not mean that false mergers of this type will never result in lexical diffusion. If two word classes remain in close proximity for any length of time, we will not be surprised if some bleeding takes place, especially with forms whose allophones are most closely juxtaposed. In Essex, for example, *point* has jumped from the *loin* to the *line* class in production, according to the spectrographic records of LYS, but this is the form most likely to have done so; in the eighteenth century, it was the form most frequently shown with a centralized nucleus.

250 : GEOFFREY NUNBERG

Labov, W., and Wald, B. 1969. Some general principles of vowel shifting. Paper presented to the Linguistic Society of America, San Francisco.

Labov, W., Yaeger, M., and Steiner, R. 1972. *A quantitative study of sound change in progress.* Philadelphia: U.S. Regional Survey.

Labov, W., and Nunberg, G. 1972. Two problematic mergers in the history of English. In W. Labov, M. Yaeger, and R. Steiner, *A quantitative study of sound change in progress.* Philadelphia: U.S. Regional Survey.

Luick, K. 1914–1940. *Historische grammatik der Englischen Sprache.* Leipzig: C. H. Tausch-nitz.

Pope, M. K. 1934. *From Latin to Modern French with especial consideration of Anglo-Norman.* Manchester: University Press.

Pyles, T. 1964. *The origins and development of the English language.* New York: Harcourt Brace & World.

Vachek, J. 1962. On the interplay of external factors in the development of language. *Lingua 11.*

Weinreich, U., Labov, W., and Herzog, M. 1968. Empirical foundations for a theory of language change. In W. Lehmann and Y. Malkiel (Eds.), Directions for historical linguistics. Austin: University of Texas Press.

Wolfe, P. 1969. *Linguistic change and the Great Vowel Shift in English.* Unpublished doctoral dissertation, University of California, Los Angeles.

Wyld, H. C. 1936. *A history of modern colloquial English.* Oxford: Oxford University Press.

Zachrisson, R. 1913. *Pronunciation of English vowels, 1400–1700.* Goteborg: W. Zachrisson.

Grammars and Dictionaries in Chronological Order

Danielsson, B. (Ed.). 1955. *John Hart's works on English orthography and pronunciation* (2 vol.). Stockholm: Almqvist & Wiksell.

Mulcaster, R. 1582. *The first part of the elementarie.* London.

Zachrisson, R. 1927. *English pronunciation in Shakespeare's time as taught by William Bullokar.* Uppsala: Almqvist & Wiksell.

Gil, A. 1621. *Logonomia.* London.

Hodges, R. 1653. *Most plain directions for true writing.* London.

Sundby, B. (Ed.). 1953. *Christopher Cooper's English teacher.* Lund: Gleerup.

Price, O. 1970. *The vocal organ.* Menston, England: Scolar Press Facsimile. (Originally published, 1665.)

Aicken, J. 1693. *The English grammar.* London.

Lehnert, M. 1936. *Die Grammatik des Englischen Sprachmeisters John Wallis.* Breslau: Priebatsch.

Jones, J. 1701. *Practical Phonography.* London.

Greenwood, J. 1711. *An essay towards a practical English grammar.* London.

Tuite, T. 1726. *The Oxford spelling book.* London.

Holmberg, B. 1956. *James Douglas on English pronunciation (1740).* Lund: Gleerup.

Rudd, S. 1755. *Prodromos.* London.

Bailey, N., and Scott, J. N. 1755. *New universal etymological English dictionary.* London.

Johnston, W. 1764. *A Pronouncing and spelling dictionary.* London.

Fenning. D. 1764. *The universal spelling book.* London.

Nares, R. 1784. *Elements of orthoepy.* London.

Walker, J. 1791. *A critical pronouncing dictionary.* London.

Adams, J. 1799. *The pronunciation of the English language.* London.

(Kenrick, 1773, and Lediard, 1725, are quoted extensively in Ellis, 1874; for Mauget, 1679, see Zachrisson, 1913.)

10

William Labov

THE SOCIAL ORIGINS OF SOUND CHANGE[1]

Introduction

The past century of phonetic research has illuminated our understanding of the production of sounds, the properties of the acoustic signals, and to a certain extent, the perception of speech sounds. But the search for the originating causes of sound change itself remains one of the most recalcitrant problems of phonetic science. Bloomfield's position on this question is still the most judicious:

> No permanent factor . . . can account for specific changes which occur at one time and place and not at another. . . . Although many sound changes shorten linguistic forms, simplify the phonetic system, or in some other way lessen the labor of utterance, yet no student has succeeded in establishing a correlation between sound change and any antecedent phenomenon: the causes of sound change are unknown [1933, p. 386].

[1] The research reported here was supported by the National Science Foundation under contracts to the University of Pennsylvania SOC-750024-1 and BNC-76-15421. A more complete account of this research is available in W. Labov, A. Bower, D. Hindle, E. Dayton, A. Kroch, M. Lennig, and D. Schiffrin, *Social Determinants of Linguistic Change,* Technical Progress Report to the NSF (1980). The work reported here is the joint product of these authors and a number of others, most notably Arvilla Payne, Bruce Johnson, Shana Poplack, Gregory Guy, Sally Boyd, and Anthony Kroch. Kroch's study of the upper class of Philadelphia, supported by a post-doctoral fellowship from the National Institute of Mental Health [MH-05536], forms an integral part of the data that this report is based on. Kroch has made a number of substantial contributions to the analysis of the Philadelphia data and the general issues of sound change, which are gratefully acknowledged here.

A condensed version of this chapter was prepared for the Ninth International Congress of Linguists at Copenhagen, August 1978.

In spite of Bloomfield's warning, linguists have continued to put forward simplistic theories that would attempt to explain sound change by a single formal principle, such as the simplification of rules, the maximization of transparency, and so on. But at the Second International Congress of Nordic and General Linguistics, King rejected his own earlier reliance on simplification (1972), and recognized the point made 50 years earlier by Meillet (1921), Saussure (1922), and Bloomfield (1933): that the sporadic nature of sound change rules out the possibility of explanation through any permanent factor in the phonetic processing system. It seems clear that any explanation of the fluctuating course of sound change must involve the continual fluctuations that take place in the structure of the society in which language is used.

The approach to the explanation of linguistic change outlined by Weinreich, Labov, and Herzog (1968) divides the problem into five distinct areas: locating universal constraints, determining the mechanism of change, measuring the effects of structural embedding, estimating social evaluation, and finally, searching for causes of the actuation of sound changes. The quantitative study of sound change in progress by Labov, Yaeger, and Steiner (1972) located three universal constraints on vowel shifting,[2] and developed the mechanism by which these chain shifts take place in phonetic space, expanding the view of structural embedding outlined by Martinet (1955). Our current studies of sound change in progress in Philadelphia (1973–1977) have developed further the measurement and mathematical analysis of vowel shifts, with the end in view of attacking the actuation problem itself. We have approached the problem of why sound changes take place at a particular time by searching for the social location of the innovators: asking which speakers are in fact responsible for the continued innovation of sound changes, and how their influence spreads to affect the entire speech community.

It is often assumed that sound change is no longer active in modern urban societies, and that local dialects are converging under the effect of the mass media that disseminate the standard language.[3] One of the most striking results of the sociolinguistic studies carried out since 1961 is to show that this is not true: On the contrary, new sound changes are emerging and old ones proceeding to completion at a rapid rate in all of the speech communities that have been studied intensively. Evidence for sound changes in progress has

[2] The three major principles state that in chain shifts, (I) tense or long nuclei rise, (II) short or lax nuclei fall, and (III), back nuclei move to the front. These principles were foreseen by Sweet (1888), but applied to individual vowel movements rather than to chain shifts, where they have much greater predictive value.

[3] This general impression is in fact reinforced frequently by the statements of dialectologists who collect data from rural areas. A journalistic account of a dialect society meeting states that "differences in the way Americans talk seem to be wearing away . . . towards the standard national blandness of a radio announcer," and cites David Reed and Frederick Cassidy to this effect (*Philadelphia Inquirer*, 15 February 1978, p. 10-E). The findings of traditional dialectology appear to reflect the general decline of rural societies with loss of population, rather than general linguistic processes.

been found in New York, Detroit, Buffalo, Chicago (Labov, Yaeger, and Steiner, 1972), Norwich (Trudgill, 1972), Panama City (Cedergren, 1973), Buenos Aires (Wolf and Jimenez, 1978), and Paris (Lennig, 1978). This evidence is provided by distributions across age levels (change in apparent time), and by comparison with earlier reports (change in real time), following the model of Gauchat, 1904 and Hermann, 1930.

Whenever these changes in progress have been correlated with distribution across social classes, a pattern has appeared that is completely at variance with earlier theories about the causes of sound change. If one looks to the principle of least effort (Bloomfield, 1933, p. 386) as an explanation, then it follows that sound change would arise in the lowest social classes. The principle of local density put forward by Bloomfield (1933, p. 476) points to discontinuities in networks of communication as a determinant of the patterns of propagation of a change: Here it would follow again that the lowest social class, which is most isolated from the influence of the standard language, would be most free to innovate in a direction distinct from the standard. If however, the theorist focuses on the laws of imitation (Tarde, 1873) and the borrowing of prestige forms from centers of higher prestige, then it would follow that new sound changes will be the most advanced in the highest social classes.

In a first approach to the mechanism of linguistic change (1965), I found no reason to favor either of these two notions about the social locus of change, and indicated that sound change could proceed from any location within the social spectrum. As Sturtevant (1948) had first suggested, the change would then follow a path determined by the social structure, adapted successively by those speakers that took the originating group as a standard of social value. However, Kroch (1978) pointed out several years later that no case had been found in which the highest social group was the originator of a systematic linguistic change, and argued that systematic (or "natural") sound changes would always be expected to originate in the working class. This insightful observation marked the beginning of a more determined search for the social location of linguistic change.

A wide variety of sociolinguistic studies carried out since 1965 showed no case contrary to Kroch's position.[4] It is true that older sound changes, like stable sociolinguistic variables, are often aligned with the socioeconomic hierarchy, so that the lowest social class uses the stigmatized variant most

[4] The cities where sociolinguistic structure has been studied systematically now include Detroit (Shuy, Wolfram, and Riley, 1966; Wolfram, 1969), Salt Lake City (Cook, 1969); Glasgow (Macaulay, 1977), Belfast (J. Milroy and L. Milroy, 1977); Bahia Blanca, Argentina (Weinberg, 1974), Buenos Aires (Lavandera, 1975), Montreal (G. Sankoff and H. Cedergren, 1971), Paris (Lennig, 1978), and Teheran (Modaressi, 1978). In none of these cities do we find systematic innovation by the highest social group. In some cases, retrograde movements will show the upper middle class in the lead; this is particularly so in Lennig's study of Paris, where women speakers show a generalized rotation that reverses the direction of the traditional working class dialect. But here of course the upper middle class began in the rear, and so in retreat is very likely to be found in the lead.

often, and the highest social class least often. But whenever age distributions and earlier reports indicate that there may be sound change in progress, the highest social class lags behind. Furthermore, it also appeared that the very lowest social group was less advanced, a finding not anticipated in Kroch's argument. In each case of sound change in progress located, the variables display a curvilinear pattern of social distribution, where the innovating groups are located centrally in that hierarchy: the upper working class or lower middle class.

Some of the data that support this observation was assembled in the general discussion of the role of socioeconomic class in linguistic change in Labov, 1972 (pp. 294–296). In New York City, the lower middle class was the most advanced in the raising of long open *o* in *lost, talk, law, etc.* (Labov, 1966, 1972). The same pattern was found in the backing of (ay) and the fronting of (aw) in that city. In Norwich, Trudgill found that the backing of short *e* before /l/ in *belt, help, etc.,* showed a rapid development among younger speakers, and was most advanced in the upper working class (1974). In Panama City, Cedergren found that one of five sociolinguistic variables studied showed an age distribution that we now know is characteristic of sound change in progress. The lenition of (ch) in *muchacha, macho, etc.,* showed a strong peak in the upper working class and lower middle class (Cedergren, 1973; Labov, 1972, pp. 293–294).

The number of cases that supported the curvilinear pattern was not very great. The quantitative data was drawn from three speech communities: New York City, Panama City, and Norwich; only six linguistic variables were involved, and for some of these [New York City (aw) and (ay)] the impressionistic data did not represent a systematic sampling. To confirm the existence of the curvilinear pattern, it seemed best to take a new community with a number of changes in progress, and develop techniques of sampling and measurement that would reduce the chances of error to a relatively low level. At the same time, the project could be designed to generate the kind of social information that would help to explain this surprising curvilinear pattern, if it were replicated. The earlier studies referred to were based on single interviews with individuals, and the reconstruction of the patterns of social communication that could lead to such a result was therefore quite limited.

Our project on linguistic change and variation[5] selected Philadelphia as a site for the further study of this problem, since it appeared that almost all of

[5] Supported by the National Science Foundation as noted in Note 1. Research conducted by this project in Philadelphia covers a wider range of issues concerning linguistic change in Philadelphia than are presented here. Payne (1974, 1977) reports the acquisition of phonetic and phonological rules by children with varying exposure to the Philadelphia dialect. Guy (1975) analyzes the constraints on consonant cluster simplification that differentiate Philadelphia from New York. Poplack examines the social influences on the English vowels used by Puerto Rican children (1976) and the functional constraints on deletion of final consonants in Spanish (1977). Experiments testing categorical perception of short *a* (Labov, 1977) show the perceptual consequences of the creation of new phonemic boundaries in mid-Atlantic dialects.

the Philadelphia vowels were in motion, and all of the basic patterns of chain shifting found in English and French could also be located in Philadelphia. The main data base for the Philadelphia investigation is a series of long-term neighborhood studies in working-class, middle-class, and upper-class areas, involving repeated interviews and participant-observation of the speech community. To this is added a geographically random survey of telephone users, with short, relatively formal interviews. Any convergence of findings from these two data bases, which have complementary strengths and sources of error, will provide strong confirmation of the results.[6]

The Measurement of Sound Change

The measurement of vowel nuclei[7] was carried out by a preliminary frequency analysis, using a real-time frequency analyzer, followed by linear predictive coding of the frequency domain to derive more exact estimates of the central tendencies of F1, F2, F3, and F0. Complete vowel analyses were carried out for the spontaneous speech of 113 subjects in the neighborhood studies and 60 subjects in the telephone survey, with 150–200 vowels measured for each subject. The mean values for each subject were then submitted to three normalization programs: uniform scaling methods using the geometric mean as developed by Nearey (1977) or vocal tract length estimate (Nordstrom and Lindblom, 1975), and a three-parameter method developed by Sankoff, Horrock, and McKay (1974).

Stepwise regression was carried out on the unnormalized and the three normalized series, deriving equations that predicted F1 and F2 mean positions from age, sex, social class, social mobility, ethnicity, neighborhood, communication patterns, and knowledge of other languages. We searched for the method of normalization that showed the maximum clustering to eliminate the effects of differences in vocal tract length, and the minimum tendency to eliminate variation that was known to be present in the data by independent means. Uniform scaling based on the geometric mean (Nearey, 1977) was selected by these criteria and will be used as the basis for the discussions to follow.[8]

---

[6] The methods followed here are in accordance with the general principles presented in Labov, 1972, pp. 208–209, which confront the fundamentally irreducible "observer's paradox": Our aim is to observe how people speak when they are not being observed. The general solution is to approach the object of investigation from radically different perspectives, so that the errors of one method of observation are not duplicated by the errors of another.

[7] The neighborhood data were recorded on a Nagra III or IVS tape recorder at 3 ¾"/sec, using Sennheiser dynamic MD214 or 404 condenser microphones. The spectral analyzer is the Spectral Dynamics 301C, synthesizing 165 filters every 16.7 msec over 3300 Hz for men, 180 filters every 18 msec for women; data is averaged over 50 msec. LPC analysis was carried out on a PDP 11/10, with programs based on Markel, 1971 and Makhoul, 1975.

[8] For further data on the normalization procedures and methods used to compare them, see Hindle, 1977; Lennig and Hindle, 1977; Lennig, 1978; and Labov et al. 1980.

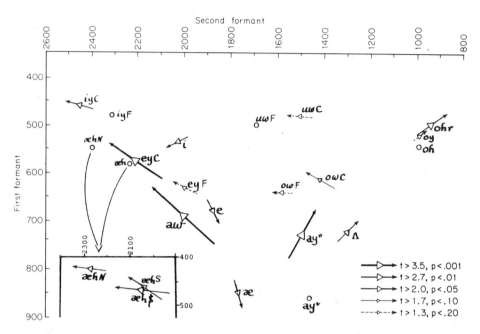

FIGURE 10.1 *Neighborhood study of 93 speakers. Regression coefficients for influence of age on F1 and F2 of Philadelphia vowels, projected 25 years ahead and 25 years behind mean values. (—F)free; (—C)checked (æh) allophones: (æhN) before nasals, (æhS) before fricatives (æh$) before stops.*

Figure 10.1 shows the mean positions of the Philadelphia vowels for 93 speakers in the neighborhood series, using the Nearey normalization. It also shows vectors representing the significant age coefficients of the regression equations for F1 and F2. The age coefficient for each formant for each vowel is multiplied by the chronological age of the subject, for example,

$$F2(aw) = 2086 - 5.39 \times Age \ldots$$

where the numbers may be read as F2 values in Herz. Thus the first and most significant coefficient shown above predicts that the difference in mean F2 positions for two speakers 50 and 25 years old will be 25 times 5.39 Hz: That is, the expected mean of F2 for the younger speaker is 135 Hz greater than for the older speaker. The vectors on Figure 10.1 represent the result of projecting the sound change 25 years ahead of the mean value and 25 years behind. The age coefficient shown above is highly significant, with a *t* value of 4.5 (*p* < .001); the significance of all age coefficients in Figure 10.1 is shown by the size of the triangles and the heaviness of the vector lines.

These age vectors fit in with evidence derived from earlier records and synchronic characteristics of the current data that allow us to set up five strata of sound change in Philadelphia:

1. Recently completed changes: for example, the backing of /ahr/ in *car*, *part*, *etc*.

2. Changes nearing completion: for example, the raising and fronting of (aeh)[9] in *man, hand, etc*.

3. Middle-range changes: the fronting of (uw) and (ow) in *too, moved, go*, and *code*.[10]

4. New and vigorous changes, not reported in earlier records: the raising and fronting of (aw) in *house, down, etc*. from [au] to [e']; the raising and backing of (ay) before voiceless consonants in *fight, like, etc*. from [ai] to a back central nucleus; the raising of (ey) in checked syllables in *made, lake, etc.*, from [eᵛⁱ] to [e^ⁱ].[11]

5. Incipient changes: for example, the lowering of the short vowels /i/, /e/, and /ae/.

Turning now to the random sample of telephone users, we have the view of Philadelphia sound changes shown in Figure 10.2. As we expected, there are fewer significant effects: Given the brief and formal character of the interchange, and the noisy and limited telephone channel, some of the minor patterns of age distribution have been eliminated. But the effects that do appear are quite consistant with the neighborhood study of Figure 10.1. The oldest level of sound changes show no age correlations (e.g., /ahr/) or only a small age vector (/ohr/). Free and checked /(ow/) are typical of the middle-range changes; they show a moderate fronting effect. The new and vigorous changes identified in the neighborhood studies are also the largest and most significant vectors here. There are some differences in the raising and fronting of (ayᵒ). The middle-range fronting and raising of (aeh) before voiceless fricatives appears to be slightly stronger in these data, and the raising and fronting of (aw) not quite as strong. But with these small differences, Figure 10.2 shows the convergence that we had hoped for. It follows that the sources of error in the neighborhood studies and the telephone survey are indeed complementary, and neither set of errors are powerful enough to prevent the consistent view of age distributions from emerging here.

The convergence of these two sets of data, combined with the earlier reports on Philadelphia phonology, allows us to conclude that we have obtained a fairly accurate portrait of sound change in progress.

[9] The parenthesis notation ( ) designates linguistic variables—phonetic units that show structured variation. Slashes / / and brackets [ ] indicate phonemic and phonetic units, respectively, where variability is not at issue.

[10] Philadelphia (ow) and (uw) are not fronted before liquids /l/ and /r/, and show no upglides before these liquids.

[11] In Figures 10.1 and 10.2, checked vowels are indicated by a following C, and free vowels by a following F. For the middle range vowels (uw) and (ow), as well the corresponding front vowels (iy) and (ey), the free vowels are lower and more centralized than the checked vowels. In the earlier stages of diphthongization under chain shifting principle II, the free vowels move more rapidly than the checked vowels. This is true in Philadelphia, but not in all of the cities where this type of chain shifting is found.

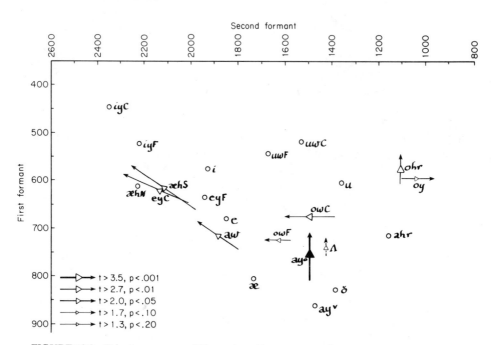

FIGURE 10.2 *Telephone survey of 60 speakers. Regression coefficients for influence of age of speaker on F1 and F2 of Philadelphia vowels projected 25 years ahead and behind the mean.*

Social Stratification

Conclusions from earlier studies would lead us to associate curvilinear social patterns with Stratum 4, the new and vigorous changes represented by the long, heavy vectors in Figure 10.1. Further terms in the regression equation show that this is the case. Extending the equation for F2 of (aw) to the three next most significant coefficients, we have:[12]

$$F2(aw) = 2086 - 5.39 \times \text{Age} + 126 \times \text{Female } [t = 3.5]$$
$$- 261 \times \text{Social Class 9 } [t = 3.1]$$
$$- 253 \times \text{Social Class 13–15 } [t = 2.5] \ldots$$

The social-class scale is a 16-point index based on education, occupation, and residence value: In the most generally used terminology, Class 9 is the "upper working class." Regression coefficients for the full range of social classes are plotted in Figure 10.3A: Here both the F1 and F2 coefficients are

---

[12] The figures shown here are based on the regression analysis with the finest division of the social class continuum. All regression analyses used a stepwise procedure (Draper and Smith, 1966) which examines each variable as if it were the last to be entered into the equation, and results are independent of the order in which the variables are presented to the program.

combined to give the resultant vectors plotted along the front diagonal, parallel to the course of sound change. At the zero level is the lowest social class group (0–3 combined), which forms the reference level for the others. The most advanced sound change is shown by the significant peak in Class 9, and the least advanced status is shown by the significant low point of the upper middle class. The less significant values show a smooth curvilinear pattern around these points.

Figure 10.3B shows the class distribution for the fronting of checked (ey) in the neighborhood studies. This is a broader curvilinear pattern with a significant peak in the middle working class (Class 7), and two other points significantly higher than the lower class reference level in groups located

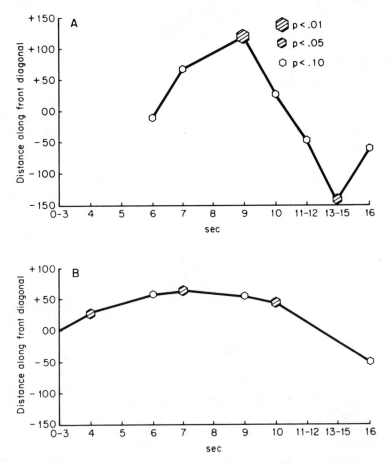

FIGURE 10.3 *Projection along front diagonal of regression coefficients for F1 and F2 (A) of (aw) and (B) of (eyC) for all socioeconomic classes compared to SEC 0–3: data from 93 speakers in Philadelphia neighborhood study.*

symmetrically above and below Class 7. Again, the less significant points form a smooth, curvilinear pattern.

It is evident that the retrograde movement of checked /ey/ is not as vigorous as the raising and fronting of (aw), and the class stratification is also not as sharp. The parallels between the two patterns can be seen more clearly by abstracting from this detailed class distribution, and dividing the social class gradient into five groups: lower working class, 0–5; upper working class, 6–9; lower middle class, 10–12; upper middle class, 13–15. The upper class, discretely separated from the others, is given an arbitrary rating of 16.

By dividing the working class and middle class into two groups each, we will be able to make the closest comparison with the various sociolinguistic studies that have documented change in progress, particularly Trudgill, 1973; Cedergren, 1973; and Labov, 1966. Figure 10.4 shows the result of this reduction. Since the F1 vectors are in general less significant than the F2 effects for the vowels considered here, F2 coefficients are plotted here without F1 to maximize confidence in the results. The patterns of F2 of (aw) and (ey) are strikingly parallel to each other and to the curvilinear results of the earlier studies. They are typical of the general pattern for all the Philadelphia sound changes: None of them show an initiative from the lowest social group or from the highest; while the most vigorous changes, that have not yet met with social correction, are advancing most rapidly in the highest sections of the working class.

The third new and vigorous change, the raising and fronting of (ay°), shows no significant class distributions of this type. It is worth noting that this is also the only change where men are in the lead (Labov, 1978b). For most of the linguistic changes that have been traced so far, we find that women are about one generation ahead of men—at least in the early stages of the process. This is true in Philadelphia as well, except in the case of (ay°). There may be a connection between the normal curvilinear class pattern and the dominance of women in the advancement of sound change, but this direction of inquiry would carry us beyond the scope of the present report.

Further Directions of Explanation

Given the confirmation of earlier evidence that systematic sound changes generally arise in centrally located social groups, we can ask how this fact bears on the causes and motivations of sound change. Instead of speculating on the psychological motivations of the upper working-class innovators, it will be more fruitful to probe more deeply into their social roles and relations to others in the community. A further investigation of the problem is based on evidence from communication networks in the neighborhoods (Labov *et al.*, 1980). Although the full results of this inquiry are again beyond the scope

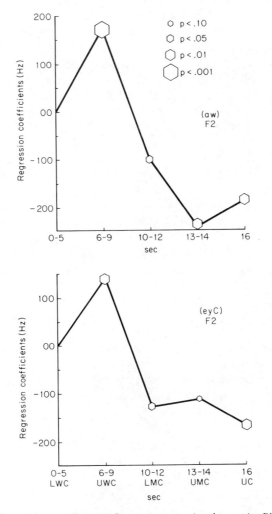

FIGURE 10.4 *Regression coefficients for socioeconomic classes in Philadelphia neighborhoods: (aw) and (eyC). 0–5 is residual class.*

of the present report, it may be helpful to indicate their general direction. It appears that the speakers who are most advanced in the sound changes are those with the highest status in their local community, as the socioeconomic class patterns indicate. But the communication networks provide additional information, discriminating among those with comparable status. The most advanced speakers are the persons with the largest number of local contacts within the neighborhood, yet who have at the same time the highest proportion of their acquaintances outside the neighborhood. Thus we have a portrait of individuals with the highest local prestige who are responsive to a somewhat broader form of prestige at the next larger level of social communication.[13] Through further studies of this process, we hope to discover how sound changes are generalized throughout the community and how local values are transmitted to create a relatively homogeneous urban dialect.[14]

The functions of language reflected in these sound changes cannot be limited to the communication of referential information. We are clearly dealing with the emblematic function of phonetic differentiation: the identification of a particular way of speaking with the norms of a local community.

The identification of the innovators of these sound changes allows us to rule out some of the explanations that have been offered in the past for the phenomenon of sound change. Their advanced social position and the high esteem they hold in the local community rule out the traditional charge of careless ignorance of the norms of society. Their reputation as vigorous and effective users of the language, combined with the nature of the vowel shifts themselves, makes any discussion of the principle of least effort beside the point. The central position that they hold in local networks of communication gives new life to the principle of local density, though we cannot project any discontinuity between these speakers and the exponents of the upper middle-class standard that they are leaving behind in their development of local sound changes. Once we are willing to refine our notion of prestige to give full weight to the local prestige associated with the Philadelphia dialect, Tarde's laws of imitation gain in respectability. But we must be ready to recognize that such a local prestige, which appears primarily in behavior and rarely in overt reactions, is powerful enough to reverse the normal flow of influence, and allow the local patterns to move upward to the upper middle class and even to the upper class.[15]

[13] These patterns in the communication of linguistic influence appear to be parallel to the two-step flow of influence isolated by Katz and Lazarsfeld (1955) in their study of personal influence.

[14] Weinreich, Labov, and Herzog (1968) argued that the basis for an empirical theory of linguistic change must be recognition of the heterogeneity of the speech community. Full competence in the use of the language requires that a speaker be able to recognize and interpret the differences within and across speakers that occur in his speech community, though he or she may use only a part of that range of variation in production. Thus the obverse of heterogeneity in production is homogeneity in normative structures, and a speech community may be defined as a group of speakers who share a set of norms for the interpretation of speech. Labov, 1966 showed that New York City was such a community. The same can be said for Philadelphia, where subjective reaction tests of native residents show internal agreement and sharp disagreement with the reactions of outsiders, and the direction of style shifting is uniform for all speakers who have been studied. But, as in New York City, these statements apply to the white community only; the black and Puerto Rican speakers form distinct communities which fail to recognize many of the norms of the white community, and show many understandings that are perceived only dimly if at all by white speakers living in the same area (see Note 16).

[15] The sample of 20 upper class speakers studied by Anthony Kroch showed a surprising conformity to the Philadelphia vowel system and clearly form a part of the speech community. Though the upper-class speakers use phonetic variants that are quite removed from the more advanced groups, it is clear that the overall rotations of the vowel system have affected upper-

None of these considerations provide an answer to the riddle of actuation. What is the force that has led to the continued renewal of sound change? Why have Philadelphians of the past few decades pushed the local vowel system even further along its traditional path, diverging even more from the dialects of other cities? The data generated by our neighborhood studies supports the earlier suggestion (Labov, 1965) that it is the entrance of new ethnic and racial groups into the community that provides the motivating forces behind this renewed diversification. In Philadelphia, as in New York, we are now witnessing a third wave of ethnic immigration. The Irish and German influx of the mid-nineteenth century was followed by a massive entrance of Italians, Jews, Ukrainians, and Poles at the end of the nineteenth century and the beginning of the twentieth; and in the middle of the twentieth century, the movement of large numbers of Southern rural black citizens into the Northern cities has created a city that is 33% black and inner city areas that are sharply divided between segregated black areas and traditional ethnic enclaves.

The renewed emphasis on local identification is accompanied by a strenuous reassertion of local rights and privileges by the ethnic groups who hold them, and a continued resistance to the pressure from black citizens of Philadelphia for their share of the jobs, housing, and political priorities in the city. The division of the city into two distinct communities by political, educational, and economic barriers is mirrored by the increasing divergence of the white and black dialects. Young black speakers do not participate at all in the evolution of the vowel system that is described here; instead, they clearly show their allegiance to a nationally based black English vernacular that is extraordinarily uniform in all the cities of the North.[16] It is unlikely that the further evolution of the Philadelphia vowel system can be understood without reference to this striking parallel between the linguistic divergence of the black and white communities, and the political, economic, and educational barriers that divide the city so sharply in so many ways.

---

class speakers, and the distributional sets used by upper-class speakers in spontaneous speech follow the Philadelphia system exactly. The oldest upper-class speaker and the oldest Irish speaker from Kensington, both born in the 1880s, show the same complex distributions of short *a* into tense and lax classes. Communities may show heterogeneity in phonemic distributions, almost inevitably in the course of mergers, tensing or laxing processes; but where we do find a resultant uniform template, it provides strong evidence for participation in a single speech community.

[16] The older Philadelphia black community appears to have participated in the Philadelphia vowel and consonant system, and it is still possible to find individual black speakers who use the Philadelphia vernacular. But the overwhelming majority of the black community now show no use at all of the Philadelphia vowel and consonant variants, or of the special grammatical features of the Philadelphia dialect. In the predominantly black high schools, there is almost no trace of the white Philadelphia vernacular described here. Instead, blacks participate in a nonlocal, nationally oriented linguistic and cultural framework; the phonology and grammar used in North and West Philadelphia appears to be identical with that used in New York, Detroit, Chicago, New Orleans, or Los Angeles.

Through the further study of communication between racial and ethnic groups, and the communication patterns that connect local neighborhoods, we hope to delineate more closely the social pressures that are responsible for the dissemination and further advance of sound change, and thus isolate the driving force behind the continuing divergence of languages and dialects. There is no reason to believe, however, that this divergence will continue indefinitely. The current linguistic situation in Philadelphia is bound to be affected by changes in job opportunities and residential patterns that affect black–white relations. We have found evidence of mutual influence of black and white speech patterns where there is daily contact and the cultural values of the opposing groups are recognized and viewed as accessible. The current divergence in the Philadelphia speech community is the product of long-standing linguistic trends and the pressures of the immediate social situation; the future evolution of the local dialect will be determined by a similar interaction between general constraints on language structure and the changing social context. The validity of any explanation of linguistic change will depend upon our ability to grasp the most relevant data in both areas and integrate our observations in a theory of language change that has the same wide scope and compelling character as the events themselves.

References

Bloomfield, L. 1933. *Language*. New York: Henry Holt.
Cedergren, H. J. 1973. *The interplay of social and linguistic factors in Panama*. Unpublished doctoral dissertation, Cornell University.
Cook, S. 1969. *Language change and the emergencee of an urban dialect in Utah*. Unpublished doctoral dissertation, University of Utah.
Draper, N. R. & H. Smith, 1966. *Applied Regression Analysis*. New York: Wiley.
Efroymson, M. A. 1966. Multiple regression analysis. In A. Ralston and H. S. Wilf (Eds.), *Mathematical methods for digital computers*. New York: Wiley.
Gauchat, L. 1905. l'unite phonetique dans le patois d'une commune. In *Festschrift Heinreich Morf*. Halle: Max Niemeyer.
Guy, G. 1975. Variation in the group and the individual: The case of final stop deletion. [*Pennsylvania Working Papers* I, 4. Philadelphia: U.S. Regional Survey.]
Hermann, E. 1929. Lautveraenderungen in der individualsprache einer Mundart. *Nachrichten der Gesellsch der Wissenschaften zu Goettingen*, Phil.-his. Kll., 11, 195–214.
Hindle, D. 1978. Approaches to vowel normalization in the study of natural speech. In D. Sankoff (Ed.), *Linguistic variation: Models and methods*. New York: Academic Press.
Katz, E. Lazarsfeld, P. 1955. *Personal Influence*. Glencoe, Ill.: Free Press.
King, R. 1972. *Historical linguistics and generative grammar*. Englewood Cliffs, N.J.: Prentice-Hall.
King, R. 1975. Integrating linguistic change. In K. H. Dahlstedt (Ed.), *The Nordic languages and modern linguistics*. Stockholm: Almqvist and Wiksell.
Kroch, A. 1978. Towards a theory of social dialect variation. *Language in Society*, 7:17–36.
Labov, W. 1966. *The social stratification of English in New York City*. Washington, D.C.: Center for Applied Linguistics.
Labov, W. 1972. *Sociolinguistic patterns*. Philadelphia: University of Pennsylvania Press.

Labov, W. 1977. Categorical discrimination along a new phonemic boundary. Paper given before the annual meeting of the Linguistic Society of America, Chicago.

Labov, W. 1978a. The measurement of vowel shifts. Paper given before the annual meeting of the American Association of Phonetic Sciences, San Francisco.

Labov, W. 1978b. The role of women in linguistic change. Paper given before the annual meeting of the Linguistic Society of America, Boston.

Labov, W., Bower, A., Hindle, D., Dayton, E., Kroch, A., Lennig, M., and Schiffrin, D. 1980. *Social determinants of sound change.* Philadelphia: U.S. Regional Survey.

Labov, W., Yaeger, M., and Steiner, R. 1972. *A quantitative study of sound change in progress.* Philadelphia: U.S. Regional Survey.

Lavandera, B. 1975. Linguistic structure and sociolinguistic conditioning in the use of verbal endings in *si*-clauses (Buenos Aires Spanish). Unpublished doctoral dissertation. University of Pennsylvania.

Lennig, M. 1978. Acoustic measurement of linguistic change: The modern Paris vowel system. Unpublished doctoral dissertation. University of Pennsylvania.

Lennig, M., and Hindle, D. 1977. Uniform scaling as a method of vowel normalization. Paper presented at the 94th meeting of the Acoustical Society of dissertation.

Macaulay, R. 1977. *Language, social class, and education.* Edinburgh: University Press.

Makhoul, J. 1975. Spectral linear prediction: properties and applications. *IEEE Transactions on Acoustics, Speech and Signal Processing, ASSP-23,* No. 3.

Markel, J., and Gray, A. H. Jr. 1976. *Linear prediction of speech.* Cambridge, Mass.: Bolt, Beranek and Newman.

Martinet, A. 1955. *Economie des changements phonétiques.* Berne: Francke.

Meilllet, A. 1921. *Linguistique historique et linguistique genreale.* Paris: La societe linguistique de Paris.

Milroy, L., and Milroy, J. 1977. Speech and context in an urban setting. *Belfast Working Papers,* 2, p. 1.

Modaressi, Y. 1978. A sociolinguistic analysis of modern Persian. Unpublished doctoral dissertation. University of Kansas.

Nearey, T. 1977. Phonetic feature system for vowels. Unpublished doctoral dissertation. University of Connecticut.

Nordstroem, P.-E., and Lindblom, B. 1975. A normalization procedure for vowel formant data. Paper 212 at the Eighth International Congress of Phonetic Sciences, Leeds.

Sankoff, D., Shorrock, R. W., and McKay, W. 1974. Normalization of formant space through the least squares affine transformation. Unpublished program and documentation.

Sankoff, G., and Cedergren, H. 1971. Some results of a sociolinguistic study of Montreal French. In R. Darnell (Ed.), *Linguistic diversity in Canadian society.* Edmonton: Linguistic Research, 1971.

Saussure, F. de 1922. *Cours de linguistique générale.* 2nd ed. Paris.

Shuy, R., Wolfram, W., and Riley, W. 1966. A study of social dialects in Detroit. Final Report, Project 6-1347. Washington, D.C.: Office of Education.

Sweet, H. 1888. *A history of English sounds.* Oxford: Clarendon Press.

Tarde, G. 1973. *Les lois d'imitation.*

Trudgill, P. 1972. *The social differentiation of English in Norwich.* Cambridge: University of Cambridge Press.

Weinberg, M. 1974. Analisis sociolinguistico de un aspecto del Espanol Bonærense: la -*s* en Bahia Blanca. *Cuadernos de Linguistica.*

Weinreich, U., Labov, W., and Herzog, M. 1968. Empirical foundations for a theory of language change. In W. Lehmann and Y. Malkiel (Eds.), *Directions for Historical Linguistics.* Austin: University of Texas Press.

Wolf, C., and Jimenez, E. 1978. A sound change in progress: The devoicing of Buenos Aires /z/ into /s/. Unpublished paper.

Wolfram, W. 1969. *A sociolinguistic description of Detroit Negro speech.* Arlington, Va.: Center for Applied Linguistics.

SUBJECT INDEX

A

Adjective conditioning, and Black English copula, 99–100, 101–102
Adverbs
  a-prefixed forms of, 111, 114, 123t
  time adverbs, 134–135
  -ing forms and, 114–115
Age spans, in language acquisition, 154–156, 157, 175–176
American English, *see also* Dialect acquisition study; English; *specific dialects*
  final /t,d/ deletion constraints in, 37–53
And in data analysis, deletion rate for, 44–45
Appalachian English, *a*-prefixing in, 107, 108–141
a-prefixed forms
  data collection on, 108–109
  frequency level for, 123t, 124
  grammatical categories of, 121–124
  historical roots of, 108
  meaning of, 139–140
  in narrative emotional contexts, 140
  phonological constraints on, 124–131
    alliterative, 131–132
  semantic aspects of, 133–141
  syntactic contexts for, 109–112, 114–117
    unacceptable, 112–114
  underlying sources of, 117–121
Articulation constraints, on deletion rule, 9
  following segments, 47–48
  preceding segments, 49–50
Articulation point, and vowel chain shift, 212–213

B

Baileyan wave model, of linguistic variables, 2–3
Be and *ing*, *a*-prefixing by, 122–124
Be deletion, in Black English, 101
Bimorphemic clusters, deletion rate for, 43–44, 47
Black English Vernacular (BVE)
  copula research in, 83, 87–89
  analytic procedures, 90
  constraint measurement, 91–94
    grammatical, 96–100
    phonological, 94–95
  field methods, 84, 86–87
  sample, 89, 90t
  West Indian creole origin hypothesis, 87–88, 101–103
  final /t,d/ deletion in, 11
  before pause, 28
  following segment, 46
  linguistic theory and, 84–86
  versus local dialect, 263–264
  research directions in, 83, 86, 104–105
  as stigmatized dialect, 86, 104

C

Cedergren–Sankoff program, 2
  output of, 13–15
  terminology of, 3–4
Consonant(s)
  in following segments, 7–8, 45
  alveolar, 50–51